THE EMERGENCE OF THE DIGITAL HUMANITIES

THE EMERGENCE OF THE DIGITAL HUMANITIES

Steven E. Jones

Routledge
Taylor & Francis Group

NEW YORK AND LONDON

Routledge
New York and London

First published 2014
by Routledge
711 Third Avenue, New York, NY 10017

Simultaneously published in the UK
by Routledge
2 Park Square, Milton Park, Abingdon, Oxon OX14 4RN

Routledge is an imprint of the Taylor & Francis Group, an informa business

Library of Congress Cataloging in Publication Data
Jones, Steven E. (Steven Edward)
The emergence of the digital humanities / Steven E. Jones.
pages cm
Includes bibliographical references and index.
1. Humanities—Electronic information resources. 2. Humanities—Computer
network resources. 3. Education, Higher—Effect of technological innovations
on. 4. Digital communications. I. Title.
AZ195.J66 2014
001.30285—dc23
2013011696

ISBN: 978-0-415-63551-6 (hbk)
ISBN: 978-0-415-63552-3 (pbk)
ISBN: 978-0-203-09308-5 (ebk)

Typeset in Bembo and Stone Sans by
Florence Production Ltd, Stoodleigh, Devon

Printed and bound in the United States of America by Edwards Brothers Malloy

CONTENTS

FIGURES

ACKNOWLEDGMENTS

This book really began as the subject of a spring 2012 graduate seminar, English 415 ("Media and Culture: The Network Is Everting"), where we all read texts and played games and thought through historical developments, technologies, and representations in ways that shaped the arguments that follow. So I'm grateful to the group of English and digital humanities graduate students who made up that seminar: Vicki Bolf, Trevor Borg, Alex Christie, Katie Dyson, Will Farina, Paul Gonter, Erik Hanson, Nathan Jung, Saira Khan, David Macey, Colin McGowan, Sean O'Brien, Maureen Smith, Cameron Phillips, Karissa Taylor, and Andrew Welch. Two of these helped with the book more directly when they served as my research assistants: Nate Jung and Will Farina. Erik Hanson provided access to an early screening of *Indie Game: The Movie* at Chicago's Music Box Theater, as well as sharing his knowledge of video games—at a level far above any I'll ever attain. Other students in the MA in Digital Humanities program were also helpful early responders, including Amy Cavender, Helen Davies, Katie Dunn, Amanda Forson, Mandy Gagel, Niamh McGuigan, Caitlin Pollok, and Adam Tenhouse.

Colleagues at the Center for Textual Studies and Digital Humanities (CTSDH) reacted to early versions of floated ideas with appropriate skepticism—Nick Hayward, Kyle Roberts, Peter Shillingsburg, and George Thiruvathukal—as did friends and colleagues who visited the Center as guest speakers, including Steve Ramsay, Ted Underwood, Kathleen Fitzpatrick, Kari Kraus, and Matt Kirschenbaum. The DH community on Twitter and the blogs was a source of everyday inspiration, ideas, and impressive hive-mindedness. Sometimes a crazy bee stood out, of course, none more so than Mark Sample, whose buzz-worthy performances online and in person always tested and provoked, and Ian Bogost, who will not want to be included under the DH umbrella (like someone standing on the train platform who'd prefer to get rained on), but who has done more than many others to make DH worth debating and understanding. Both generously checked portions of the manuscript draft as it was in progress, as did Matt Kirschenbaum and Bethany Nowviskie, but all errors and shortcomings are of course mine, not theirs. Bethany Nowviskie also gave a moving talk at MLA 2013 that helped to inspire Chapter 7 and then kindly responded at length to my emailed questions. Artist Kelly Goeller took the time to discuss her work in email exchanges and granted permission to reproduce her photo of her own iconic *Pixel Pour* in Chapter 2.

To Matthew Gold I'm grateful for the opportunity to present a version of the argument as part of his open-access *Debates in the Digital Humanities*, where comments from peer-to-peer reviewers, especially Jentery Sayers, Tanner Higgin, Claire Warwick, and Dave Parry, were very helpful. Similarly, anonymous reviewers for the DH 2013 conference at the University of Nebraska offered useful evaluations of a proposal based on the introduction. I'm grateful too for the feedback provided in person at conferences and talks over the past year, including at University of Illinois Chicago—at the invitation of (the other) Steve Jones, who also answered a number of questions specific to the arguments—and Marie Hicks and Carly Kocurek at the Illinois Institute of Technology (IIT), who also kindly took me on a quick, impromptu tour of the Idea Shop at IIT's University Technology Park, as I recount in the Introduction.

The usual thanks to my family have to include, in this case, more specific forms of recognition, as this book benefitted a good deal from the touchstone of Heidi's computer-science expertise (and general worldliness), and from Hannah and Emi's insights into education and the arts and chicken farming (as they contribute to Appalachian Maker culture). I remain inspired by the amazing Henry's ever-resurgent creativity in multiple media, and I'm grateful for the time we worked downstairs together in adjacent rooms. I thank them all for listening to me read aloud the new bits, about which I was least uncertain, but especially for leaving me alone in the mornings to write, then joining me later at the beach for beer and grouper sandwiches.

A note on sources: On a topic so embedded in the present digital network, it has been necessary to cite a good number of online sources, including potentially ephemeral ones, individual blogs and Twitter among them, but also project Wikis and experimental publications on CommentPress and similar platforms. References to online sources by URL or DOI were accurate at the time of writing. Neither the author nor the press is responsible for URLs that may have changed or expired since the manuscript was completed. I also make use of e-books in many cases, so I declare the format (usually Kindle) and cite by location or page (where available) in my copies, but, of course, as is often the case these days, text search may be a more efficient way to locate cited passages. Because of their practical ephemerality, wherever possible I cite Twitter exchanges in the body of the text using screen captures.

INTRODUCTION

On a cold March day in Chicago, I crossed the heavily designed campus of IIT. I had just given a talk (on this very book, then in progress) and had enjoyed coffee in the dramatic campus center designed by architect Rem Koolhaas (with the Green Line train running through it). But my hosts from the Humanities department had also arranged for me to drop in to see the fabrication and rapid-prototyping lab, the Idea Shop at the University Technology Park.[1] In one empty room we looked into, with schematic drawings on the walls, a large tabletop machine jumped to life and began whirring, as an arm with a router moved into position. A minute later, a student emerged from an adjacent room and adjusted something on the keyboard and monitor attached by an extension arm to the frame for the router, then examined an intricately milled block of wood on the table. Next door, someone was demonstrating finely machined parts in various materials, but mostly plastic, wheels within bearings, for example, hot off the 3D printer. At the table where he stood, a box full of colorful 3D-printed prototypes or experimental objects (it was hard to tell the difference just by looking) was laid out, like interesting toys. Most had been built up out of melted polymers squirted onto a base, extruded according to the specifications of CAD (computer-assisted design) and STL (stereolithography) files.

What exactly, again, was my interest as a humanist in taking this tour, one of my hosts politely asked? Why was I so eager to visit this kind of combination machine shop and design lab, where "technology transfers" and start-up companies shared space with students, interns, and faculty members (some of whom were creating those start-ups)? It was a very good question. The answer is the subject of this book, really, and I'll come back to 3D printers throughout the chapters that follow, with a special emphasis in the final chapter, Chapter 7. But to begin, let's just say that I'm convinced that the newer forms of the digital

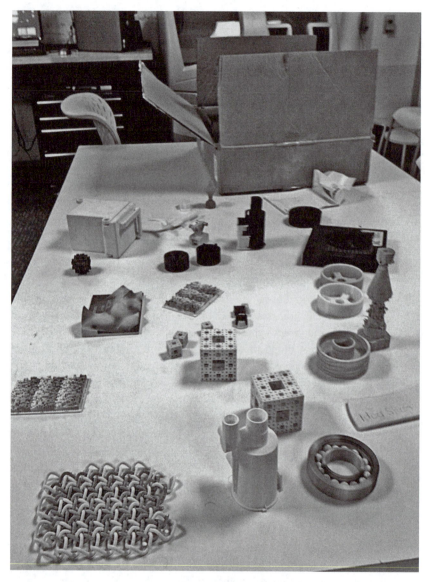

FIGURE I.1 3D printed prototypes, IIT Idea Shop

humanities have as much in common conceptually with those working in the Idea Shop as they do with the great libraries and seminar rooms elsewhere on that campus (and on other campuses). The whole point of the digital humanities today, I think, is manifest in this weirdly suspect interest of mine (I'm by no means unique in this regard) in the whole idea of extruding physical objects from digital files, as well as going the other way around: digitizing physical objects in our archives and collections. Our walk from Humanities to the Idea Shop was, for me, resonantly symbolic of the situation of the digital humanities at the moment, as the chapters that follow will make clear.

This book is about the digital humanities and how it emerged in the past decade as an influential field of study. I'm aware, of course, that a tradition of humanities computing extends back quite a bit further, at least to the middle of the twentieth century. I was working in forms of humanities computing myself (digital textual editing, for example) by the early-to-mid 1990s. But my focus here is on the more recent emergence of a newly prominent form of digital humanities that goes by that name (or by DH; I'll use the terms interchangeably throughout the book, as most practitioners now do). The new-model DH grows out of the longer tradition and is continuous with it, but it also extends the tradition in new directions, in part because of changed cultural contexts, which were, in turn, produced partly in response to material changes in networked technology.

Surely one precondition for these changed contexts was the bursting of the dot-com bubble, starting in March 2000, an event that can be taken as marking the end of the *cyberspace* era, the end of the idea (though some have not yet relinquished it) that technology was an autonomous, unstoppable force. Within a few years, but gaining noticeable momentum between 2004 and 2008, a cluster of new digital products and platforms was introduced—often in a somewhat chastened, post-bubble tone—new software and hardware technologies and new cultural conventions associated with them, frequently based on relatively down-to-earth ideas of what networked technology could do. In place of the Singularity, "the social"; in place of cyberspace, check-ins; in place of immersive virtual reality (VR), Web services and targeted mobile apps. Taken in the aggregate, all those changes mattered. Something important happened during those years.

This was not an inevitable development, and it was certainly not the end toward which the network was always tending, but the related changes gained momentum from one another and added up to a consequential shift in the way most people perceive and relate to the Internet and its bundle of related networks, in particular the cellular + satellite networks as they're integrated with the Internet—in other words, the "network" as most people experience it. Now, I have to pause here to say that the "most people" who "experience" networked technology are, of course, specific subsets of people in general, a kind of convenience for the sake of my argument. Though it's not my topic in this book, and I've deliberately restricted my focus to the already-networked world, I don't mean to gloss over the uneven distribution of these technologies around the world, or the serious social and political problems associated with manufacturing and discarding the devices and maintaining the server farms and cell towers on which the network depends. Some portion of the world is simply not on the grid that theorists argue is becoming "ubiquitous." Even a person in the developing world with only a cheap cell phone will "experience" the "network" very differently from a relatively affluent North American who owns or has access to an array of devices—smartphones, tablets, and desktop computers, as well as an environment increasingly saturated with sensors and processors. I do think it can be too easy to assume a qualitative *hierarchical* difference in the impact of networked technology, too easy to extend the deeper biases of privilege into binary theories of the global "digital divide," which can serve the purposes of globalization (in arguing for closing the "divide" so constructed). But differences of privilege are nonetheless real.[2] So I want to make it clear at the outset that my focus is on a recent shift experienced by the already-networked portion of the world.

Where it was experienced, this shift in technology went well beyond the so-called Web 2.0, with its emphasis on Web services and social software and crowdsourcing, although at the time that was one way of trying to summarize and make sense of the changes.[3] But the shift was propelled by the popularity of social-network platforms, most obviously with the appearance of MySpace in 2003, Facebook early in 2004, and Twitter by 2006. Then a cascade of other changes in the network followed closely, in both commercial and noncommercial applications, frequently crossing over from one to the other, and often deliberately tied to the new social-network platforms. Google Books was introduced late in 2004 (a development of particular interest to humanists). GPS for mobile phones was introduced in a viable way in 2004; selective availability of satellite data was turned off in 2000, but the Google Maps application programming interface (API), which allowed for the mashups and apps with which most people were able to experience geolocative data, was introduced mid 2005. Twitter made micro-blogging available to a mass audience in mid 2006. The iPhone was previewed in 2006 and released mid 2007; the Android OS and phones followed within a year. Although 3D printing—the fabrication of physical objects from software models—was developed earlier and was available in relatively expensive forms by the 1990s, the idea of do-it-yourself (DIY), inexpensive 3D printing as part of a networked media ecology and a culture of hands-on fabrication dates from the same years as the other changes I've been listing, and the company most associated with the new fabrication, MakerBot, was founded in 2009. None of these developments in itself amounted to a major shift, but the sum total of these changes, and in a compressed span of so few years, created a new context within which to imagine the network, and within which to imagine new ways to use computers in humanities research.

Indeed, a new-model digital humanities emerged more or less concurrently with the new context associated with these developments in technology. The term digital humanities itself was solidified in a collection of essays published online in 2004 and as a hardcover book in 2005 (Blackwell's *Companion to Digital Humanities*). The National Endowment for the Humanities (NEH) introduced an initiative for the digital humanities in 2006, leading to the establishment of the NEH Office for the Digital Humanities in 2008. By 2009, the massive Modern Language Association (MLA) conference was host to a number of buzz-worthy meetings that led the public as well as academic press to identify DH as "the next big thing."

The appearance on the scene of the new-model DH around 2004–2008 wasn't a paradigm shift—in Thomas Kuhn's sense of that overused term—in which competing models within a discipline lead to a new dominant view.[4] It was more like a "fork" of humanities computing (already an interdisciplinary field of practice) that established a new "branch"—to use terms associated with version-control platforms popular with many DH practitioners. Or, to apply another set of metaphors: DH *emerged* in those years, not as in "out of the primordial soup," but as in "into the spotlight." The emergence was the effect of a shift in focus, driven, as I've said, by a new set of contexts, generating attention to a range of new activities. These new forms of DH emerged in conjunction with, and often in response to, changes in the culture, especially changes in how people perceive and relate to the digital network, what author William Gibson has called the *eversion* of cyberspace. My thesis is simple: I think that the cultural response to changes in technology, the eversion, provides an essential context for understanding the emergence of DH as a new field of study in the new millennium.

Even that term, field of study, is itself contested within DH.[5] It's still not clear whether digital humanities should be thought of as a field or an (inter)discipline, or just as a label of convenience for the moment for what all humanists will be doing relatively soon. But in this book, let *field* mean something like "energy field" across various disciplines, in and out of the academy—the excitement and intellectual curiosity (and funding and syllabi and programs) that the newly emergent, new-model DH has generated. To shift the metaphor: Like many contributing to the field (in that capacious sense), I understand digital humanities as an umbrella term for a diverse set of practices and concerns, all of which combine computing and digital media with humanities research and teaching. Admittedly, it's a big umbrella, and a shelter of convenience. One recent "short guide" to digital humanities declared that DH is "not to be understood as the study of digital artifacts, new media, or contemporary culture in place of physical artifacts, old media, or historical culture," and it generated a good deal of controversy.[6] I think it's likely the authors meant that DH is not *merely about replacing* "old media" with "new media," that an attention to the relationship between the two media regimes is an important feature of digital humanities work. At any rate, the sentence touched a nerve among some in the field because the study of new media *is* sometimes excluded from definitions of digital humanities. Media scholar Nick Montfort (of MIT) has recently said that, "work in the digital humanities is usually considered to be the digitization and analysis of pre-digital cultural artifacts, not the investigation of contemporary computational media."[7] But Montfort's own work on the formal features of games, on platform studies, and on electronic literature, for example, seems to me to belie the distinction. The Electronic Literature Organization itself, an important center of gravity for the study of computational media in which Montfort has been instrumental, was for a time housed at the Maryland Institute for Technology in the Humanities (MITH), a preeminent DH center where Matthew Kirschenbaum served as faculty advisor.[8] Though these kinds of newly forming disciplinary affiliation are made by people and their shared interests and institutions, and are clearly still shifting, for me, it's important to recognize that the umbrella term does cover some portion of new-media studies and media archaeology projects. *Of course* not all of media studies is or should be covered by the term digital humanities. But there is a rich area of overlapping interests and methods, especially at the more experimental edges of DH. On a panel with media-studies scholars at the Society for Cinema and Media Studies meeting in Chicago, March 6, 2013, I suggested in response to this question about media studies, DH, and other fields that an ideal Venn diagram, with overlapping disciplinary circles, would produce a kind of flower shape at its center, just slivers of overlap where the fields intersect (the petals), but which nevertheless, like a fractal coastline, if you look closely enough, amounts to an interesting shape—with a surprisingly long and interesting perimeter or border to explore. After all, it's often along such complex boundaries, the multi-petalled borders of intersecting academic disciplines and practices, that the most interesting developments in methods and new questions emerge.

The relationship of "digital" and the "humanities"—whatever both terms are taken to mean precisely—operates in both directions. Just as traditional humanities research both made use of the medium of print and turned its investigations (in the practices of book history and textual studies) on the medium of print, so computing is both means and matter for the digital humanities. Besides using computers to research literature or art or history, self-identified practitioners doing DH have also, as a matter of course, applied the methods, insights, and research questions of the humanities to the study of computing and digital media. Using computers to encode and represent, archive and preserve, make accessible and/or analyze, say, eighteenth-century historical documents remains central to DH; but analyzing video games, for example, or other born-digital cultural objects, using combined humanities and computational approaches, is also part of the field. Various intellectually fruitful combinations of computing and the humanities are possible, and I don't see the advantage of ruling out some in advance. Moreover, when it comes to the question of new media, just considered historically, one of the most influential institutional digital humanities centers, founded in 1994, is George Mason University's Roy Rosenzweig Center for History *and New Media* (my emphasis);[9] one of the most influential contributions to the field is Matthew Kirschenbaum's award-winning book, *Mechanisms: New Media and the Forensic Imagination* (2008); and other media archaeology or media history work by Lisa Gitelman, for example, or Noah Wardrip-Fruin, Nick Montfort, or Lev Manovich, along with many others, has continued to influence DH in its current forms.[10] As Jussi Parikka has pointed out, archival practices are "worthy of investigation in the context of media archaeology," and in this area media archaeology "has affinities with the recent interest in *digital humanities*"[11] (emphasis in original).

The meaning(s) and parameters of digital humanities remain contested, to the extent that defining DH is a known rabbit-hole problem from which one may never return. However, in *this* book, some areas of media studies—including especially video games—will be treated as potentially part of DH. This isn't merely a gesture of inclusiveness, or, worse, an attempt at colonization. Media studies is a large field, extending far beyond the portion that falls under the DH umbrella, and game studies has its own autonomy as a field. But the alternatives of autonomous fields versus "flowered" overlap are not mutually exclusive. As I'll show in the chapters that follow, DH emerged in association with, sometimes borrowing from, developments in "vernacular" as well as academic new media and media studies, including especially in the areas of art, publishing, and video games. Some of what it borrowed it kept. And some topics and approaches simply live at the fractally uncertain border between the two fields. That's fine, I think. Many of those associations and borrowings, topics and approaches are significant within established DH practices, and they're definitely worth following out and exploring further.

As I mentioned above, the digital humanities really emerged into the spotlight, came to the attention of academic departments, university administrators, and people outside the academy, when it was reported a few years back in *The Chronicle of Higher Education* and *The New York Times* as "the next big thing" and "Humanities 2.0,"[12] just after the establishment of an Office of Digital Humanities (ODH) at the NEH. Since then, interest in DH has risen so fast that there's already talk of a DH bubble, as if the digital humanities were all start-up hype and hot air. This is not the case—although there is a certain amount of hype, and this will inevitably subside or collapse, as hype does. DH is, of course, a socially constructed phenomenon, along with every academic field and intellectual movement. That doesn't mean it's an aery nothing, mere hype. Especially as a set of strategic practices, some of which I'll explore throughout the book but especially in the final chapter, DH is more than hype, and it will, I think, outlast (in some form) the current bubble. For one thing, as I began by indicating, the newly popular DH is a kind of efflorescence growing out of a longer tradition. The new DH descended from, and is still in some ways continuous with, a 60-plus-year tradition of humanities computing, starting with lexical and linguistic work on mainframes in the mid twentieth century and continuing through the birth of the Internet and the World Wide Web at the end of that century, which focused attention on the need to digitize our so-called cultural heritage, the stuff of our aggregate archives. That work continues in new ways, in fact at an accelerating pace as the datasets grow, and there is a need for area specialists to intervene in this process, for teams of textual scholars and computer scientists to create thoughtful digital texts, for example, or to create tools for studying them, from very simple viewers and collation software to the application of quantitative methods to large corpora of texts and other archives, forms of humanities data mining, topic modeling, or text analysis that are extensions of the earliest lexical processing of humanities computing, the building of concordances, and experiments in stylometrics and attribution studies.

If DH did not burst on the scene around 2004 as a completely new thing in the world, nonetheless *something* happened at around that time, and I think it was something significant, something significantly more than just a rebranding of humanities computing. Director of the Scholars' Lab at the University of Virginia, Bethany Nowviskie, put her finger on one likely proximate and "disruptive" cause outside academe that appeared around 2004: Google Books.

> Least-common-denominator commercial digitization has had grave implications not only for our ability to insert humanities voices and perspectives in the process, but also for our collective capacity and will to think clearly about, to steward, and to engage with physical archives in its wake. A decade on, as a community of scholars and cultural heritage workers, we have only just begun to grapple with the primary phase change of digitization-at-scale.[13]

However, as her own work demonstrates, and as I summarized above, the mass digitization of Google Books itself came along at the same time as a wave of other disruptive and stimulative material technologies—the rapid rise of mobile computing and cellular communications, GPS and GIS, social-network software on the Internet, augmented reality (AR) displacing the earlier ideal of virtual reality (VR), as well as experiments in new media, including video games in particular, that accompanied, stimulated, and reflected these changes. Cumulatively, these changes amounted to a major shift in people's everyday experience of the Internet and related technologies during the first decade of the twenty-first century. This shift in the general attitude toward the network, how it's viewed and how it affects everyday life—what William Gibson has called the *eversion* of cyberspace, its turning itself inside out—happened at roughly the same time as the emergence of the new digital humanities and with the simultaneous rising profile of this newly recognized, newly formidable, newly fundable academic field of practice. Both sets of changes got underway around 2001 but crystallized around 2004–2008, and I don't think this was mere coincidence. The emergence of the academic field was not an isolated phenomenon, unconnected to the jostling world outside the academy.

This is not a question of technological determinism. It's a matter of recognizing that DH emerged, not in isolation, but as part of larger changes in the culture at large and that culture's technological infrastructure. The changes I enumerated above and that Gibson has called the eversion were themselves intertwined with culture, creativity, and commerce—just as the emergence of DH was. It should not be surprising that the emergence of the new academic field and the larger cultural shift in relation to the network were themselves intertwined events. But cultural norms both inside and outside the walls of the academy often work against such recognition. In recognizing the importance of the changes Gibson calls the eversion, I assume that today's network is significantly different in various material ways from the Internet of the 1980s–1990s, in terms of scale, speed, access, and ubiquity. Some of the key differences were instituted 2004–2008. The most important effect of these differences is in the way people experience the network every day—in material terms, yes, as they use smartphones and cloud services and expect to be always connected, for example, but also emotionally and imagi-natively, and this aspect of their experience is often revealed in metaphors, figures through which they think about and represent their experience. Those metaphors are collectively constructed and experienced, as they're shared and altered in the sharing. So I take seriously the effects of these new collective *perceptions* of the network's eversion, as well as perceptions that a new form of digital humanities has emerged as an academic field of study. Such perceptions are real things in the world, and they're worth understanding.

I was trained a literary scholar, and so my first instinct when it comes to understanding collective imaginings or shared (and sometimes symptomatic) metaphors is to look to the arts, where such representational thinking is practiced by experts. That's one reason I cite examples from imaginative and speculative fiction throughout this book. William Gibson called cyberspace a "consensual hallucination," and what he now calls the eversion of cyberspace is likewise a consensual, collective imagination, a set of shared perceptions about the world. Cyberspace mattered, in culture and in numerous technological inventions, in art but also in funding for business and the military. And so does the eversion matter, in significant material and cultural ways. Likewise, the connotative differences between humanities computing and digital humanities, even if we take them to be mostly differences in emphasis and point of focus, are more than mere semantics. If only as a tactical term, the name change has already had real institu-tional and intellectual consequences that often go well beyond the immediate tactics with which they began.[14] The shift to DH has become for many a frame-work for imagining the humanities today, a way of imagining what might be done, but also an institutionalized framework of support within which to do it.

Of course, the relationship between culture and power, imagination and practice, is often complicated (to say the least). More than ever, it's necessary to remain skeptical in our age of the effortless and banal sublimity of always having location-aware computers in our pockets—and of the exploited labor and environmental costs that underwrite that possibility. Historically, especially since the industrial era, the idea of the irresistible power of new technologies, especially when linked to expanding capital, has been used by those in power to increase or consolidate that power, from the suppression of the original Luddite rebellion in the early nineteenth century to the creative destruction of today's global corporations. Some who administer universities have surely pricked up their ears at the appearance of what looks like a humanities upgrade ("2.0") that comes with the promise of (at least relatively) increased funding and more demonstrable practical uses to society. Adding "digital" to the humanities sounds to some like just the thing for shoring up the liberal arts and humanities during the latest version of the long crisis in higher education, and this shoring up is not without implications for the increased precariousness of academic labor. DH practitioners I know are well aware of these complications and complicities, and they're often busy answering, complicating, and resisting such opportunistic and simplistic views. Recently, for example, many have had to explain that the latest versions of online courseware—MOOCs (massively open online courses), about which there has been much talk—are not simply synonymous with DH. Digital humanities scholars are well positioned to address these kinds of developments, not just because they tend to support open access to knowledge, and because they're often the people who create platforms, such as Omeka, for example, which might serve as alternative examples to more broadcast-based lecture-delivery systems, but also— as I show in Chapter 6—because they're engaged in what I call "platform thinking" in general.

As will emerge from the chapters that follow, DH is sometimes associated with the kind of playful, sometimes seemingly arrogant, confidence common among computer programmers, a kind of DIY hacker attitude (in the sense of the term associated with experimental tinkering) that believes in altering the immediate chunk of code at hand, if not the overall infrastructure of a system, at least for the purposes of experiment and demonstration. Now it's true that the overarching effect of such coding may be severely limited, especially these days, when programmers may work on small modules of larger projects and have little direct effect over the shape of any whole. But I find that hands-on experimentalism, even a willingness to maybe break something in order to see how it works, remains part of coding culture. This isn't the same as under-theorized optimism, or naive instrumentalism (though those are always dangers worth guarding against where powerful technologies are concerned). It's more a kind of pragmatic Archimedean sense that you might be able to move some subset of the world connected to any system on which you have root access or any project for which you're building a key component—from the leverage point of the command line. The sometimes world-weary and condescending skepticism common in some segments of the humanities often finds itself at odds with—and in fact deeply suspicious of—this kind of confident hacker ethos, which can seem naive or deluded. But those outside DH often underestimate the theoretical sophistication of many in computing, who deal every day, for example, with gaps between complex data-mining algorithms and the practical sources of those data, or with the production of multiple, sometimes contradictory, visualizations from the same dataset. They know better than many of their humanist critics that their science is provisional and contingent, and that the results of research require interpretive acts. They deal in profound uncertainties as a matter of course, and they have seen first hand the multiplicity of models and representations that can be constructed in any given case. Or, to cite a more mundane example, coders who have spent many hours designing and tweaking, breaking and fixing a content management system (CMS) platform better understand the limitations of such technology, and have fewer illusions about what it can do, than most self-identified neo-Luddites do. Even in complex computing systems, things don't just happen (as the programmer's old joke goes) *automagically*. They can always be tweaked (or broken), shaped by human agents or events in the world. Legendarily, the very metaphor of the computer bug is based on acknowledging the inevitable contamination of technological systems by stubbornly recalcitrant, physical, real-world objects. (A real bug, an insect, can unexpectedly gum up the works.)

That's why the confusion of DH with an uncritical, idealized boosterism for the limitless power of the "disruptive" educational technology of MOOCs is particularly galling to many in the field, as many digital humanities scholars have been among the more vocal critics of existing course management software platforms, as well as the lecture-based information-delivery model associated with MOOCs. They're more often advocates instead for labs and workshops, a collaborative, hands-on model in which students learn to code or build their own online exhibits of digital objects, run sophisticated scanners and edit digital image files, or make their own hybrid physical–digital objects involving sensors and Arduino circuit boards. They're more likely to be interested in a mixed curricular design, including the idea of "flipping the classroom," for example (putting mere informational lectures online and using class time for active projects and discussions), and the hands-on making of prototypes that are closer theoretically to the prototyping of "design fictions" than to traditional humanities work, as Kari Kraus has pointed out.[15] The emphasis by DH on making things is not a flight from theory (or, anyway, it's not usually that, in my experience, and it's certainly not *necessarily* that). In fact, DH making can be profoundly theoretical, a way of resisting what many see as enervating and disenfranchising ideologies of cyberspace, medial and social ideologies based on the supposed immateriality of the digital.

My perspective on all of this is inevitably shaped by my own experiences. As I said, I was working in humanities computing by the mid 1990s, specifically in the construction of the Romantic Circles Website, a platform for publishing digital textual editions, archives, study tools, and its own gamelike space, a dedicated MOO (multi-user dungeon, object-oriented), in which a simple object-oriented programming language allowed almost any user to learn to create virtual objects. I helped to make the site along with Neil Fraistat (who would later direct the influential DH center, the Maryland Institute for Technology in the Humanities), Donald Reiman, and Carl Stahmer (who would later serve as Associate Director of MITH), at around the same time as related projects, such as the William Blake

Archive and the Rossetti Archive, were going online. My c.v. used to list among my scholarly interests "humanities computing" and "digital textuality." Around 2009–2010, I altered it to read "digital humanities" instead, reflecting the rise, not just of a new term (I had been using the term for some years by then), but of a new way to frame the work I was doing and the scholarly community with which I identified in that work.

That same year, 2009, I became founding co-director, with a computer-scientist colleague, George Thiruvathukal, of a new, modestly sized interdisciplinary center at Loyola University Chicago, the Center for Textual Studies and Digital Humanities. As the name suggests, we deliberately linked the kind of textual-studies work many of us had already been doing for decades with the newly emergent field of DH. The founding of the CTSDH also coincided with the hiring of Peter Shillingsburg as the first Martin J. Svaglic Chair of Textual Studies, and he helped spearhead initial research projects, including two that were funded by start-up grants from the NEH's then-new ODH. There had been much larger and massively funded centers already, of course, including first IATH and later the Scholars' Lab at Virginia, CHNM at George Mason, and MITH at Maryland, among others. And that's just in the US and does not mention extremely important centers in Europe and Canada (at the University of Victoria and the University of Alberta, for example), and elsewhere around the world.[16] These pre-dated the shift that brought DH to the attention of so many departments and university administrations around 2009 (and that has led to a second wave of centers and programs). Our smaller endeavor was a product of the beginning stages of this new wave, a collaborative effort by the Departments of English and Computer Science, and with an advisory board representing multiple disciplines and schools, as well as off-campus institutions such as the Newberry Library. The result is a center inhabiting a space between the usual "centers" of institutional resources and organization structure. Unlike some larger centers with longer traditions and more significant funding, ours was conceived of from the start as a strategic response to this newly emerging field, as a research center, yes—it has sponsored multidisciplinary projects in history, the libraries, and communication, as well as textual studies, literature, and computer science—but also as the home of a professional MA program in DH.

Students seeking that degree study programming, markup, HCI (human–computer interaction), and new media, as well as textual scholarship and book history. They create projects in textual editing, archives and library collections, historical GIS Websites, and data visualization tools, including one tool for analyzing the pathways players take through video games. They have come from a range of disciplines, backgrounds, and experiences, but they all come to do project-based work in DH. Faculty work in the CTSDH sometimes includes graduate students as team members and reveals the same range of multiply-materialist methods and topics, from a Web-services infrastructure for collaborative scholarly textual editing (HRIT) to a digital archive of the works of Virginia Woolf

(WoolfOnline), to a custom CMS designed for that kind of textual and DH work (Mojulem), to the digitization of a special collection of nineteenth-century prints, including mobile tools for accessing and annotating them. Our currently dedicated faculty member in the MA program, Nicholas Hayward, has a PhD in ancient history, as well as an MS in computer science. He's at home as much among runes and stone artifacts as he is coding in Ruby or Python. Growing out of conversations, collaborations, and gameplay sessions in the center, my co-director George Thiruvathukal and I wrote a book on the Nintendo Wii for the Platform Studies series at MIT Press (2012)—which we both understood as a digital humanities project.

Every center or informal cluster of DH faculty and students has its own character and scale, and programs and centers in DH are proliferating as I write. I describe my own merely to suggest up front how my institutional contexts led me to write this book. It's my premise that what sets DH apart from other forms of media studies, say, or other approaches to the cultural theory of computing, ultimately comes through its roots in (often text-based) humanities computing, which always had a kind of mixed-reality focus on physical artifacts and archives, the things of the humanities, on the one hand, and digital representations, models, and analysis of those things on the other hand. For the DH scholar, the archival objects on which humanities discourse is based, the material things that, in a very real sense, prompt that discourse and afford that knowledge, were always already saturated in data. Any manuscript, copy of a printed book, or ancient carved fetish is made by our framing attention and the human history of the thing into a research object, which is to say a thing + data (broadly conceived). For me, DH is the intellectual arena where such things are made as well as studied, where the very condition of data-rich archives and objects—and their significance for culture—is investigated, theorized, experimented with. DH is a fundamentally mixed-reality arena: It deals with the multiple materialities of our archives, as these are shaped and augmented by the increasingly ubiquitous digital network.

So, in that context, while ramping up the initiatives that would lead to the CTSDH a year or two later, I read William Gibson's *Spook Country* in 2007 and heard him speak after that about the *eversion* of cyberspace, and something crystallized for me. I saw the metaphor as a way to understand connections between a wide and diverse range of cultural, intellectual, and technological changes that I was experiencing in my own work and everyday life. In fact, I had an experience something like what Gibson identifies in the Blue Ant trilogy to which *Spook Country* belongs: pattern recognition. In the first novel in the trilogy, *Pattern Recognition*, the protagonist, Cayce (whose name ironically echoes that of Gibson's first cyberpunk "console cowboy," Case, who had jacked into cyberspace in 1984's *Neuromancer*), is so attuned to patterns in the data all around her that she fears she suffers from apophenia, the paranoid "recognition" of patterns that may not be there. In this way, she resembles an earlier female protagonist caught up in a web of suspected conspiracies—or paranoia—Thomas Pynchon's Oedipa Mass.

So I should make it clear at the outset: I am not claiming in paranoid fashion that everything is connected: cell phones, satellites, social networks, ubiquitous computing, e-books—and DH. (Although, now that I think about it, the posthorn signs that are everywhere in *The Crying of Lot 49*, in graffiti marking the physical environment for Oedipa as she wanders the city in search of connections, do nicely anticipate those later ubiquitous signs of a glimpsed and desired network of meaning: QR codes. Like the posthorns, they also may mean not much at all. But they may be signs of a collective desire for more meaningful connections.)

But seriously, I take Gibson's eversion for what it is: a rich metaphor. In fact, I think it's a useful master trope that partly highlights existing connections and partly makes connections (as to connect two data points is both constitutive and revealing of potential meanings), many of them connections Gibson recognized but that resonate with me in a slightly different context. The shift in attitude toward networked technology that I've been discussing has been noticed by a number of people writing from different perspectives, as the augmented has displaced the virtual, and computing has gone mobile and locative. (I cite a number of them in the next chapter.) The purpose of this book is to bring these wider changes together under the concept of the eversion and reveal their meaningful conjunction with the emergence of the digital humanities.

The definition of the digital humanities itself remains contested, and this book makes no attempt to pin it down. It isn't a survey of, or an introduction to, DH. It's an extended essay, really, exploring how new questions and practices have arisen out of the combination of digital and physical dimensions of experience, what has been called AR or mixed reality. These new questions and practices address the social, locative, embodied, and object-oriented nature of our experience in the networked world. The eversion provides a context out of which the new DH has emerged, but it's also a context to which DH has contributed, and which it has the potential to help shape in the future.

Plan of the Book

This book has seven chapters. The first two explore key metaphors for recent shifts in our experience of the digital network—the Eversion (of cyberspace) and (multiple, physical and digital) Dimensions. The next three chapters look at specific aspects of the everted network that are also relevant to the newly emergent digital humanities: the ways in which the network is social, geolocative, and enmeshed with material objects in the physical world (People, Places, and Things). Finally, there are two more chapters on what DH does: publish, in various senses of that term (Publications), and mediate between the academy and the world, the physical world and the world of digital media (Practices).

Chapter 1 explores the metaphor of the eversion—the idea that cyberspace is turning itself inside out—as a way to understand both broader changes in our experience of the network and the emergence of DH at around the same moment (2004–2008). Prompted by William Gibson's imaginative fiction, the chapter revisits cyberspace, including looking at its origins in arcade video games, and then examines the shift from that notional nonspace to the everted space of the contemporary networked world. Appropriately enough, given that they inspired cyberspace, video games also provide examples of complex, mixed-reality systems and their responses to the realities of the ubiquitous network. In fact, throughout the book, video games offer concrete examples of dynamic models of the eversion and its effects.

Chapter 2 characterizes one of those effects: The experience of the eversion as taking place between multiple dimensions, in the figurative sense, ultimately figures for the common experience today of the network as linking the different dimensions of the physical and the digital. Without accepting any essential, ontological separation of the two, I do take seriously the many phenomenological reports, including those grouped together by the so-called New Aesthetic, of the sense that we are living surrounded by portals, irruptions, uncanny perceptual awakenings of other dimensions. These are often metaphors for what it feels like to experience the process of eversion, the perceptual shift that characterizes the culture's changing relationship to networked technology and the data it conveys, now that we're soaking in it (as it were).

Chapter 3, "People," turns to the fundamentally and self-consciously social nature of the everted network, pointing to the increased visibility of collaborations between humans and machines, as a key feature of the newly recognized imminence of data. What began with Web 2.0 social-networking software and crowdsourcing, for example, now looks more like another aspect of the fundamentally mixed-reality nature of today's networked world. In Chapter 4, I look at the conceptual impact on the shape of the new DH of the geolocative turn in networked technology. This turn includes in its effects the eversion of virtual places, and their replacement in many cases with today's data maps, which are designed to be used out in the world rather than as a parallel, alternative world. The object-oriented "thingness" of DH, its preoccupation with material objects as good to think with, as well as being prompts for humanities discourse, is the focus of Chapter 5. Digitization is a process for producing augmented data objects, spime-like combinations of material things and data, networked things that embody the already-hybrid nature of our overall experience of inter-networked technology in the era of the eversion. And the preoccupation of DH with building things, making things, even software things, is therefore a potentially serious form of theoretical engagement.

DH experiments in the forms of publication, making humanities research and discourse public, are the subject of Chapter 6, set in the context of the momentous changes in commercial and academic publishing associated with the digitization of books and the rise of e-readers and electronic text in general. These experiments involve the use of platforms previously identified with software development, for example, as well as blogging, but underlying them is a kind of platform thinking. The form of this mindset that's characteristic of DH is, I suggest, a productively Frankensteinian response, in the mixed-reality moment, to the crisis in publishing that Kathleen Fitzpatrick has captured in the uncanny figure of the undead scholarly monograph. As humanities scholars, we are responsible for making our hybrid, sometimes stitched-together platforms, and we're ultimately responsible for recognizing their fundamentally social makeup and uses. Chapter 7 highlights some key digital humanities practices, based in each case on fruitful interaction with vernacular media in the extramural world of the arts, letters, and computing. From 3D printing to reconceptions of the book in the age of mixed reality, creative inspiration as well as practical technologies flow in both directions, through portals in the supposed wall between the humanities and the world—both the physical world and the social world outside the boundaries of the academy. DH has the potential to facilitate these productive breaches, to afford the kinds of cultural exchange that have shaped the new DH since its emergence. In this sense, the digital humanities is the humanities everted.

★

Notes

1. http://ipro.iit.edu/ideashop. My thanks to Marie Hicks and Carly Kocurek for extending my visit on that cold day.
2. From the point of view of the technology industries, see Allan Swann, "Report: Global Digital Divide Getting Worse," *Computer Business Review*, April 5, 2012, http://cbronline.com/news/report-global-digital-divide-getting-worse-05–05–12. Compare the somewhat different view from a United Nations Telecoms Agency report, October 11, 2012, http://un.org/apps/news/story.asp?NewsID=43265&Cr=digital+divide&Cr1=#.UUNMkqXufGc.
3. Tim O'Reilly, "What is Web 2.0: Design Patterns and Business Models for the Next Generation of Software," author's blog, September 30, 2005, http://oreilly.com/web2/archive/what-is-web-20.html.
4. Thomas S. Kuhn, *The Structure of Scientific Revolutions* (Chicago: University of Chicago Press, 1962). Kuhn's term has by now become a cliché, and there are problems with the original argument, but the model of competing paradigms as one way that peer-reviewed fields change (and thus, by extension, one way new fields emerge) remains useful in general.
5. For a good, brief summary of the issues involved, including consideration of the terms used to identify DH, see Alan Liu, "Is Digital Humanities a Field?—An Answer From the Point of View of Language," author's blog, March 6, 2013, http://liu.english.ucsb.edu/is-digital-humanities-a-field-an-answer-from-the-point-of-view-of-language/. References to more detailed histories of the field and debates about its meaning are found in the chapters that follow.
6. The *Short Guide to DH* was extracted from the multi-authored book, *Digital_Humanities*, by Anne Burdick et al. (Cambridge, MA and London, UK: MIT Press, 2012). It was made available online in January 2013 at http://jeffreyschnapp.com/wp-content/uploads/2013/01/D_H_ShortGuide.pdf. As David Golumbia pointed out in "Digital Humanities: Two Definitions," *Uncomputing*, January 20, 2013, http://uncomputing.

org/?p=203, the guide's apparently exclusionary definitions are contradicted by the more capacious view of the full book.

7. Nick Montfort, "Beyond the Journal and the Blog: The Technical Report for Communication in the Humanities," *Amodern* 1 (2013), http://amodern.net/article/beyond-the-journal-and-the-blog-the-technical-report-for-communication-in-the-humanities/.

8. Electronic Literature Organization Website, http://eliterature.org/about/.

9. As pointed out on Twitter, January 17, 2013 by Brett Bobley, Chief Information Officer and Director of the ODH for the NEH.

10. Lisa Gitelman, *Always Already New: Media, History, and the Data of Culture* (Cambridge, MA: MIT Press, 2006); Noah Wardrip-Fruin and Nick Montfort, eds., *The New Media Reader* (Cambridge, MA: MIT Press, 2003); Lev Manovich, *The Language of New Media* (Cambridge, MA: MIT Press, 2001).

11. Jussi Parikka, *What Is Media Archaeology?* (Cambridge, UK: Polity Press, 2012), 15, 115.

12. William Pannapacker, "The MLA and the Digital Humanities," *The Chronicle of Higher Education* Brainstorm blog, December 28, 2009, http://chronicle.com/blogPost/The-MLAthe-Digital/19468; *New York Times* series, "Humanities 2.0," November 17, 2010–July 27, 2011, http://topics.nytimes.com/top/features/books/series/humanities_20/index.html.

13. Bethany Nowviskie, "Resistance in the Materials," author's blog, January 4, 2013, http://nowviskie.org/2013/resistance-in-the-materials.

14. Matthew G. Kirschenbaum, "Digital Humanities As/Is a Tactical Term," in *Debates in the Digital Humanities*, ed. Matthew K. Gold (Minneapolis and London: University of Minnesota Press, 2012), 415–28.

15. Kari Kraus, "Introduction: Rough Cuts: Media and Design in Process," The New Everyday, July 28, 2012, http://mediacommons.futureofthebook.org/tne/pieces/introduction.

16. See the lists, information, and interactive global map of DH centers at the centerNet Website: http://digitalhumanities.org/centernet/.

1

EVERSION

> Cyberspace, not so long ago, was a specific elsewhere, one we visited periodically, peering into it from the familiar physical world. Now cyberspace has everted. Turned itself inside out. Colonized the physical.
>
> (William Gibson 2010)[1]

The eversion of cyberspace, or the shift in perception it metaphorically describes, has actually been going on for some time, now. When Gibson coined the term cyberspace in 1982–1984, it was a metaphor for the global information network, but, in the decade that followed, it made a material difference in technology and culture, and in the perceived relation between the two. Now, as Gibson and others have recently noted, the term has started to fade like an old photograph, to sound increasingly archaic.[2] In a Twitter exchange on November 27, 2011, @scottdot asked "Who the hell says 'cyber'-anything anymore?" and in a few minutes Gibson himself (@GreatDismal) responded: "I have said that myself, many times." The notable exceptions, perhaps significantly enough, are uses of the term by the military and governments, as in cyber-attack and cyber-warfare, and in the analogous case of cyber-bullying. In all of these cases, one might imagine that there's a resistance to acknowledging the (frightening) breakdown of the distinction, the interpenetration of what had been conceived of as separate worlds. Even in this case, the Department of Homeland Security Deputy Secretary Jane Holl Lute began her testimony before a congressional committee on cybersecurity in March 2013 by observing that "cyberspace is woven into the fabric of our daily lives," and she has said repeatedly (in a paradoxical-sounding metaphor) that cyberspace "functions as the very endoskeleton of modern life."[3] No longer a place apart (some other "space"), it's now seen as the infrastructure inside the "body" of everyday

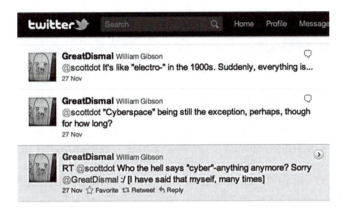

FIGURE 1.1 Twitter conversation, Gibson

existence. For some years now, Gibson has been pointing out that "cyberspace is everywhere now, having everted and colonized the world. It starts to sound kind of ridiculous to speak of cyberspace as being somewhere else."[4] Although she continues to use the term, Secretary Lute would agree with Gibson that cyberspace has everted, turned inside out (and outside in).

In one sense, Gibson is just overwriting his own earlier metaphor (cyberspace) with a newer one (eversion). But, despite his claim that "cyberspace is everywhere, now," in fact, as one of his characters says in the 2007 novel, *Spook Country*, there never was any cyberspace, really. It was just a way of understanding the culture's relationship to networked technology, in other words, a metaphor. As that relationship changed, so did the metaphor. Of course, most of the time people don't go around measuring in figurative terms their shifting attitudes toward technology. Everyday technology is experienced in more literal, concrete terms. For increasing numbers of people, networked technology is becoming an integral part of everyday life they take for granted—and that's the point. The metaphor of eversion is particularly resonant, particularly useful, because it articulates a widely experienced shift in our collective understanding of the network during the last decade: inside out, from a world apart to a part of the world, from a transcendent virtual reality to mundane experience, from a mysterious, invisible abstract world to a still mostly invisible (but real) data-grid that we move through every day in the physical world.[5] If cyberspace once seemed a transcendent elsewhere, someplace other than the world we normally inhabit, that relationship has *in*verted as the network has *e*verted. In a 2009 interview, Gibson described the eversion in this way:

> The ubiquitous connectivity that we're all taking very much for granted, and are increasingly depending on, has become our Here. And the disconnected space, you know, when you can't get your WiFi to link up, or when your cellphone won't work, that's become our There.[6]

The network is no longer normally imagined as a place you jack into in order to upload your disembodied consciousness, a place you "visit" as if it were another planet. It's right here all around us, the water in which we swim. Moreover, we made it, or at least we contribute our own data to it daily, whether fully aware or fully consenting or not.

The term *eversion* is unusual, with medical and surgical associations appearing early (in which inner surfaces—of the eyelid, for example—are turned inside out), and as the term for a rhetorical figure in the seventeenth century (also called *eparedos*), in which a sequence of words or phrases is turned around and repeated in reverse order (according to the *Oxford English Dictionary* (OED)). Gibson himself first used a form of the term in print in a poem published in 1992, "Agrippa" (as we'll see in Chapter 3). There it simply described an umbrella turned inside out by the wind in Japan ("umbrella everted in the storm's Pacific breath"). It's perhaps interesting, however, that Gibson's initial use of the word was to describe a physical object out in the weather. By 2007, he used it as a metaphor for the digital network's turning-out into the physical, out into the world.

In 1999, Marcos Novak, who is a theorist and practitioner of "virtual architecture," used the term eversion in roughly the same way as Gibson later would.[7] Novak begins with the premise that "we are tending toward a culture of ubiquitous virtuality," a state beyond cyberspace and VR. Novak argues, however, that the concept of immersion by itself is incomplete, that it "lacks a complementary concept describing the outpouring of virtuality onto ordinary space" (309, 311). That missing concept is eversion—"the obverse of immersion" (311). Novak's anticipates Gibson's use of the term in a number of ways, even before the implications of newer networked technologies in the new millennium were fully evident. He uses the same spatial metaphor, for example: "Eversion . . . signifies a turning inside–out of virtuality, a casting outward of the virtual into the space of everyday experience" (311). And Novak grasps what will become in the 2000s the crucial point of the eversion of cyberspace—the shift of focus to the everyday and to physical space: "the phenomena we are familiar with in cyberspace will find, indeed are finding, their equivalent, everted forms in ordinary space" (312).

For Novak, at the time, the shift was primarily conceptual. He had not yet seen the eversion embodied in the banal ubiquity of mobile technology, or even of widespread and free, or inexpensive, fast wireless Internet connections. As a visionary architect, however, Novak was used to modeling and thinking with imaginary objects, design fictions, including in his case hyperspatial or multi-dimensional structures that figure eversion in graphical terms. Furthermore, he was interested in design based on metaphors, and in what he calls the "poetics of new technologies" (309). For Novak, eversion is a concept for *more precisely imagining* "the cultural and poetic circumstances brought about by the exponential growth of information technology" (312). Since those early speculations, in a 2008 exhibit for example, Novak has explored the idea "that we live in a new sort of space, encompassing the actual and the virtual, and using the invisible as a bridge and interface between the two"—a formulation that sounds much like the mixed-reality state of the eversion as I'll be characterizing it.[8] Again, as an architect working in an auspicious time, Novak connects that experience to objects in space, what he calls "turbulent topologies," and a sense of being surrounded by "strange geometries." I'll come back in the next chapter to that sense of the eversion as exposing weird, heretofore hidden dimensions of experience, and to the seemingly contradictory sense that the network is mundane, a fact of life all around us, but somehow still redolent of an otherness associated with its former existence as cyberspatial. This double sense is what characterizes our moment of transition, of the eversion still in the process of working itself out and becoming more widely distributed.

In fact, William Gibson is often credited with saying that the future is already here, it just isn't evenly distributed.[9] There's a way in which what Novak sensed with his future-oriented theoretical antennae around the turn of the century took a few years to be experienced by a preponderance of users. And that process continues. But I think we can roughly date the watershed moment when the preponderant collective perception fundamentally changed to 2004–2008. At about that historical moment, the quintessential virtual world, Second Life, arguably peaked. It was more or less taken for granted just as it began to decline, in terms of number of users and—more importantly—in terms of the publicity surrounding it as *the* paradigm platform for the future of the Internet as a whole.[10] At around the same time, the idea that the network itself was essentially a virtual world, a *second* life, lost some of its power, as network technology became increasingly intertwined with everyday activities. The MMORPG (massively multiplayer online role-playing game) *World of Warcraft* was taking off at the same time as a mainstream entertainment, but the interface for that game was decidedly video gamelike in its mixed menus, chat, and 3D graphics. The experience of playing it for many people, with their headsets on, talking to their guild, was closer to using social-network software than to immersive VR as it had been imagined in the era of cyberspace during the 1990s.

Speaking of games, at about the same time, Nintendo's motion-control Wii was introduced (2006), helping to usher in an era of mixed-reality casual gaming, matched only by the rapid rise of mobile gaming. The same massive increase in the use of mobile technologies contributed to the success of the so-called Web 2.0 social-network platforms introduced at the time, especially Facebook. As I pointed out in the Introduction, Facebook first appeared around 2004 (MySpace had preceded it by about a year), but it came into its own, reaching a mass user base, in 2006–2007—just in time to be joined by the microblogging platform Twitter in 2006. Geolocative social-network platform Foursquare, in which users check in to real-world locations using GPS, debuted in 2009. Indeed, as the work of Jason Farman (among others) has shown, the rise of mobile computing is in itself another way to characterize the shift I'm calling the eversion.[11] Farman sees the rise of mobile media as a significant "cultural shift" and a force that produces and reconfigures "social and embodied space"; his work focuses on "the embodied and spatial actions to which our devices contribute" (1, 5, 2). The timeline of eversion, therefore, is marked by the appearance of Apple's iPhone, for example, which was previewed in 2006 and introduced in January 2007; the Android OS and phones followed within a year.

Early in 2007, William Gibson's novel *Spook Country* was published, in which he first articulated the eversion of cyberspace.[12] Set in 2006, its story is based on the rise of mobile network access (though everyone in the book still flips their cell phones open and closed, rather than poking at a multitouch interface, a telling detail that dates the writing to the just-pre-iPhone era), and on the related confluence of AR, locative art, viral marketing, pervasive surveillance, and the total security state. Like what happens in the novel (and the one that preceded it in the trilogy, *Pattern Recognition*), the novel itself is an act of "coolhunting," a report from the interface of culture and networked technology. Characters in the novel execute works of art (and a direct-action protest) by leveraging the cellular data networks, GPS satellite data, and the mobile and wireless Web to tag or annotate the physical world, overlayering locations with data of various kinds, including surreal 3D artists' images. The novel presents a media landscape in which the mundane trumps the transcendent, but it's a mundane with a difference, and the difference is distributed and mobile networked data. In *Spook Country*'s vision of 2006, already there isn't any cyberspace out there, because the network is down here, all around us. The book is about streets and buildings, shipping containers and remote-control drone aircraft, pills, guns, and religious fetish objects, objects of all kinds, because that's where the network lives, now, as data and sensors and connections, built into and surrounding the myriad physical objects that make up the ambient world.

This condition, what Gibson calls the eversion of cyberspace, corresponds to a shift noted by a number of media-studies specialists working in different disciplines, what Katherine Hayles, for example, has identified as a fourth phase in the history of cybernetics (which began in its modern form with information theory in the mid twentieth century), from "virtuality" to "mixed reality," to "environments in which physical and virtual realms merge in fluid and seamless ways."[13] This is the most recent shift in what Hayles sees as the history of cybernetics: moving from homeostasis (1943–1960), to reflexivity (1960–1985), to virtuality (1985–1990s), and now, to mixed reality: "A decade or two ago there was much talk of virtual realms as 'cyber' locations distinct from the real world," she says, as embodied in the VR helmet of the 1980s. Such rigs have been replaced, now, by the graphical user interfaces (GUIs) of computers of various form-factors, increasingly experienced via the "pervasiveness, flexibility, and robustness of ubiquitous media."

> Instead of constructing virtual reality as a sphere separate from the real world, today's media have tended to move out of the box and overlay virtual

information and functionalities onto physical locations and actual objects. Mobile phones, GPS technology, and RFID (radio frequency identification) tags, along with embedded sensors and actuators, have created environments in which physical and virtual realms merge in fluid and seamless ways. This fourth phase is characterized by the integration of virtuality and actuality that may appropriately be called mixed reality.

(Hayles 2010, 148)

The history of cybernetics, for Hayles, began with information being separated from its material "body," being treated as a mathematical abstraction. This has had the effect of a general emphasis on disembodiment that Hayles' earlier work explicitly addressed. The mixed-reality model, however, emphasizes the role of human and machine within complex environments "though which information and data are pervasively flowing" (149). In other words, like Gibson, she recognizes in this 2010 essay that what was once imagined as a realm apart is now discovered all around us in the physical world, as information and data are seen as complexly material phenomena, everywhere embodied.

To cite another example: In 2006, at the time that Gibson was writing *Spook Country* (just before it was published, although excerpts had appeared on his blog), Adam Greenfield used terms much like Gibson's to describe what he called the condition of "everyware," a "paradigm shift" around 2005 to ubiquitous or pervasive computing.[14] This new distributed network offers a radical alternative to "immersing a user in an information-space that never was"—and amounts to "something akin to *virtual reality turned inside out*" (73; my emphasis). Writing from the point of view of technology design, Greenfield cites *Neuromancer* for the earlier paradigm. In cyberspace, he says, the "nonspace of the interface" made it feel as though "each of our boxes [personal computers] [was] a portal onto a 'consensual hallucination' that's always there waiting for us" (72). By contrast, so-called everyware works by "instrumenting the actual world, as opposed to immersing the user in an information-space that never was" (73). Moreover, the new everyware network "happens out here in the world" and is a social phenomenon (16). Science fiction like Gibson's still plays an important role. Greenfield notes, "in everyware pop culture and actual development have found themselves locked in a co-evolutionary spiral," and he cites, for example, movies and science fiction novels, as well as literary fiction, such as work by David Foster Wallace and Don DeLillo, as imaginative representations of ubiquitous computing of the kind actually being developed in the 2000s (93–95). Recognizing this effect doesn't require subtle cultural-studies methods. As he reminds us, sometimes audience members of imaginative films representing technology, for example the interfaces of *Minority Report*, "go on to furnish the world with the things they've seen"; in that way, the "fantastic" is quite literally "made real" (95). In fact, as I'll argue in the chapters to come, the central role of fictional designs or deliberate "design fictions," together with their closeness to being translated into actual, physical prototypes, is one of the features of the eversion, one of the ways the (imagined) virtual and physical are linked; not dual, separate realms, but two possibility states, always already available.

In a Foreword to Beth Coleman's *Hello Avatar,* Clay Shirky praises her analysis of the network as finding a "means to escape the seeming incommensurability of two competing models"—the network as cyberspace and the network as a medium for social communication in the real world.[15] Her preferred framing concept, which sets aside or avoids the presumed dualism, is "x-reality," "x-media," or "cross-media," a "landscape" held together for us by our construction of identities (avatars), and, as Shirky says, it "crosses from the real to the mediated world and back" (xiii). In her own words, Coleman declares that she sees "an end of the virtual and the acceleration of the augmented," due to "the growing phenomenon of pervasive media engagement" (2–3). Augmented or "x-reality," Coleman says, "traverses the virtual and the real" (3).

One more important example is the public writings by sociology student Nathan Jurgenson (a PhD candidate in sociology at the University of Maryland), who in the past few years has argued in various venues against what he calls "digital dualism," the fallacy that "the digital and the physical are separate," and in favor of recognizing instead that "the digital and physical are increasingly meshed" in AR.[16] Jurgenson's arguments about the network overlap with my own in many ways. He writes in response to what he sees as "the fetishization of the offline," which he associates with retro fashions for analog media, and a persistent ideology of cyberspace as a place apart.[17] Against the analog backlash based on digital dualism, Jurgenson asserts that:

> Our lived reality is the result of the constant interpenetration of the online and offline. That is, we live in an augmented reality that exists at the intersection of materiality and information, physicality and digitality, bodies and technology, atoms and bits, the off and the online.
>
> ("The IRL Fetish")

This argument by Jurgenson (and others at the Cyborgology blog in particular) attracted the criticism of Nicholas Carr, author of *The Shallows: How the Internet Is Changing the Way We Think, Read and Remember,* who wrote his own blog post February 27, 2013 against what he called the "digital dualism denialism."[18] Carr equates offline existence with a pre-technological, more natural way of life: "We should celebrate the fact that nature and wilderness have continued to exist, in our minds and in actuality, even as they have been overrun by technology and society." The constructedness of the idea of "nature" for the past 200 years—especially in reaction to the industrial revolution—and the presence in the "wilderness" of machines and technologies of various kinds for much longer than that are glossed over in Carr's account, revealing the very kind of idealization of "offline" life Jurgenson was addressing in the first place. But Carr's call for "thinking more deeply about people's actual experience of the online and the offline and, equally important, how they sense that experience" is, I think, useful. It's true that, at times, Jurgenson's rhetoric can sound like simple debunking rather than deconstruction, as if it's merely a matter of exposing digital dualism as a silly illusion. He has, I think rightly, said that "the clear distinction between the on and offline, between human and technology, is queered beyond tenability" ("IRL Fetish"). But, as with other forms of queering, that doesn't mean that the relational constructions of digital and physical suddenly come to an end and are resolved into a unity, now that they are less stable, fixed, or natural categories. It certainly doesn't mean that *people no longer experience them as mutually co-constructed*, as defined by differences that cannot quickly be resolved into easy unities. In one marginal note to one of the essays I've been citing, Jurgenson qualifies his own polemic: "To be clear, the digital and the physical *are not the same*, but we should aim to better understand the relationship of different combinations of information, be they analog or digital" ("The IRL Fetish"). Agreed. In this book, I'm deeply interested in pursuing that kind of better understanding of the relationship of digital and analog, in part by looking (as Carr suggests) at how people "sense" their experience of this relationship. I begin by reading the metaphorical significance carried in expressions of digital dualism, and by interpreting the *shift* from one dominant metaphor (cyberspace) to another. That shift characterizes the eversion for me, the move toward what Jurgenson calls enmeshed or AR, what Coleman calls x-reality, what Greenfield calls everyware, and what Hayles calls mixed reality. So, as I further explain in the next chapter, I'm less interested in debunking cyberspace as a transparent illusion than I am in exploring what, after having had such a profound cultural influence, cyberspace's dissolution and ongoing eversion might mean, now, for culture and the humanities. If cyberspace was a "consensual hallucination," then that consensus was widespread (and remains in effect for some people), and the eversion therefore represents a significant but still unfolding shift in the collective imagination. Such a shift calls for interpretation.

I think the changes observed by authors such as Jurgenson, Coleman (and Shirky), Greenfield, Hayles, and others, all writing from different disciplines and different perspectives, reflect a broader cultural change whose effects we are still experiencing, a multi-platform shift in the nature of the collective experience of networked technologies. My focus is on that shift, as an ongoing process, and on its significance as a context for understanding the emergence of the digital humanities. It's not that (to borrow a phrase from Virginia Woolf) on or about December 2006, say, the character of the network changed. Nothing that sudden and clear cut took place, of course. But I do think that, between about 2004 and 2008, the cumulative effect of a variety of changes in technology and culture converged and culminated in a new consensual imagination of the role of the network in relation to the physical and social world. In other words, the network was everting.

At about that same moment, the digital humanities rather suddenly achieved a new level of public attention, as I sketched out in the Introduction, emerging out of a decades-long tradition of humanities computing and marked by the term "digital humanities" itself—which seems to have been coined in 2001 but reached a kind of critical mass, in terms of public awareness and institutional influence, ranging from the publication of the influential *Companion to Digital Humanities* (2004), to notices in the press, to the establishment of an Office of Digital Humanities (ODH) at the NEH, between 2004 and 2007.[19] While the earlier established practices of humanities computing continued, the new-model digital humanities emphasized new methods and new media, the analysis and visualization of large datasets of humanities materials, for example, including for the purposes of what Franco Moretti named "distant reading" (2005); it continued to engage in building digital tools and Websites and archives, but also began to experiment with using 3D printers and making wearable processors and other devices; and it responded to the geospatial turn across the disciplines.[20] The new digital humanities also increasingly turned its attention to new media, including born-digital media, and, to a greater extent than has been fully recognized, began to study game theory and even to build video games and alternate reality games (ARGs). So the concurrent eversion of cyberspace and the rise of the new DH was no mere coincidence. In one sense, the new digital humanities—the product of the same changes marked by the eversion—is arguably humanities computing everted.

In its newly prominent forms, DH is both a response to and a contributing cause of the wider eversion, as can be glimpsed in the substitution performed at a crucial moment (by John Unsworth and Andrew McNeillie, in titling a collection of essays) from *digitized* to *digital* humanities: from implying a separation between the stuff of the humanities—manuscripts, books, documents, maps, works of art of all kinds, other artifacts—and computing, to more of a mixed reality, characterized by two-way interactions between the two realms, physical artifacts and digital media.[21] Instead of only digitizing the archives of our cultural heritage in order to move them out onto the network (though that work continued of course), many practitioners began to see themselves putting the digital into reciprocal conversation with an array of cultural artifacts, the objects on which humanistic study has historically been based, as well as new kinds of objects, including born-digital artifacts. In new media, this kind of reciprocal interaction between data and artifacts, algorithm and world, has been effectively modeled for decades in video games. So, throughout this book, I'll cite games as the best examples of some of the problems of new media that are especially relevant to the rise of DH.

Transcendent Network, Mundane World

First, to revisit cyberspace: Combining "cybernetics" and "space," William Gibson coined the term in a 1982 short story, "Burning Chrome," as an imaginary brand name for a network device set in the 2030s, but it became famous in his 1984 cyberpunk novel *Neuromancer*. He later said that his vision of cyberspace— a disembodied virtual reality, a transcendent other world made up of "clusters and constellations of data. Like city lights receding"—was inspired by watching arcade video game players as they leaned into their machines, bumping the cabinets and hitting the buttons (in the novel, a fictional documentary says that the "matrix," the network, "has its roots in primitive arcade games").[22] Gibson, who, significantly, was not himself a gamer, imagined that the gamers were longing to be immersed in, and to disappear into, the virtual world on the other side of the screen, longing to transcend the body in physical "meat space" and be uploaded as pure consciousness into the digital matrix of cyberspace.[23] Thus, Norbert Wiener's 1948 use of cybernetics, which was etymologically about "steerage" or human control of machines, was mutated by Gibson in 1984 to suggest a willing relinquishment of the bodily and the material in order to go to another place, another plane.[24] In fact, the Other Plane was Vernor Vinge's term for the 3D virtual world he imagined a few years before Gibson's *Neuromancer* introduced the world to cyberspace, in the novella *True Names*.[25] Vinge based his imagined Other Plane on his experiences logging on to a PDP-11 in 1979 through a dial-up connection; creating the virtual world was a matter of "scaling up from that and imagining consequences" (Frenkel, 16, 18).

> One of the features of *True Names* is the notion that a worldwide computer network would be a kind of *place* for its users. I needed a word for that place, and the best I came up with was "the Other Plane." Alas, that is a lightning bug compared with the lightning bolt that is "cyberspace."
>
> (Frenkel, 20)

(Vinge is referring to an idea he attributes to Mark Twain, that "the difference between the right word and the almost right word is the difference between lightning and a lightning bug.") Both Vinge's and Gibson's metaphors had to be spatialized. As Katherine Hayles has said, Gibson created cyberspace by "transforming a data matrix into a landscape"—a place apart from the physical world—"in which narratives can happen."[26] This newly 3D imagined place, which Gibson characterized from the beginning in idealist terms as "a consensual hallucination," looked like a glowing abstract grid, as seen in 1982's TRON, for example, where, as in Plato's world of the Forms, the contingencies of material reality and the body have been burned away, sublimated into green and amber phosphor.

This notion of cyberspace informed general perceptions of the Internet and of the user's experience of digital media for most of the decade that followed. In 1996, *Wired* magazine's style guide defined cyberspace as "information space. The ether. The place between phones, between computers, between you and me," before citing Gibson in *Neuromancer*.[27] The *Wired* style guide was already calling "cyber" a "terminally overused prefix for all things online and digital," while itself serving as further evidence of that overuse. The idea of cyberspace carried with it a series of assumptions about the real network for which it served as a metaphor. For example, it was often taken for granted that the ultimate goal of users interfacing with the network was total immersion, meaning the loss of body-consciousness as one disappeared into the digital world on the other side of the screen. Only imperfect technology stood in the way. This assumption owed much to 1980s and 1990s experiments in VR, in which a helmet or wraparound goggles replaced your physical sensorium, as you literally buried your head in cyberspace. Some of these early environments were in turn directly inspired by Gibson's vision of cyberspace. Katherine Hayles has said that his novels "acted like seed crystals thrown into a supersaturated solution," causing inventions of user interfaces and VR applications to crystallize.[28]

However, in the first decade of our new century, as I've said, Gibson overwrote his own metaphor, first and most explicitly in *Spook Country*. Over 20 years after inventing cyberspace, he imagines in the novel a scene in which a journalist, a curator, and a locative artist are sitting in a booth in the restaurant of the Standard Hotel in Los Angeles, discussing art and new media and observing that, in 2006 (when the story is set), cyberspace "is everting," turning itself inside out and flowing out into the world (20). Significantly, the artist dates the beginning of the change from May 1, 2000, when the United States government turned off selective availability to GPS satellite data, making a larger set of those data available to the general public, not just the military, for the first time. Google Maps (for which the API was released in June 2005) and better automobile navigation systems were the most immediate and widely experienced results, but the implications were profound. In the decade that followed, with the marked increase in the use of mobile devices and other pervasive processors and sensors, a cluster of activities emerged, circulating from artists' and hackers' subcultures to mainstream awareness and back again, practices that first came to prominence about six years ago but are still evolving: geocaching, hyperspatial tagging or spatially tagged hypermedia, locative installation art based on AR, all overlapping with a larger trend, the pervasive use of embedded RFID tags and other markers such as QR codes, as well as cheaper sensors, in and on everyday physical objects. This amounts to the beginnings of an infrastructure for the kind of widespread AR many people first became aware of when Google announced Project Glass, an AR application using a field-of-vision lens supported by a glasses-like frame and with location-aware networking technology. As I write it's still in developer prototype stage, but reportedly it will contain a GPS chip and connection through WiFi to Google services, and Bluetooth connection to a cell phone, though not its own cellular radio receiver, and will provide access via touch and voice control, with voice as well as visual feedback—a hands-free, heads-up AR display.[29] Marketing has stressed the ability to capture and then upload video and photos from a first-person perspective, all with voice commands, but has also shown AR features such as real-time location-aware data from various Google services. These developments emerged from long-pursued work in ubicomp (ubiquitous computing) or the Internet of Things. The larger trend involves bringing together the data grid with the physical and social world—not leaving the one behind to escape into the other, but deliberately overlayering them, with the expectation that users will experience data (and data-enriched media) anywhere, everywhere, while moving through the world—and mobility is a key feature of the experience. By definition, such technologies afford dynamic hybrid experiences, taking place at the literally shifting border, where digital data continually meet physical reality as the user moves through the world and its everyday objects. Although Gibson has characterized this as the colonization of the physical by the digital, this would *seem* too pervasive a vision of the network in our lives, now, too mundane a reality to be experienced with a dark cyberpunk *frisson*. It's just how increasing numbers of people move around in and inhabit the world. In *Spook Country*, a GIS-trained hacker who facilitates locative art projects explains that, once cyberspace everts, "then there isn't any cyberspace," and that, in fact,

> there never was, if you want to look at it that way. It was a way we had of looking where we were headed, a direction. With the grid, we're here. This is the other side of the screen. Right here.
>
> (64)

As mundane as this new networked reality might seem, in the next chapter, I'll explore some signs and metaphors that suggest that it is still haunted by a lingering sense of the uncanny, of contact with a hidden dimension ("the digital") that we once consensually experienced as cyberspace—and the status of which, as reality or hallucination, we remain unsure.

The Emergence of the (New) Digital Humanities

It's the *process* of moving from one dominant metaphor to another, a direction or trajectory, from cyberspace out into the data-saturated world, that characterizes our sometimes tense and ambiguous relationship to technology at the moment. That's why I value Gibson's figure of eversion, a term for a complex process of turning. As a metaphor, eversion calls attention to the messy and uneven status of that process—the network's leaking, spilling its guts out into the world. The process remains ongoing, and the results continue to complicate our engagements with humanities archives *and* new media. It's an often disorienting experience, like looking at a Klein bottle, affording a sense of newly exposed overlapping dimensions, of layers of data and cultural expression combining with the ambient environment via sensors and processors, with a host of attendant risks to privacy and civil liberties. This complex sense of promise and risk also applies to the changing infrastructural networks of traditional as well as new digital humanities practices. New-media scholar Ian Bogost has challenged the humanities to turn itself outward, toward "the world at large, toward things of all kinds and all scales,"[30] and, indeed, I think that's the trajectory of the digital humanities in the past few years, as the infrastructure of humanities practices, from research on various fronts, to teaching, to publishing, peer review, and scholarly communication, is increasingly being exposed to the world, turned inside out. In that sense, the larger context of the eversion itself provides a hidden (in plain sight) dimension that helps to explain all the fuss—first documented for many outside the field of DH in William Pannapacker's 2010 declaration in his *Chronicle of Higher Education* blog that the digital humanities was "the next big thing," or in the coverage in *The New York Times* of "culturomics" and new digital humanities work in the "Humanities 2.0" series (2010–2011).

The eversion provides a context, as well, for some debates within digital humanities. This book will be concerned with one such debate in particular: If the eversion coincides with the rise of the digital humanities in the new millennium, the increased emphasis on layerings of data with physical reality can, I believe, help us to distinguish some aspects of the new-model digital humanities from traditional humanities computing. The two are clearly connected in a historical continuum, but the changes in the past decade open up a new range of activities and new problems for digital humanities research. It's not a question of accepting the 1990s opposition between humanities computing and new media, but of recognizing the new imperatives emerging from changes in network technologies and cultural responses to those changes.[31] Digital humanities scholars have responded to the eversion as it has happened (and continues to happen). This is reflected on many fronts, including work with (relatively big) data, large corpora of texts, maps linked to data via GIS, and the study and archiving of born-digital and new-media objects. These were various responses on the part of the digital humanities to the changes of the eversion, but the forms they took were also often *effects* of the wider eversion, were in the air, as they say, at the very moment the digital humanities emerged into public prominence. A series of simple juxtapositions is suggestive: Franco Moretti's influential book, *Graphs, Maps, Trees: Abstract Models for a Literary History*, was published in 2005, the same year that the Association of Digital Humanities Organizations was founded—and the same year the Google Maps API was released. The open-access online journal, *Digital Humanities Quarterly* (DHQ), first appeared in 2007, the year of the iPhone, the publication of Gibson's *Spook Country*, and the completion of Kirschenbaum's award-winning *Mechanisms* (published 2008). The NEH office dedicated to the field (the ODH) and its funding was established in 2008 after a two-year staged development process. So Brett Bobley and others were working on establishing the ODH at the very moment Gibson was writing about the eversion and Kirschenbaum was applying his digital-forensics methods to, among other objects, Gibson's earlier artist's book (and harbinger of the eversion),

Agrippa. Also in 2008, the first THATCamp (The Humanities And Technology Camp) "unconference" was sponsored by the influential Center for History and New Media at George Mason University. I could go on. But I want to stress that these juxtapositions have nothing to do with technological determinism. They're just meant to demonstrate that the emergence of the new digital humanities isn't an isolated academic phenomenon. The institutional and disciplinary changes are part of a larger cultural shift, inside and outside the academy, a rapid cycle of emergence and convergence in technology and culture.

Father Roberto Busa, S.J., who is frequently cited as the founder of traditional text-based digital humanities for his work with computerized lexical concordances, wrote in his 2004 Foreword to the groundbreaking *Companion to Digital Humanities* that humanities computing "is precisely the automation of every possible analysis of human expression . . . in the widest sense of the word, from music to the theater, from design and painting to phonetics."[32] Although he went on to say that its "nucleus remains the discourse of written texts," a qualification still being debated by digital humanities scholars, the capaciousness of "every possible analysis of human expression" should not be overlooked, especially in the context of the moment in which it was published (xvi). Rather than divide the methodological old dispensation from the new in ways that reduce both (such as opposing humanities computing to studies of new media, or merely "instrumental" to more truly "theoretical" approaches), I'll suggest throughout this book that we'd do better to recognize that changing cultural contexts in the era of the eversion have called for changing emphases in digital humanities research, some of which have surely effected changing cultural contexts in turn.

It seems clear to me that some of the newer forms of supposedly practical or instrumental digital humanities, which are central to the field, were produced in the first place by younger scholars working with a keen awareness of the developments I'm grouping under the concept of the eversion, and with a sense of what these meant at the time for various technology platforms of interest to humanists. Leading digital humanities scholars had their ears to the ground, and some worked as programmers or designers in technology industries or new media, or in what are now called "alt-ac" (alternative academic) positions within the university, often in collaboration with researchers and vendors in advanced sectors of IT. Influence, like an infection, spreads among people. In the era of social networks, casual gaming, distributed cognition, AR, the Internet of Things, and the geospatial turn, one segment of new digital humanities practitioners were early adopters and observers of these new developments and, often deliberately, brought them into their university research centers and projects. This is largely the reason for the central role of a hands-on, practical turn in the new digital humanities ("more hack, less yack," as the notorious THATCamp motto goes), a spirit borrowed from the vernacular Maker movement. But this practical turn, arguably based on theoretical insight, was often, I think, a kind of deliberate rhetorical gesture—a dialectical countermove to the still-prevailing idealisms associated with the cyberculture studies of the 1990s. Much of the practical digital humanities work during the decade that followed, which formed an important core of the newly emergent field of activity, was undertaken, not in avoidance of theory or in pursuit of scientistic instrumentalism, but against disembodiment, against the ideology of cyberspace. The new digital humanities often aimed to question "screen essentialism," the immateriality of digital texts, and other reductive assumptions, including romantic constructions of the network as a world apart, instead emphasizing the complex materialities of digital platforms and digital objects. New digital humanities work, including digital forensics, critical code studies, platform studies, game studies, not to mention work with linguistic data and large corpora of texts, data visualization, and distant reading, is a collective response by one segment of the digital humanities community to the wider cultural shift toward a more worldly, layered, hybrid experience of digital data and digital media brought into direct contact with physical objects, in physical space, from archived manuscripts to Arduino circuit boards.

In this context, the digital humanities looks less like an academic movement and more like a transitional set of practices at a crucial juncture, on the one hand moving between old ideas of the digital and of the humanities, and, on the other hand, moving toward new ideas about both. The new DH starts from the assumption of a new, mixed-reality humanities, complicated and worldly, mediating between the physical artifacts and archives on which humanities discourse has historically been built, and the mobile and pervasive digital networks that increasingly overlay and make those artifacts into data-rich, tagged and encoded, sensor-enhanced things, what author Bruce Sterling (Gibson's friend and collaborator) calls spimes.[33] From its origins in the early modern era to today, the humanities has been, in part, a collective effort by scholars and others to discover, edit, archive, interpret, and understand our cultural heritage as it has been transmitted—which is to say in the forms of inherited material objects, stone tools, runes, artifacts and works of art, manuscripts and books, new media and software. Encoding and decoding, augmenting, commenting on and interpreting the layers of data that surround those objects and make them culturally significant have historically formed the agenda (or call it the calling) of the humanities. Within the past decade, humanities work and cultural heritage itself have been digitized, just as the larger, collective understanding of everything that digitization means has undergone a major conceptual and practical shift. This process isn't over yet, and the outcome remains uncertain, as anyone following news about Google Books (and HathiTrust), or shifting policies at Apple's App Store, or traditional publishing in the e-book era, will recognize. As William Gibson remarked in one recent interview, "the eversion continues to distribute itself, and here we are."[34] That distribution itself is inevitably uneven and not always well understood. One job for the *digital* humanities going forward might be consciously to engage with, to help make sense of, and to shape the dynamic process of that ongoing eversion (and its distribution) out in the world at large. The digital humanities should be about this work, as I'll argue in the rest of this book, because the digital humanities is, in fact, the humanities everted.

The Example of Video Games

As I've said, in almost every chapter of this book, I'll cite video games as examples. For one thing, given the role of games in the history of computing, it would be surprising if I didn't. Humanities computing and digital humanities work have often involved games and gamelike environments, from early multi-user dungeons (MUDs) and MOOs, to the experimental *Ivanhoe* game developed at the University of Virginia (the work of Johanna Drucker, Jerome McGann, Bethany Nowviskie, Stephen Ramsay, and Geoffrey Rockwell, among others), to Matthew Kirschenbaum's inclusion of video games among the objects of his digital-forensics approach (2008), including the project on Preserving Virtual Worlds.[35] This is not to mention explicit video-game studies by specialists in information studies, new media and digital media, or electronic literature—not all of whom always see themselves as working in digital humanities, but whose work has unquestionably contributed to the field.

For another thing, video games are simply the most prominent and influential form of new media today, and so it should not be surprising that they help to illuminate the larger culture's relationship to technology. Unfortunately, anxiety about treating games as a serious academic subject, and the need of a newly emergent field such as digital humanities to be taken seriously by administrators and the public, have meant that the study of games is often situated at the very far end of the spectrum from more traditional, text-based humanities computing. My own interest in games met with resistance from some anonymous peer reviewers for the program for the DH 2013 conference, for example (though in the end, the enthusiasm of positive reviews won the day). I think it's safe to say that games are at least recognized by many digital humanities scholars as belonging in the continuous spectrum of their area of practice. Again, I want to assert: As a medium, video games are significant cultural expressions, worthy of study in their own right. But I also believe that digital humanities approaches, alongside approaches from other fields and disciplines, have much to contribute to that study. And, to turn the relationship around, computer-based video games embody procedures and structures that speak to the fundamental concerns of the digital humanities. They are based on much-tested forms of creative, algorithmic, formally sophisticated systems, many recent examples of which model in interesting ways the general dynamics of the eversion. Games are designed to structure the fluid relationships between digital data and the game world, on the one hand, and between digital data and the player in the physical world, on the other hand. A number of recent fictional works in various media have explored the ways in which video games model the multidimensional relationships between data and the world, including, for example, David Kaplan and Eric Zimmerman's short film *PLAY* (2010), Ernest Cline's novel *Ready Player One* (2011), and Neal Stephenson's novel *Reamde* (2011), along with theoretical game studies by Jane McGonigal, Ian Bogost, or Mary Flanagan, for example. McGonigal, the creator of several of the most influential cross-platform ARGs—played collectively across the Internet, phone landlines and cell-phone networks, television, other media, and in real-world settings, as well, using GPS coordinates to locate clues revealed on Websites, on TV, in trailers to films, etc.—has argued that we should apply the structures of games to real-world personal and social problems. As a result, she has been accused of indirectly abetting the "gamification" trend, most notoriously associated with Facebook games such as Zynga's *Farmville*, which critics see as colonizing players' everyday lives for commercial profit by reductive, exploitative, and addictive games blatantly designed according to principles of operant conditioning. Gamification is bullshit, as Bogost says, a transparent kind of "exploitationware," based less on persuasion than on outright manipulation.[36] But even this trend has unwittingly responded to larger changes in media and culture. It's significant that the underlying premise shared by both McGonigal's idealistic, world-saving games and the most crass kind of gamification—and shared as well by critics of gamification—is that video games are now "busting through to reality" as never before (as Jesse Schell said in one notorious talk),[37] crossing over from the game world to the player's real world. In its own unwitting way, gamification is yet another sign of the eversion.

Cyberspace was always gamespace in another guise, gamespace *dis*placed. Not only was Gibson inspired by arcade gamers when he came up with the concept, he interpreted the gamers' desires in terms of popular misconceptions about the motivations and effects of playing video games, in an example of what Katie Salen and Eric Zimmerman have called the "immersive fallacy," the assumption that the goal of any new media experience is to transport the user into a sublime and disembodied virtual world.[38] On the contrary, Salen and Zimmerman argue, most gaming has historically taken place at the interface of player and game, the boundary of physical space and gamespace, where heads-up displays (HUDs), controllers and peripheral devices, and social interactions are part of the normal video-game experience. Salen and Zimmerman see a "hybrid consciousness," a sense of being simultaneously in the game world and in physical reality, as the norm, not the supposed "pining for immersion" that many assume is driving the experience (458, 451–55). However deeply engaged players become, however riveted their attention, the experience of gameplay has always been more mixed reality than VR. In other words, the relation of gamer to game world is more cybernetics than cyberspace, literally more mundane, more in the (physical) world than has been imagined by many, especially many non-gamers.

In the past six or seven years, a major development in gaming has borne out this multilayered view of gaming and has undermined the cyberspatial ideology of total immersion: what game theorist Jesper Juul calls a "casual revolution."[39] Though we now often associate the idea of casual games with mobile platforms,

Nintendo's Wii console, introduced in 2006, led the way into casual gaming by tapping into the mass market of first-time gamers or non-gamers and shifting attention by design from the rendering of realistic, 3D virtual game worlds to the physical and social space of the player's living room.[40] The Wii is all about the mixed-reality experience of using a sometimes klugy set of motion-control peripherals, connected in feedback loops that evert the gamespace, as it were, spilling it out into the living room, creating a kind of personal area network for embodied gameplay. It's that hybrid, everted gamespace where Wii gameplay takes place—with a coffee table at the negative center of it, and perhaps other people playing along, as well as various peripherals beaming data to and from the console—not some imaginary world on the other side of the screen. When Microsoft's Kinect appeared in 2010, it was marketed as gadget-free, a more transparent version of a somatic motion-control interface. It actually works, however, by taking the sensor system's gadgets out of the user's hand (or out from under her feet) and placing them up by the screen, looking back out at the room. In practice, Kinect play is a lot like Wii play in its focus on the player's body and the physical space in which she's moving around. A flood of hacks and homebrew applications for Kinect have, for the most part, focused on it, not as a VR machine, but as a system for connecting digital data and the physical world via the embodied player.

In this regard, the Wii and Kinect, and casual gaming in general, have only re-emphasized a fundamental aspect of all digital games. Writing about text-based adventure games and interactive fiction (IF), generically among the earliest examples of computer games, Nick Montfort has said that the two fundamental components of such games are the world model—"which represents the physical environment of the IF and the things in that environment"—and the parser— "that part of the program that accepts natural language from the interactor and processes it."[41] Although he is careful not to extend this model to video games in general, it offers an important general analogy. All computer games are about the productive relationship of algorithmically processed data and imagined world models—which include representations of place (maps, trees) and artifacts (weapons, tools, other inventory). One plays in collaboration or competition with other players, non-player characters (NPCs), or the "artificial intelligence" that is the overall design of the game, negotiating between the two: data and world. At the same time, one plays from an embodied position in the real physical world. That betweenness is the condition of engaged gameplay, the "hybrid consciousness" that Salen and Zimmerman refer to. Even a game with an apparently immersive game world, whether realistically rendered (*Skyrim*) or iconically rendered (*Minecraft*), is *played* between worlds, at the channels where data flow back and forth in feedback and feedforward loops. That's why HUDs, representing maps and inventories and statistics of various kinds, and other affordances of gaming persist—not to mention discussion boards, constantly revised Wikipedia articles, and other paratextual materials surrounding gameplay—even in games that emphasize the immersive beauties (or sublimities) of their represented game worlds.

The digital humanities could do worse than look to games for examples of complex mixed-reality systems that reflect the contingencies of the network at the present moment. It's hard to think of a more widely distributed and widely experienced set of models of the larger process of eversion that we're now in the midst of than video games. And games are also useful models of the combined human-computer interactions by which all meaningful computing gets done. In the broader sense, the network doesn't evert by itself. It's not really turning *itself* inside out. That requires human agency, actors out in the world, just as games require players, and just as digital humanities research requires scholar–practitioners, working in the channels of the eversion, where the data network meets the world in its material, artifactual particulars.

★

Notes

1. William Gibson, "Google's Earth," *New York Times*, August 31, 2010, http://nytimes.com/2010/09/01/opinion/01gibson.html.
2. See, for example, Clay Shirky, *Here Comes Everybody: The Power of Organizing Without Organizations* (New York: Penguin Press, 2008), 195–96, who echoes Gibson on the term cyberspace and its fading from use. The notable exceptions, perhaps significantly enough, are uses of the term by the military and governments, as in cyber-attack and cyber-warfare, and in the analogous case of cyber-bullying. In all of these cases, one might imagine that there's a resistance to acknowledging the (frightening) breakdown of the distinction, the penetration of what had been conceived of as separate worlds.
3. Jane Holl Lute, written testimony before House Committee on Homeland Security, March 13, 2013, http://dhs.gov/news/2013/03/13/written-testimony-dhs-deputy-secretary-jane-holl-lute-house-committee-homeland. She has used the endoskeleton metaphor for years, for example, in an op-ed co-authored with Bruce McConnell, "A Civil Perspective on CyberSecurity," *Wired*, February 14, 2011, http://wired.com/threatlevel/2011/02/dhs-op-ed. (Thanks to Erik Hanson for cc'ing me in a retweet of Lute's latest remarks.)
4. "The Art of Fiction No. 211: William Gibson," *The Paris Review* 197 (Summer 2011), 106–49 (109).
5. By "the network," I refer to the notional composite that combines (and popularly confuses) the Internet, the Web, cellular data networks, the GPS satellite network, over copper, fiber optics, radio waves—in other words, the network as it's experienced by most people in their daily lives.
6. William Gibson interviewed by Robert Hilferty, 2009, YouTube (aitchayess), http://m.youtube.com/?reload=9&rdm=mfca6baq#/watch?v=GXaU_FLaSzo&desktop_uri=%2Fwatch%3Fv%3DGXaU_FLaSzo.
7. Marcos Novak, "Eversion: Brushing Against Avatars, Aliens, and Angels," in *From Energy to Information: Representation in Science and Technology, Art and Literature*, eds. Bruce Clarke and Linda Dalrymple Henderson (Stanford: Stanford University Press, 2002), 309–23. A version of the essay first appeared in *Hypersurface Architecture AD* 69 (London: Academy Editions, 1999), 9–10.

8. Marcos Novak, in exhibit sponsored by UCSB's Media Arts and Technology program, 2008, "Turbulent Topologies," http://mat.ucsb.edu/res_proj5.php.

9. Gibson has said this in various interviews, including on the radio in 1999. For one tracing of the saying, see Brian Dear, Brianstorms blog, October 16, 2004, http://brianstorms.com/archives/000461.html.

10. On the decline of Second Life, see Dan Heath and Chip Heath, *The Myth of the Garage and Other Minor Surprises* (New York: Crown Business, 2011), http://heathbrothers.com/the-myth-of-the-garage.

11. Jason Farman, *Mobile Interface Theory: Embodied Space and Locative Media* (New York and London: Routledge, 2011); and Eric Gordon and Adriana de Souza e Silva, *Net Locality: Why Location Matters in a Networked World* (Chichester, West Sussex, UK: Wiley-Blackwell, 2011).

12. William Gibson, *Spook Country* (New York: Putnam, 2007).

13. N. Katherine Hayles, "Cybernetics," in *Critical Terms for Media Studies*, ed. W. J. T. Mitchell and Mark B. N. Hansen (Chicago: University of Chicago Press, 2010), 144–56 (147–48).

14. Adam Greenfield, *Everyware: The Dawning Age of Ubiquitous Computing* (Berkeley, CA: New Riders, 2006), 73. One of the virtues of Greenfield's book is that it considers the legal and ethical implications for agency, privacy, and security of newly pervasive systems.

15. Clay Shirky, Foreword to B. Coleman, *Hello Avatar: Rise of the Networked Generation* (Cambridge, MA, and London, UK: MIT Press, 2011), iv–xiv.

16. Nathan Jurgenson, "Digital Dualism versus Augmented Reality," Cyborgology blog, February 24, 2011, http://thesocietypages.org/cyborgology/2011/02/24/digital-dualism-versus-augmented-reality.

17. Nathan Jurgenson, "The IRL Fetish," *The New Inquiry*, June 28, 2012, http://thenewinquiry.com/essays/the-irl-fetish.

18. Nicholas Carr, "Digital Dualism Denialism," Rough Type blog, February 27, 2013, http://roughtype.com/?p=2090.

19. The advantage of the metaphor of *coining* is that it suggests bringing a term into currency, rather than that more elusive thing—invention and first use. Though some may have used "digital humanities" before 2001, I follow Matthew Kirschenbaum's account of the term's coming into currency in "What is Digital Humanities and What's it Doing in English Departments?," in *Debates in the Digital Humanities*, ed. Matthew K. Gold (Minneapolis, University of Minnesota Press, 2012), 3–7. See also Patrik Svensson, "Humanities Computing as Digital Humanities," *DHQ* 3.3 (2009), http://digitalhumanities.org/dhq/vol/3/3/000065/000065.html.

20. Stephen Ramsay and Geoffrey Rockwell, "Developing Things: Notes Toward an Epistemology of Building in the Digital Humanities," in *Debates*, ed. Gold, 75–84; Bethany Nowviskie, "Eternal September of the Digital Humanities," in *Debates*, ed. Gold, 243–48.

21. This was for the collection, ed. Susan Schreibman, Ray Siemens, and John Unsworth, *A Companion to Digital Humanities* (Oxford: Blackwell, 2004), http://digitalhumanities.org/companion. On this shift from "digitized" to "digital," see Kirschenbaum, "What is?," in *Debates*, ed. Gold, 5.

22. William Gibson, *Neuromancer* (New York: Ace Books, 1984), 51.

23. In a conversation with Timothy Leary in 1989 that was later edited for *Mondo 2000*, Gibson suggests that the cyberpunk protagonist of *Neuromancer*, literally addicted to cyberspace, has an orgasmic epiphany at the end of the novel, a "transcendent experience," in which, interestingly, he recognizes the body, the "meat," from which he has been estranged, "as being this infinite complex thing." In the novel, it's referred to as "the flesh the cowboys mocked" (239). Intriguingly, at the time, Gibson and Leary were discussing the development of a video game based on *Neuromancer*. R. U. Sirius, ed., "Gibson and Leary Audio (*Mondo 2000* History Project)," Accerler8or blog,

December 23, 2011, http://acceler8or.com/2011/12/gibson-leary-audio-mondo-2000-history-project.

24. Norbert Wiener, *Cybernetics: or Control and Communication in the Animal and the Machine* (Cambridge, MA: MIT Press, 1948).

25. Vernor Vinge, *True Names*, first published in *Dell Binary Star* 5 (1981), reprinted in James Frenkel, ed., *True Names and the Opening of the Cyberspace Frontier* (New York: Tom Doherty Associates, TOR, 2001), 239–330, and available online at http://ny.iadicicco.com/Finished/20,000%20Ebooks/Vernor%20Vinge/Vernor%20Vinge%20-%20True%20Names.pdf. Vinge's story is set in the year 2014. Later, Neal Stephenson's *Snow Crash* (New York: Bantam, 1992) would imagine the Metaverse, which inspired the developers at Linden Lab to create Second Life in 2003. Both Vinge's and Stephenson's worlds are more explicitly gamelike than Gibson's. Fittingly, Vinge's more recent *Rainbows End* (New York: Tor, 2006) is set in a world of AR, an environment closer to the actual 2014.

26. N. Katherine Hayles, *How We Became Posthuman: Virtual Bodies in Cybernetics, Literature, and Informatics* (Chicago: University of Chicago Press, 1999), 38.

27. *Wired Style: Principles of English Usage in the Digital Age*, ed. Constance Hale (New York: Hardwired, 1996), 66–67.

28. Hayles, *How We Became Posthuman*, 35.

29. See https://plus.google.com/+projectglass. And see Joshua Topolsky, "I Used Google Glass: The Future, With Monthly Updates," *The Verge*, February 22, 2013, http://theverge.com/2013/2/22/4013406/i-used-google-glass-its-the-future-with-monthly-updates.

30. Ian Bogost, "Beyond the Elbow-patched Playground," author's blog, August 23 and August 25, 2011, http://bogo.st/xy.

31. Kirschenbaum, "Digital Humanities As/Is a Tactical Term," in *Debates*, ed. Gold, 415–28 (418).

32. Roberto Busa, S.J., foreword to Schreibman et al. eds., *Companion*, http://digitalhumanities.org/companion.

33. Bruce Sterling, *Shaping Things* (Cambridge, MA: MIT Press, 2005).

34. August C. Bourré, "An Inteview With William Gibson," *Canadian Notes & Queries* (CNQ), August 17, 2011, http://notesandqueries.ca/an-interview-with-william-gibson.

35. Jerome P. McDonough, Robert Olendorf, Matthew G. Kirschenbaum, Kari Kraus, Doug Reside, Rachel Donahue, Andrew Phelps, Christopher Egert, Henry Lowood, Susan Rojo, *Preserving Virtual Worlds Final Report*, 2010, https://http://ideals.illinois.edu/handle/2142/17097.

36. Ian Bogost, "Gamification is Bullshit," author's blog, August 8, 2011, http://bogost.com/blog/gamification_is_bullshit.shtml.

37. Jesse Schell, "Design Outside the Box," presentation, DICE (Design, Innovate, Communicate, Entertain), February 18, 2010, http://g4tv.com/videos/44277/DICE-2010-Design-Outside-the-Box-Presentation.

38. Katie Salen and Eric Zimmerman, *Rules of Play: Game Design Fundamentals* (Cambridge, MA: MIT Press, 2004).

39. Jesper Juul, *A Casual Revolution: Reinventing Video Games and Their Players* (Cambridge, MA: MIT Press, 2009).

40. Steven E. Jones and George K. Thiruvathukal, *Codename Revolution: The Nintendo Wii Platform* (Cambridge, MA: MIT Press, 2012).

41. Nick Montfort, *Twisty Little Passages: An Approach to Interactive Fiction* (Cambridge, MA: MIT Press, 2003).

2

DIMENSIONS

The digital network and the physical world are still sometimes talked about as if they were separate, parallel universes, or different "dimensions" of reality, in the popular or science-fiction sense of the term. But in recent years, the metaphors behind the term have been foregrounded, made obvious, because their premises have been everywhere disrupted. That way of thinking about the digital and the physical has begun to lose its transparency, as it were, so that, newly opaque and in front of us, the idea of the dimensional divide has been exposed. That explains, I think, the often-reported sense that a rift has opened between the supposedly separate worlds of the digital and the physical. Not that people consciously believe the divide is real, necessarily, but that the divide has in the past *felt* real, and that it feels now as if we're living at the breach.

So the language of two dimensions, and therefore of the possibility of interdimensional experience, persists, often paradoxically arising at just those places where the doubleness of digital and physical is breaking down. James Bridle, designer and leader of the New Aesthetic movement, has said, "The Internet is not a space . . . the network is not a space—it's like a whole other dimension."[1] I think he means that the digital network is an already available perspective on the existing world, just one that has been difficult to perceive as such, but is now increasingly breaking into our field of perception. Contemporary networked environments, city streets or airports or workplaces or homes, often feel interdimensional, as if points of contact with digital data were wormholes or tiny rifts in the fabric of everyday life, revealing (sometimes with a chill of uncanny recognition) how close the digital dimension has been for some time now. If the network has everted, as William Gibson says, has "colonized" the physical world around us, then we know this because signs of increasingly ubiquitous data are everywhere we look. In the words of another science-fiction author,

H. P. Lovecraft, "strange, inaccessible worlds exist at our very elbows," but the increasing presence of the digital network all around us in the world has begun to "break down the barriers" between what had *seemed* separate realms of existence, the digital and the physical.[2]

The Semiotics of QR Codes

It may sound surprising, but I think there may be no better example of this interdimensional experience in everyday life than QR codes, those inscrutable little squares printed on everything that you scan with a smart phone, "quick-response" triggers or gateways between physical objects or places and the data of the Internet (see Figure 2.1). They're like a (one-dimensional) bar code with an added second dimension, their marks laid out on a 2D x–y grid instead of in a line. The darker squares in three corners are visual anchors that allow the scanning phone's camera to properly align the view, and various regions inside the larger square are set aside by the conventions of the ISO standard for the encoding of different kinds of data, using the tiny black tile-like or pixel-like squares in varying patterns. More than the older bar codes, at least in their most familiar uses, QR codes face outward, toward the public. So far, they've been less about inventory management, for example, than about marketing, taking people to the URLs of products or companies. They became widespread shortly after the introduction of smartphones in 2006–2007 gave large numbers of people a way to scan them wherever they were encountered. You see them in shop windows, on real-estate yard signs, on business cards, paper cups, stickers on your bananas, flyers for campus events, the back of business envelopes, badges at conferences. They mark up the world and link it to data. However, at least so far, they have stopped short of creating what Bruce Sterling calls "spimes," fully networked objects, with metadata attached to them, that can be tracked and managed (*Shaping Things*). They offer some real affordances, at least theoretically. They scale efficiently and can encode data at fairly high densities, for example; a tiny square can contain a great deal. And, of course, they do save time spent typing URLs (and are more accurate than typing).[3] But so far, more often than not, the little squares have seemed to function as magical talismans of connectedness, expressions of the *desire for* connectedness, really. They say "this thing or place is networked," or "data are here," but often in the predictable, simplified form of opening a URL on your phone. Often their appearance and display betray the general uncertainty surrounding their use, the suspicion that they're nothing but a gimmick. For example, some are given an image shadow, so the cryptic square itself looks like a 3D object, as if they were large black and white stamps stuck on the posters or print ads of which they're a part. Sometimes you see them printed on an 8.5 × 11 inch sheet of paper with instructions added in large black type, just in case users are still unfamiliar with the concept: "Scan This With a Mobile Phone App." (Just printing the URL would be easier and save toner.) Maybe it's assumed that, at this stage, the relative novelty of QR codes will entice some people to try scanning them in situations where they'd never stop to type in or write down a URL. Advertisers are always interested in any attention-getting device. There's a Guinness pint glass with a QR code on it that can only be seen when beer fills the glass (and can be seen most clearly when the beer is dark stout). Scanning it links to a Foursquare check-in link and additional Web content advertising Guinness. Some companies have incorporated them into printed logos—in print ads, the department store Macy's red star, for example, sometimes has one in the center—so that every act of branding is also linked to online data, or the public's awareness that some such data exist.

Many complain that the codes are pointless, non-functional, as they are so often used as short-cut substitutes for printed URLs. Sometimes they're placed on a Website as a link to yet another Website, when a simple HTML hyperlink would do, or on in-store displays linking to the store's own Website. Web designers denounce them, people seem baffled by their sudden proliferation, but, as I write this, QR codes show no signs yet of fading away. If anything, they seem to have become more accepted, more mundane, just another banal feature of the data-soaked urban environment.

FIGURE 2.1 QR code for this book's Tumblr

FIGURE 2.2 QR code with instructions

Like other banal found objects that send interestingly mixed messages, QR codes have, of course, been picked up by artists. They look like etched tattoos and, like UPC (universal product code) barcodes before them, they have been turned into tattoos, which when scanned show an animated GIF or the wearer's most recent tweet. Whether they come with some of the (cyber)punk anti-consumerist associations of the barcode tattoos is another question. An article on the Style Blog of *The Washington Post*, December 19, 2011, condescendingly advised that,

> when it comes to tattoos, which will be on your body presumably forever, an emerging technology that is almost certain to become obsolete within

your lifetime may not hold up over the years. When the bearer of a QR code tattoo is 60 and the scanners have long been replaced with something more efficient, that tattoo will be a quaint but non-functioning reminder of simpler times in the first decade of the century.[4]

But surely the point of such tattoos in most cases is to flaunt the friction between permanent and ephemeral, to mark one's body with a cryptic-looking, fast-changing sign of rapid change itself. The irony is being engraved in the flesh with a mark of the technological present, already looking a little dated, like a body augmentation in a 1980s cyberpunk story. The desired effect may be, not the conventional, fashionable "cool" that the article assumes, but the darker irony of using a permanent marker for such a fleeting link to ephemeral (and presumably etherial) data.

Dutch new-media artist Sander Veenhof combined the format of the QR code with a working animation of John Conway's *Game of Life* simulation program. An actual URL can be typed in to produce the source-image QR code, which immediately begins to mutate as tiny square dots appear or disappear, the pattern shifting algorithmically.[5] At the top of the Web page, the results of each new mutation—new codes—are printed in rapid succession: mostly bad, random-string URLs. This creates an odd feedback system, between (working and nonworking) URLs and (typed and generated) QR codes. The whole work suggests a metaphorical association between the little dots of artificial life, representing the emergent complexity of evolving organisms in a constrained ecosystem, and the little dot matrices of data encoded all around us in our own environment, on signs and packaging and museum walls, signs of emergent data that may evolve into something more compelling if allowed to run their course.

One of the most dramatic uses was at the 2012 Venice Architecture Biennale, where Russia constructed its national pavilion, made up of multiple buildings, the surfaces of which were covered in QR codes, like hundreds of intricate tiles.[6] Visitors walked around inside the large, sometimes domed structures pointing mobile devices at the walls and ceilings in order to access materials on a planned futuristic, real-life city, Skolkovo, which has aspirations to become a kind of Silicon Valley near Moscow.

And, of course, each new Google Books page includes a QR code with that book's bibliographic information. At present, in the examples I've tried, the code on the page links to . . . the same page, so that scanning it produces a mobile version of the page on one's phone, complete with a smaller version of the same QR code, an infinite regress with no apparent purpose. But, as part of the metadata record of a book, the code could conceivably be repurposed in any number of ways. An advance video for Google's Project Glass, the HUD and camera application for reading AR tags and accessing the network out in the world, showed a user wearing the product, which looks like a pair of glasses with no lenses, supporting the device over one eye.[7] The user finds the music section in New

York's Strand Bookstore, then locates a book on playing the ukulele. All very physical, except for the directions to the store and the right section. What this video doesn't show, but Google's own earlier Goggles project has been used for, is the user scanning the book's QR code and being taken to a detailed information page about the title. This would presumably make it even easier and less obvious to engage in what book retailers bitterly call "showrooming," using the brick-and-mortar store to shop for what they buy online. Or you might go to the information page in order to see if there are newer titles in a popular series before buying a paper copy of the volume displayed in the store. Either way, the use of the QR code in such displays of books, as with any physical merchandise, would save time and keystrokes (and thus make it more likely the customer would bother looking up additional information). And, perhaps more significantly from Google's point of view, it would control the results of the search, linking directly to whatever data file, image, or URL is encoded in the little printed square. If Google Books' QR codes were actually used in such a scenario, the online destination would be the Google Books page, where the e-book might be on sale. The same device that scans the code displays the data that the code contains, all in a couple of seconds.

The significance of all these proliferating encrypted marks, like little canceled postage stamps stuck on various things in the environment, is worth thinking about. Even fetish objects can mean something—maybe especially fetish objects, and most especially when their practical uses are not clear. They are usually about desire. For example, just in terms of design, it's intriguing that QR codes go the bar code one dimension better with their matrix layout—as if this might indicate something about the complexity of the data to which they're linked (no longer just an inventory number, say, but an entire Website or image, and in some sense the open possibilities of the Web as a whole) and the trajectory of those data's emergence into the world. One example in Seoul, Korea, was created by sculpted objects out on the street, like a sideways architectural model of a cityscape, all in white, with obelisks of various heights standing out from the square surface. When the sun is at its height—during the downtown lunch hour—the shadows of the shapes form a matrix of squares that is a QR code and can be scanned for special sales offers in the surrounding businesses. Blatantly commercial, this is nonetheless an interesting example of the metaphor of dimensional transit that I think also helps to explain the semiotics behind QR codes: A 3D white object, in the right light, casts a shadow of itself as a 2D code that when scanned directs you to the surrounding physical buildings (which are modeled in an abstract way in the all-white 3D object with which you started). QR codes *encode* in more than one sense—they stand as signs for an unspoken idea, the idea that the network and its data are connected to the grid of the physical world, and that those connections can be revealed by way of readily available, cheap, and ubiquitous acts of dimensional translation. People pointing and scanning is how they work, and that may be the point for now: to get people to engage with the link in that relatively active way. You have to stop and point your phone and scan a QR code. This is weirdly redundant, and it annoys many people, but from a marketing point of view it may be superior to the infamous *Minority Report*-style micro-targeted AR ads that many now predict. You have to do something to reveal the data, so you're already at least minimally engaged. And what you're doing is triggering a translation from one code to another, and then to another, practicing the process, exploring the possibilities of such acts of decoding and encoding in today's mixed-reality environment.

One example I saw was a QR code on the back of a white panel van for a construction company, but accompanied by a little glyph, the image of a cell phone emanating a series of nested curved lines, a semi-universal sign for WiFi signal or other radio waves, in this case the wireless connection of phone with code (see Figure 2.3). It looked like a strange version of the iconic pictograms you see on warning signs ("falling rocks!") or painted on lanes in the street ("no bikes") or in instruction booklets ("nut connects to bolt"). In this case, the QR code came with pictographic instructions saying, "scan using your cellphone's radio waves." I know that, like other pictograms, it's meant to be ergonomically efficient, a faster way to communicate ("dispose of trash here" or "don't walk!"). But for whom is a glyph + QR code like this intended, really? Potential customers of this contractor who happen to be following the van but don't know how to use their phones to read the code?

The image on the van made me think of the Pioneer spacecraft or Arecibo radio telescope message icons that Carl Sagan helped develop in the 1970s for

FIGURE 2.3 QR code with glyph

communicating with aliens, etched plates with line drawings that "said" something like "male and female humans on the third planet from the Sun," sent to eldritch Others who would be capable of decoding the semiotics of the images. The QR code is an encoded protocol for accessing data, and is in that sense an act of encrypted transmission. With it included in the image, alongside the little picture of a cell phone, the whole thing is reminiscent of the related Arecibo message, which was also beamed out into space, but in the form of a binary string to be decoded into a pixelated pictogram saying the same sort of thing: "We are Earthlings." In a sense, that is what QR codes like this are doing: beaming out encoded messages to unknown but nominally intelligent life out there on the streets—somebody with a cell phone who can figure out how to scan with it and thus link the truck to the less terrestrial realm of digital data (in this case, just a Website).

I'd submit that QR codes *are* an interesting phenomenon, in part because they're so basic, because they so nakedly reveal the gesture of connecting data with the physical world, in fact reveal *the cultural desire to make* that gesture. QR codes such as the one on the van are in effect visible glitches, signs of the uneven process of eversion itself. Sometimes they're nothing more than glitches, nothing more than failed gestures. But they're everywhere, reminding us what's at the heart of the eversion of cyberspace: the process of encoding/decoding, of linking the world to a world of data. The QR code + pictogram I saw on the van is a symptom of a more general anxiety about the acts of decoding/encoding/decoding, the acts of translation, involved in this process—from digital to physical to digital again. That process is ultimately the point of the codes, the deeper purpose lying behind the explicit goal of getting someone who is parked behind the van at a stoplight to point their cell phone at the image in order to open the company Website. QR codes make more sense if we interpret them as a cultural symptom—mundane signs that someone is trying to communicate with invisible, unknown intelligences out there somewhere in the ether—in "the digital realm."

New Aesthetic Irruptions

If QR codes are the simplest, most blatant signs of the eversion out in the world (maybe with the exception of those tall, fabric teardrop banners standing on sidewalks that seem designed to look like flags in Google Maps), there are subtler signs everywhere, increasingly. One group of designers and artists looking for these signs goes under the umbrella term New Aesthetic. In an essay on a panel presentation by some of those associated with the group at the South By Southwest conference in 2012, Bruce Sterling both praises the potential and critiques the limitations of what he calls the design fiction of this movement or aesthetic, and especially as represented in James Bridle of London's Really Interesting Group, whom Sterling calls "the master of the salon."[8] Sterling is particularly questioning the group's implicit focus on a kind of artificial intelligence (AI), on how machines see the world, on the nostalgia of 8-bit or 16-bit imagery, and he judges that, so far, the movement has mostly collected an under-curated "heap of eye-catching curiosities." But it's clear from the ongoing collection and from Bridle's talks in particular that the New Aesthetic is about spotting something emerging in a variety of cultural representations, about noticing signs of "something coming into being," as artists and designers give "the real world the grain of the virtual."[9] These two worlds, Bridle recognizes, were once seen as separate but are now "eliding" everywhere you look, representing an "irruption of the digital into the physical world." In other words, they are signs of the eversion.

Indeed, Bridle has said in a blog post that, "the network is not space (notional, cyber or otherwise) and it's not time (while it is embedded in it at an odd angle), it is some other dimension entirely."[10] But, he adds, "meaning is emergent in the network," and the New Aesthetic is about this emergence, which I take to be Gibson's eversion under another name. Its signs are irruptions from this "other dimension," as Bridle says, whether pixelated designs on clothing, umbrellas, or on the tail sections of airliners, or the increasing presence of flying drones over-head, whether for art, for surveillance, or for warfare, musical compositions using audio glitches, or works of 8-bit street art that look like objects from old video games that show up on a wall or the sidewalk. One vivid example of street art Bridle has included in his slideshow presentations is a piece called *Pixel Pour* by Kelly Goeller, made by converting a mundane curved black pipe on a New York street into a spout from which pixelated blue water with white foam appeared to be pouring. It was created in mid April 2008 on a sidewalk on 9th Street between 2nd and 3rd Avenues—and was quietly removed within a few days.[11] Goeller created a second version, *Pixel Pour 2.0*, installed in SoHo, on Mercer Street between Howard and Grand. Goeller made the "pixels" (or "voxels," really; they're 3D, though the painted surfaces are meant to *look* 2D from a distance) from MDF particleboard squares, then painted them with acrylic and pieced them together with wood glue. The illusion of a 2D pixelated irruption of the digital from the 3D black spigot in the physical world was, of course, created using mundane physical materials, the artist picturing in an imaginative overlay the "digital" water.

The 2008 work resonated widely. Besides Bridle's (anonymous) use of it to illustrate the New Aesthetic, media-studies specialist Julian Bleeker photographed it in three stages—when it was new, after it was tagged with graffiti, and the empty sidewalk and spigot after the work was removed—and his Flickr set was noticed with a positive comment ("Dang") by science-fiction author Bruce Sterling (brucesflickr).[12] Eventually, a promotion for the animated feature film with a retro video-game setting, *Wreck-It Ralph*, turned a London street (Brick Lane) into a display of constructed 3D "8-bit" objects, including a knock-off (and unattributed) version of Goeller's *Pixel Pour*.[13] The effectiveness of the original work depended on the play between 2D and 3D, pixelated and "normal," objects from a digital

FIGURE 2.4 *Pixel Pour* by Kelly Goeller, http://kellotron.com

dimension out in the physical world. It worked so well because, as spontaneously installed (and uninstalled) street art, it figured, like a particleboard metaphor, the feeling of encountering sudden, unexpected irruptions of digital realities into the everyday physical environment.

Bridle also cites in his litanies of New Aesthetic irruptions another example so mundane you see it every day online, the CAPTCHA security tests when you sign on to Websites, in which machine-read texts, one or two words at a time, are offered up as gateways for supposedly human readers (that's the point). These are all, for Bridle, examples of our

> collaboration with technology, and a useful visual shorthand for that collaboration has been glitchy and pixelated imagery, a way of seeing that seems to reveal a blurring between "the real" and "the digital," the physical and the virtual, the human and the machine. It should also be clear that this "look" is a metaphor for understanding and communicating the experience of a world in which the New Aesthetic is increasingly pervasive.

Nowadays, it feels as though the digital network is breaking through to the physical world, to the everyday physical dimension in which we live, as if through cracks that have opened in the fabric we once believed separated the mundane world from cyberspace. The result is irruption, eversion, a new mixed reality in progress, still haunted by the earlier metaphor of different dimensions.

Multidimensional Game Worlds

It's not all about retro-style 8-bit or pixel art for James Bridle and others interested in the New Aesthetic, but Bridle does remark that the game *Minecraft*, with its game world constructed by players out of volumetric blocks (more voxels than pixels, therefore, but with a similar aesthetic effect), "has a lot to answer for" ("Waving"). For me, games and game platforms offer particularly suggestive examples, not necessarily (as Bridle implies) because games teach us how machines see the world, but because games have for so long deliberately experimented with modeling the world, and have done so from a media perspective that takes as given the constitutive role of digital technology. For obvious reasons, game designers tend to assume that digital technology constructs worlds, and they've often been highly self-conscious about the implications of that assumption. In fact, because the evolution of game worlds, crudely speaking, has been associated with increasing dimensions, from text-only forms—which might be thought of as 1D because they are experienced in a linear fashion—to 2D and then 3D worlds, game designers have had to think about dimension as a design problem. In recent years, art games, such as *Braid* or *Fez*, along with some mainstream commercial titles (especially Nintendo's Mario games) have self-consciously focused on dimensions and navigating their differences as themes. *Braid* and other platformer games with which it shares a family relation are obviously about movement through 2D gamespace, left to right, mostly, jumping or climbing up and down. The fact that 2D side-scrolling game worlds have in some cases been supplanted by 3D versions, and in other cases have been crossed with them, making strange hybrids, suggests that the whole genre has continued to be about exploring the problem of dimensionality. The Mario franchise embodies the history of this exploration, from *Donkey Kong* to *Super Mario 64* to *Super Mario Galaxy*. *Super Paper Mario* famously built in the ability to toggle between dimensions—the player can switch from 2D to 3D views for brief periods, adding a fresh perspective (literally) on its puzzles—and *Super Mario Galaxy* 1 and 2 made sandbox puzzles out of planetoids, each of which is a (game) world of its own, with sometimes weird physics the player has to deal with.

The preoccupation of indie art games with 2D side-scrolling platformers is in part about employing a knowing, lo-fi, retro aesthetic, often using an 8-bit graphic style, and is in part about what's practical or even doable by a single person or small team on a limited budget. Either way, it's a way of making a virtue of necessity. But it's also often a way to return to foundational questions about game worlds, starting with the question of what happens when you add a dimension (literally) or are aware of multiple dimensions as possibilities for gameplay.

New media have always experimented with the border where different medial "dimensions" meet, with points of eversion. Think, for example, of early experiments with mixing animation and live-action film—Gene Kelly tap dancing with Jerry the cartoon mouse in *Anchors Aweigh* (1945), or Winsor McCay morphing from live performer on the vaudeville stage in front of the screen to realistic animated image of himself on the screen in one of the earliest animated theatrical hits, *Gertie the Dinosaur* (1914). When the live McCay stepped up to the screen, slipped behind it, and was replaced by his filmic image (in the same tuxedo and at the same scale), the illusion suggested that he had stepped through the looking glass, crossed over from the real world to the virtual world of animated cartoons (still in their infancy as a medium). Toying with the imagined portal between the real world and the virtual world was a very early device in film. One of the most famous stories in the history of cinema—in fact, a story with the status of founding myth—concerns the Lumière brothers' 1895 short film, *L'arrivée d'un train en gare de la Ciotat*, in which a train comes into a crowded station, aiming out toward the audience as if the viewers were standing on the platform. According to legend, the moving image so terrified the original audience, who could not tell illusion from reality, that they leapt from their seats in a panic. The story is almost certainly apocryphal, but it still tells us something about the historical imagination of media. In 1935, the Lumière brothers exhibited a remake of *L'arrivée d'un train* in a stereoscopic 3D format.[14] Knowing this, one might be tempted to read the traditional legend as proving that movie fans have always sought more and more realistic forms of total immersion. The legend assumes that the uncanny realism of the original film was its attraction and thrill —to the naive audience unfamiliar with cinematic conventions, the train appeared to be coming out of the screen and out into the room—and that thrill remained the point of the remake four decades later, only more so. But what if, instead, the story reveals that movie audiences, and audiences for other media, have been for 120 years fascinated by the ambiguity between 2D and 3D, compelled by the irruption of elements of an artificial world into the real world (and, potentially, vice versa)? What if the point of the train and Gertie the dinosaur was imaginative play, experimental probing, at the permeable membrane between worlds, real and artificial, physical and virtual?

I think something like this experimental, exploratory urge motivates the design of many of today's indie art games. But they possess a new urgency because today's version of the boundary between worlds is volatile and porous—and it's where we live, as we see all around us signs of the irruption of the virtual into the physical, of a mixed reality in which we're called to negotiate between dimensions.

That's how I understand the apparent design of Marc ten Bosch's promised game *Miegakure*, for example, which has so far only been seen in preview glimpses. It's an art game about adding a fourth *physical* dimension, rather than just thinking of time as the fourth. In *Miegakure*, the experience of multidimensionality is narratively or figuratively structured: as the irruption of one dimension into another, in other words, as a kind of eversion. The player swaps between dimensions, but usually the purpose is to cause a block or other object to protrude into a dimension where it was previously invisible or inaccessible. Warps, wormholes, cracks in the fabric separating one dimension from another are where strategy unfolds and the key moves are made. In this respect, Valve's *Portal* games can be seen as a related experiment: You play by discovering ways to tunnel through the 3D maps as if they had been folded or warped. The portals you shoot with your portal gun are, in effect, dimensional wormholes. But gameplay in *Miegakure*—and in many related indie platformers—is explicitly about negotiating the extrusions of one dimension into another.

Jonathan Blow's much-celebrated game *Braid* (2008), though it toys with some 2D and 3D spatial transits, is most significantly focused on the fourth dimension of time. The game was prototyped using an avatar in blue with a red hat—clearly Mario—and its roots in classic platformers run deep. You play as Tim (whose name is close to Time), and you are trying to rescue a princess from an abducting monster. But the story feels more serious, based on the portentous soundtrack and layered background art, than the *Donkey Kong* plot might lead you to expect. In fact, Blow's rather serious personality and the heavy thematics of *Braid* led one wit to create a video in which various indie platformer avatars run into Mario in a bar.[15] Mario calls attention to all that he and his game have in common with Tim and *Braid*, while Tim, a stereotypically pretentious hipster, protests that he's much too cool for the comparison and rails against *Super Mario Bros.* as a "sellout" and a "mainstream kiddie game." Tim insists that Mario "wouldn't understand," as he's "just another suit." Bemused, Mario objects: "But you are *literally* wearing a suit right-a now!" The story of *Braid*, looming ominously behind the platform and puzzle gameplay, involves hidden emotional and plot dimensions, murky depths in the relationship between Tim and his princess, who can be read as an allegory for the atomic bomb, or the elusive ultimate knowledge of the universe— combined with extreme secrecy—that made the bomb possible.[16] Ultimate questions seem to lurk just behind the fabric of the game's universe, so that the mechanic that allows you to rewind game time in order to recover from a fall, try again to make a jump, or back your way into a puzzle, has philosophical resonances, even early on in the game. At the end, however, the payoff comes in the form of a level in which Tim runs along the bottom of the screen, pursued by a wall of flames but aided in overcoming the various obstacles by the Princess, who is moving along above him, as he attempts to save her from the abducting monster. When you then must rewind the entire level, however, you are shocked to find yourself experiencing the chase in reverse: The Princess is running *from* Tim (you) and desperately attempting to throw roadblocks in his way (rather than aiding him). The monster becomes her rescuer, as she leaps into his arms to escape from Tim. There have been intimations that the relationship was troubled all along, and these come to the surface as the final reversal plays out. Happening on one level of the game, this personal story is also allegorical of the larger story— about the fabric of the universe, ultimate knowledge, and its pursuit. The simple mechanic of rewinding the action of a platformer game becomes (as Patrick Jagoda has persuasively argued) a procedural, playable representation of the meaning of reality and what might be concealed behind what is taken for reality (18–19).

Braid is one of the games featured in the 2012 documentary, *Indie Game: the Movie*, which also looks at the development and release of *Super Meat Boy* and *Fez*.[17] At one point in that film (a moment that's included in the trailer), *Fez*'s developer Phil Fish describes the effect of being absorbed in making his own art game as a problem of perspective: "All we've been doing for four years is look at this—like this close, like [holds his hands right in front of his eyes]—you can't see anything else." It's an appropriate comment about a game that's all about the need to see from different perspectives the possibilities that remain hidden in plain sight, possibilities you can't see or take advantage of until you (literally) turn the problem around, using the left and right triggers of the Xbox controller to rotate the whole game world 90 degrees in one direction or the other, shifting from 2D to 3D—or back to 2D. As the opening of the game says, you rotate the game world in order to change your perspective—in more than one sense.

Fez was announced in 2007, while *Braid* was still in development. It won awards in advance but was not released (on Xbox Live Arcade) until April 2012. You play as Gomez, a small, all-white cartoon character in a colorful, pixelated universe of giant tower-worlds floating in the sky, which, whether they're styled as villages or castles, water gardens or islands in a sea, are often reminiscent of Magritte's famous, surreal painting of a castle in the Pyrenees, perched atop a giant rock floating suspended above the sea. (*Fez*'s worlds often incorporate temples or altars or pavilions at their peaks.) But the pixel-based, cubic forms of the worlds also invoke the tiled landscapes of *Super Mario Bros.*, for example, or the birds-eye maps of early adventure RPGs such as the Zelda or Final Fantasy franchises. Doors take you to interior rooms or other levels, cubes hover overhead until you grab them by jumping up to hit them. Negative-space niches, ledges, and overhangs look as if they were created by removing or rearranging the basic cubes with which the game world was created. (According to the interviews in *Indie Game: The Movie*, that's often precisely how they were created in Fish's image editor.) *Fez* sometimes looks almost as blocky as *Minecraft*, and, as in that game, the blocks are metaphors for pixels or bits (there are 8 "cube-bits" to find in the first level and 64 cubes and anticubes in all), figurative, primitive particles of the digital realm. The opening cutscene that follows your getting the magic red fez hat, with beautiful animated graphics, is glitchy in what we'd now call a New Aesthetic sort of way, revealing in sputtering glimpses the digital realm behind the visible game world, then shifting to a "reboot" of the game, complete with logos. Fish has said that the game world is essentially a "computer world . . . and every now and then the universe becomes unstable and has to defragment itself and reboot" (*Indie Game: The Movie*). Though he describes the game world as existing inside a computer, of course gameplay takes place at the boundary of the imaginary computer game world and the player's physical world. Every time you flip dimensions, you call attention to that perspective on the boundary. The glitchy moments are thus moments of self-consciousness that recall for the user at the controls, whose triggers change the dimensions of *Fez*'s world, that the larger gamespace of *Fez* is a hybrid digital and physical space, and that the game is a kind of allegory of the glitchy and interfused relationship of that hybrid space, which is to say, a lot like everyday reality.

Once you get the fez hat and reboot, you start once again in the same bedroom that opened the game, but this time wearing the magic fez that allows you to toggle between dimensions. You navigate in the usual platformer way, by running, jumping, and climbing, looking for shiny golden cubes and the invisible anticubes that are their counterparts. The story goes that the cubes are the remnants or shards of a larger cube destroyed in a catastrophic explosion—that destabilizing catastrophe mentioned earlier. If you don't find them all and put the fragments back together, according to the opening dialogue with the multicolored NPC helper-sprite, Dot, "the universe collapses with you in it. No pressure!" This is a pretext to gameplay, ironically inflected, of course. But the idea that the multidimensionsal fabric of the universe—of our hybrid digital/physical reality— is the object of the game's exploration *and deliberate construction* is also the serious thematic premise behind this art game.

Until that fabric collapses, there are no serious consequences for merely falling and dying as you jump and run on the rotatable platforms. You just respawn immediately, at or near your latest perch. And there are no real enemies or bosses to battle in *Fez*. You just explore, collect, reconstruct, and reveal the dimensions of the problem. At the very beginning of the game, you encounter a glowing Hexahedron, "a strange and powerful sentient artifact," that "reveals to [you] the mysteries of the third dimension" by granting you the magical fez, which floats down from above in a column of light. The artwork is whimsically pretty—lighter in style, less pretentious, than the lush layers of *Braid*—from the shifting colors of the sky to the tiny details, including tributes to Mario and Zelda in the form of tiny mushrooms and treasure chests that emanate light when opened, vines you climb from one level to another, floating platforms you jump to and from, and cubes above your head you jump to collect. There are also animated birds (seagulls?) calling and walking around in niches in the sides of towers, and tiny inchworms moving along the ground—lots of clever animated touches. The soundtrack music modulates in response to gameplay, and the sky cycles through multiple hues and shades, with abstract line-drawing clouds drifting by.

Playing *Fez* on an Xbox attached to a high-definition television screen is an aesthetically pleasing experience. But, especially for a first-time player or uninitiated watcher, the most noticeable thing about the game—the visual feature that most stands out—is the repeated shifting in perspective triggered by the player as she searches for a platform to jump to or a way around an obstacle. And the rotation is striking precisely because it causes an alternation between 3D and 2D views. Click and, whoosh, everything is flat like a classic side-scrolling platformer. Click again and, whoosh, the same structure has depth, and the two square platforms you just jumped between are revealed in another dimension to be many feet or meters apart, one floating behind another in space. In that new, third dimension, the same objects are transformed, either expanded or reduced, along with what they afford or constrain in the way of your gameplay. The most interesting thing about the mechanic is that the 3D world often affords *fewer* options for movement than the 2D world. What we think of as the optical illusion—that the two square ends of platforms viewed straight on appear to be alongside one another when aligned along the horizontal y-axis, even though they are "actually" cubes and are very far apart along the z-axis (once you can visualize depth)—turns out to be a navigable reality within the game, a kind of viable parallel universe of only two dimensions. Toggling with the controller triggers has a leveling effect, relativizing the 2D and 3D worlds, revealing them as interpenetrating dimensional realities, alternatives always available, despite the evidence of your senses, accessible with a simple but world-altering shift in perspective. Even your square heads-up inventory frame, which shows the number of cube shards and keys you've collected, can be rotated using the triggers to reveal that it's actually itself a cube, with space to store other items—a treasure map, for example. And that map, in turn, though it looks flat at first, can be rotated to reveal its edges and the slight accordion fold of its paper surface.

It's no accident that one of the devices you encounter in *Fez* is—what else?—giant QR codes. The game was in early development at around the time the codes first began to show up out in the world, and so it stands to reason programmers and developers might want to play with them in a new indie game. But it's interesting that Phil Fish and his then programmer partner, Renaud Bédard, saw them in the same context as other devices in the game: as puzzles linking different dimensions, based on encoding and decoding. Users later discovered that even the soundtrack of the game, when opened in an editor that graphically reveals the audio waveforms, contains QR codes at the end of sound files![18] (They reportedly encode a series of four-digit dates, the meaning of which is unknown.) In the game itself, you find the image of one giant QR code embedded in a kind of temple wall between tall pillars, for example, as if it were an enigmatic glyph left by a lost civilization, partially obscured by what looks like scaffolding. When completed, the code is scannable. You point a smartphone at the TV screen, and the reader application opens up a simple text file containing a cryptic string of LTs and RTs—a controller-pad button combo code that, when enacted, flips and re-flips the game world several times in a pattern and moves your avatar Gomez in order to reveal a previously invisible multicolored anticube, glowing and rotating in the air in front of the QR-code wall.

Fez is a puzzle platformer, and most of its puzzles that are not directly about jumping involve decoding of one sort or another, from the QR codes to a cryptic secret alphabet you first glimpse in the opening cutscenes on tablet-like slabs, as if they were the dialog boxes through which the giant yellow Hexahedron speaks to you. The characters of the alphabet are clearly reminiscent of the Tetrimino shapes from the ur-puzzle game, *Tetris*. *Tetris* patterns are sculpted into surfaces throughout the game world, as Fish admits (*Indie Game: The Movie*). As with the 8-bit graphics, the tribute to *Tetris* is part of the game's retro aesthetic, but it also calls attention to the importance in games, and in the digital world as a whole, of puzzles, acts of encryption and decryption—of encoding and decoding. When combined with the game's central mechanic, rotating the game world, the puzzles reinforce the sense that *Fez* is about the need to decrypt the world in order to reveal its digital foundations. In the context of the New Aesthetic, which appeared on the scene just as it was (finally) released, *Fez* looks like a meditation on the cryptic but ultimately meaningful relationship between different dimensions of the world, and the need to navigate between those dimensions in order to make meaning. The pixelated style, all the blocks, tiles, or bits in increments of 8, 16, 32, and 64—as well as its epiphanic glitches revealing the hidden digital infrastructure—suggest that the dimensions you must navigate are the physical and the digital, already intricately combined within a tricky, mixed-reality environment.

Art games such as *Fez*, as well as the unreleased *Miegakure* and the critically acclaimed *Braid*, can be seen as exploring in procedural terms some of the same metaphorical territory as literary fantasy fiction, such as Mark Z. Danielewski's *House of Leaves*, Thomas Pynchon's *Against the Day*, Haruki Murakami's *1Q84*, China Miéville's *The City & The City*—or works by Borges and Calvino before that—but also traditional science fiction such as *Flatland*, in which denizens of a 2D world learn to grasp the weirdness of 3D existence, and, perhaps most immediately, just in terms of its cultural influence on games and digital media in general, H. P. Lovecraft's stories. Of course, science fiction has always explored alien worlds, parallel universes, time travel, and the counterfactual worlds that are Earth's own imagined futures. But I have in mind a more specific variation of these themes: the paradox of living in two worlds at once, two overlapping realities, imaginings metaphorically based on what it's like to grasp the multiple dimensions of space–time that we *do* live in all the time. I think, in the past decade, such imaginings have often taken on an added significance, have often become allegories of the perceived overlapping realities that now characterize our own present moment—the digital and the physical.

This significance is discernible even in older works that were not, of course, intended to be read in this way, none more so than those by H. P. Lovecraft, whose fiction of the early twentieth century has for decades, now, been reread as relevant to emerging digital technologies. Lovecraft's stories contain a repeated motif of "eldritch" horrors from another dimension, "from beyond," that are only partly glimpsed when they break through briefly and extrude themselves into everyday reality: "strange, inaccessible worlds exist at our very elbows, and now I believe I have found a way to break down the barriers," one character declares, then reports, "I felt the huge animate things brushing past me and occasionally walking or drifting through my supposedly solid body." Passages such as the following one resonate in unexpected ways in our current media climate, a climate that includes New Aesthetic irruptions:

> Suddenly I myself became possessed of a kind of augmented sight. Over and above the luminous and shadowy chaos arose a picture which, though vague, held the elements of consistency and permanence. It was indeed somewhat familiar, for the unusual part was superimposed upon the usual terrestrial scene much as a cinema view may be thrown upon the painted curtain of a theatre. . . . I saw to my horror that they *overlapped* . . . the newly visible world that lies unseen around us.
>
> (Lovecraft, "From Beyond," loc. 2001–2011)

The augmented reality revealed in this horror story takes the form of overlapping worlds, momentarily inter-transpicuous, experienced with a frisson or chill of recognition, as having inhabited the same space all along.

If it seems odd that fantasy fiction from the 1920s would read so well as an allegory of our own technological moment, the moment of eversion, consider that our cultural relationship to the network has historically been partly defined by creative artists and writers, and by inventors and engineers who were inspired by artists and writers, and that many of those artists and writers were directly influenced by Lovecraft in particular, and by the fictional traditions he represented and to which he contributed in general, running from Mary Shelley through Jules Verne to Hugo Gernsback, and including Vernor Vinge, William Gibson, and Neal Stephenson. In his DH work on graphing the discourse of the Website TV Tropes, Elijah Meeks associates the Lovecraftian uncanny, this breaking-through from a parallel dimension, with "the weird geometry of the Internet" itself.[19] Lovecraftian dimensionality, "weird geometry," was, I suspect, baked into conceptions of the network at its inception, when it was often discussed as a sometimes uncanny mirror world—culminating in the dominant metaphor of cyberspace. Lovecraft's fiction now returns because it usefully figures the more recent eversion of the network, as the image of cyberspace fades. What had been relegated to another dimension is now colonizing this one, irrupting into our everyday reality. The connection is particularly clear in the case of AR—or its mundane instantiations in mobile maps and QR codes, which, to use Lovecraft's terms, superimpose digital realities—a "newly visible world that lies unseen around us"—on "the terrestrial scene," suggesting that a weird geometry connects the two worlds, especially at points of extrusion, places where the unseen reveals itself as a potential layer of experience.

The idea of weird geometry is evident throughout Lovecraft's work, but it's probably most fully represented in a 1926 short story, "The Call of Cthulhu." In that tale, a mysterious statue points to aliens who colonized the earth eons ago, The Great Old Ones, but are hidden in secret cities and waiting for their cue, the call of Cthulhu, to rise. *Fez* may not have been intentionally modeled on Lovecraft's descriptions of the uncanny cityscape; the images are by now overdetermined in games, films, and literature. Nonetheless, certain passages in Lovecraft read like detailed descriptions of the game's worlds. For example: "an unprecedented dream of great Cyclopean cities of titan blocks and sky-flung monoliths, all dripping with green ooze and sinister with latent horror. Hieroglyphics had covered the walls and pillars" (loc. 6217). Of course, on the surface, *Fez* may seem light rather than dark, cartoony rather than horrific. (The revelation of shadowy horrors is, by contrast, obviously at the heart of *Braid*, where time is the dimensional difference. The difference between the tones of the two games is reflected in their artwork and soundtracks.) But a closer look and more gameplay reveals Lovecraftian undertones everywhere in *Fez*'s iconic game worlds, some of which are tinged with undersea green light or darkened with thunderstorms, or look like abandoned temples etched with occult hieroglyphics. Actually, the game's dimension-flipping mechanic and initially sunny style can be read as attempts to counteract or keep at bay the anxieties represented by the fragmented, glitchy universe at the heart of its story. "The Call of Cthulhu," like *Fez*, represents this sometimes-anxious confluence of worlds in terms of weird geometry:

> broad impressions of vast angles and stone surfaces—surfaces too great to belong to anything right or proper for this earth, and impious with horrible images and hieroglyphs. . . . He said that the *geometry* of the dream-place he saw was abnormal, non-Euclidian, and loathsomely redolent of spheres and dimensions apart from ours . . . crazily elusive angles of carven rock where a second glance shewed concavity after the first shewed convexity.
>
> ("From Beyond," loc. 6598)

The weird geometry emerges more and more as the story is told, exemplified in details such as the "monstrously carven portal" that presents "a phantasy of prismatic distortion" (loc. 6617). Lovecraft inspired an important strand of fiction, films, and the popular imagination when it comes to the uncanny irruption of intuited but hidden dimensions of reality. No wonder the stories sometimes seem like premonitions of games like *Fez*—and of the larger metaphorical context of our present moment.

That context helps us see that the fascination of independent game designers with the side-scrolling platformer is more than simple nostalgia or convenience. It may have something to do with a desire to explore the theme of multidimensionality in a procedural, playable way. The weirdness of Lovecraftian geometry is the result of uncanny paradoxes. What seems outside is actually inside, what should be depth is surface (and vice versa), difficult to grasp aspects of dimensional space that were likely inspired in the first place by mathematical models of topology such as the Klein bottle, that mind-bending object whose inner and outer surfaces are one, a curved continuous surface always already turned inside out.

Another video game, Valve's acclaimed *Portal* (2007), makes this kind of geometry the basis of its celebrated gameplay mechanic, in which you shoot entrance and exit portals into the surfaces of the giant buildings of the game world, creating wormholes you can navigate through folded space. In a 2009 paper, Patrick LeMieux and Stephanie Boluk place *Portal* (and *Braid*) at the center of a genre or taxonomic family that they call "eccentric games." Against the trend in the game-design industry toward ever-increasing realism, eccentric games, they say,

> employ spatiotemporal effects which give the player access to logics indigenous to digital environments. . . . These logics often reference pop-physics theories and paradoxes such as those related to time travel, parallel realities, navigating multiple dimensions, folding time and space, quantum mechanics, probability engines, and the conflation of virtual and actual space.[20]

They connect the famous portal gun (the Aperture Science Handheld Portal Device) to the then-recently-emerged iPhone, when used as a handheld AR viewer. In particular they cite the Trover social-network app, which makes available people's photos and videos linked to geographic locations. Trover tells you when you're at a physical location that was the site of a recorded video, say, and allows you to play the video associated with that street corner or park or public building.

> Thus, if positioned consciously, the iPhone transforms into a temporal window or portal linking the viewer to multi-layered past and embedding the present with a feeling of historicized place. Instead of folding space as seen in the Aperture Science Handheld Portal Device, Trover folds time.
> (Ibid.)

The authors go on to discuss ARGs, as well as AR. The links between indie games that explore interdimensionality, ARGs taking place out in the world as well as on the Internet, and AR applications that connect data (such as crowd-sourced videos) to the physical world are, I believe, highly significant. What LeMieux and Boluk are describing is, I think, a media efflorescence around 2007–2008, including games and mobile apps, that was part of the larger phenomenon of the eversion, the collective sense that a kind of portal has opened up between hitherto separate dimensions, "the conflation of virtual and actual space." As they conclude, "These objects colonize a new home in what was once uncanny borderland."

As my earlier references to literary science fiction and the imaginative worlds of games should make clear, I'm using the term "dimension" in a broadly metaphorical way. The history of the word itself gives the term from mathematics, meaning "a mode of linear measurement, magnitude, or extension, in a particular direction," these broader associations. The basic geometrical sense of the term is the basis of *Flatland*, a story that turned the difference between 2D surfaces and the 3D depth in which our own bodies live into a fable of different worlds, different perspectives on reality, parallel universes, and imagined worlds. But, as the story and the OED remind us, even in geometry, when thinking about these differences, "the notion of measurement or magnitude is commonly lost, and the word denotes merely a particular mode of spatial extension," of different ways of being in the world. Figuratively, different *dimensions* refer to different possible aspects or ways of looking at a given situation or abstract object. We speak of exploring the multiple dimensions of a problem, for example, or discovering a new dimension in a relationship. When an art game such as *Braid* or *Fez* explores points of contact or portals of transition between dimensions, it means more than 2D vs. 3D. It encompasses the figurative and emotional meanings of the term as well, the sense that dimensions are meanings, that the irruption of a new dimension into a game world, or the real world, offers new ways of seeing. Of course, Lovecraft and interdimensionality in video games have been around a long time, but the renewed and intensified focus on them around the time of the eversion—on this theme of interdimensionality as expressed across a variety of cultural forms—is, I think, illuminating.

Multidimensional Texts

As Elijah Meeks suggests, Lovecraftian weird geometry is an apt metaphor for the new dimensions opened up via the vast data of the Internet itself. On the Humanist online discussion list, Meeks wrote in mid January 2012, "I'm a fan of Lovecraft's work and his concepts and think they are useful in framing our attempts to grapple with all manner of extremely complex digital objects." As I've been arguing, the biggest and most complex such digital object at present is the network itself. Willard McCarty has suggested as much (also on the Humanist listserv dedicated to humanities computing and DH), connecting Lovecraft's eldritch worlds with the emerging "vistas" of "total digitization" and the possibilities opened up by big data.[21] As I mentioned earlier, Meeks's remarks were in the context of a data-mining project in which he was engaged, a form of digital humanities research. Exploring the interdimensional nature of our mixed-reality moment is something art games share with the digital humanities, especially the new forms of digital humanities work that have emerged in the 2010s.

Contemporary video games offer vital examples of digital humanities in practice, creative works of cultural expression in digital media, living examples of the contemporary liberal arts, not just born digital but created to be experienced on the latest software and hardware platforms. But the digital humanities, at least in some quarters, has been somewhat slow to embrace the study of games, even though many DH practitioners and scholars are themselves avid gamers, fans, and collectors of games. Part of my purpose in this book is to bring the relationship of games and digital humanities out into the open, where its potential can continue to be explored.

I also believe games have much to teach the digital humanities about today's digital platforms and their cultural meanings, even in areas of specialization that may seem at first not at all gamelike, such as textual editing, text encoding, and the digitization of print texts and archival documents. All kinds of text, including literary texts, poems, plays, novels, and stories originally produced in the medium of print over the past 500 years, are now being digitized. But "digitized" can mean many things, and I'll have more to say about the way we conceptualize digitization in the next chapter. For now, digitizing sometimes just means being keyed in or scanned as digital files, more or less accurately transcribed, usually to be uploaded to the Web; sometimes it means that useful metadata are attached, sometimes not; sometimes such texts are made freely available, sometimes they're bundled as part of collections, commercial products sold by subscription or outright to university libraries. In the more scholarly versions of the process, digitization involves thoughtfully considered metadata, markup, or encoding, most likely these days according to a standard such as the text encoding initiative (TEI), or according to one or another experimental methods of standoff markup, or in more granular form as proper database records. At any rate, scholarly digitization should involve reconceiving of inherited literary works as they take on a digital mode of existence, not just transcribing the lexical content, the words of a text, but in effect "porting" a print text to digital platforms to be read and studied in potentially new ways, from different perspectives—in ways that may reveal its hitherto hidden dimensions. Note that the text already contains within itself innumerable possible dimensions of meaning, as textual theorist and digital humanities scholar Jerome McGann has argued for years.[22] All texts, but most vividly those with a literary or imaginative role in the culture, are multidimensional, in the sense that they prompt innumerable performances, ongoing rereadings and re-interpretations, but also in the sense that their potential meanings can be accessed from many different (sometimes contradictory) perspectives. The simplest example is that a text can be read for its narrative content, poetic effects, or expository argument—or it can be accessed backwards, as it were, through an index or concordance that first atomizes that lexical content into its separate words (with some excluded) and then rearranges the results alphabetically or in a digitally searchable format, reordering the text as a verbal matrix. The same text, different dimensions. As I pointed out in the previous chapter, the digital humanities is often said to begin with the computer-assisted concordance of the works of St. Thomas Aquinas, produced starting in the 1940s by Jesuit scholar, Father Roberto Busa. As Stephen Ramsay has suggested, there is a direct line between that foundational example of humanities computing and more experimental examples of textual interpretation in today's DH.[23] A text's—any text's—interpretive possibilities are always manifold, measured along different axes of relationship. Digital technologies can open up new views of those axes, those possibilities. So the goal of digital humanities work with texts is not simply to translate texts from print to digital environments, moving them from one world into another, and, as it's often feared, relegating the husk of the physical object to the darkness of storage stacks. It's to digitize texts in ways that reveal new dimensions and open up portals, modes of transit, between physical books or manuscripts and the digital transcriptions and metadata attached to them. The dimensions of texts include and are revealed by networked data, derived directly from texts or their various contexts. Such data now address themselves to texts as a matter of course, constituting a new dimension of textuality in the digital era.[24]

Jerome McGann argued, in a piece reprinted in the influential *Companion to Digital Humanities* (2004), for expanding the scope of digital textual practices, such as markup and archiving, but also visualization and analysis, in order to better represent the *n-dimensional* nature of texts (imaginative texts in particular).[25] Standard text encoding schemes (such as the TEI), he argued, are inadequate to represent the "markup" of various kinds, mostly in the form of invisible conventions and structures, that "pervades paper-based texts." For one thing, such digital encoding schemes focus primarily on the presumed structure of texts as determined by their linguistic features, whereas paper-based literary works "organize themselves along multiple dimensions, of which the linguistic is only one." McGann proposes a partial ontology of his own, a list of six "dimensions" that should ideally be considered in the process of digitization and markup. Besides the linguistic dimension, these include the graphical, documentary, semiotic, rhetorical, and social. Obviously, other lists could be produced. The broader point is that digitization should highlight and make accessible as many as possible of the multiple dimensions of literary texts and their meanings. A markup system such as TEI, according to McGann, is essentially two-dimensional: a map of discrete "content objects" arranged as nested trees (in an ordered hierarchy). But texts—especially imaginative texts—are *autopoetic* systems for generating their own possibilities, their own performed meanings, in a cybernetic/hermeneutic loop involving readers. In an experimental search for ways of representing (or triggering) that process in digital formats, McGann and his collaborators, including Johanna Drucker, Bethany Nowviskie, and others, made a significant decision: They designed a game. *Ivanhoe* was a role-playing game focused on texts as discourse-generating systems. It was first played via a text-only platform—in email exchanges. Although a number of designs were considered for interfaces, it finally appeared in playable form as a set of pie-chart-style visualizations of "moves" made by players within a "discourse field" spun out of a shared text. Gameplay involved writing and rewriting, with every move tracked and visualized by the digital environment. Walter Scott's romance-adventure novel, *Ivanhoe*, was just the first major work around which the game was played. As McGann says, the best models for this kind of self-conscious collaborative interpretation "descend to us through our culture in games and role-playing environments."[26]

In the *Companion to Digital Humanities* essay, McGann replaces the term dimensional with "dementianal"—a strategic and ludic act of linguistic play influenced by the work of Alfred Jarry, whose "'Pataphysics" McGann takes as model for performance (or, the term he prefers, "deformance") of critical discourse. But I want to stick to the vernacular first term, here, "dimensional," in order to make a point of my own. McGann's influential digital humanities work from this era treated the advent of digital technology as a productive irruption into print culture. Digital technology, he suggests, opened up a new perspective on the multidimensionality of texts, and it afforded an opportunity to more self-consciously and extensively represent and reveal sometimes hidden dimensions of the textual archive.

The areas of academic specialization, even within a multidisciplinary field such as the digital humanities, often obscure larger trends. If we zoom out, as if to get a satellite view of the field, the concerns of the digital humanities in recent years appear to be part of a set of broader contours, not confined to the academy. That metaphor, of the new perspectives opened up in a long zoom, is itself a reminder of an important adjacent area of literary history now often understood as being part of the digital humanities, Franco Moretti's call for a distant reading (as opposed to the close reading that has been central to literary studies since the late nineteenth century). In his influential 2005 monograph, Moretti defines for literary history "a new object of study: instead of concrete, individual works, a trio of artificial constructs—graphs, maps, and trees—in which the reality of the text undergoes a process of deliberate reduction and abstraction."[27] The key shift in method is from *texts* to *models*—in part because modeling is what computers do best[28]—so that Moretti's distant reading is, in effect, an affordance of digitization and the consequent possibility of treating large bodies of texts as data to be modeled, mined, and analyzed. Moretti anticipated by some years the public interest in Google Books, or other large, digitized corpora of texts, as a kind of (relatively) "big data" to be mined and graphed, whether using simple NGrams for frequency of words or more sophisticated techniques such as probabilistic topic modeling. The 2D line graphs of Moretti's literary history and the dynamic pie-graphs of *Ivanhoe* share an interest in revealing other dimensions of literary texts (though they focus on different dimensions or sets of dimensions). They both assume that the techniques usually associated with mathematics or engineering or the quantitative social sciences might provide the humanities with valuable insights.

Johanna Drucker (as we've seen, McGann's collaborator in the creation of *Ivanhoe*) has more recently sounded a cautionary note. She warns that the quantitative techniques taken from the sciences and social sciences are ultimately inappropriate for humanistic inquiry: "the ideology of almost all current information visualization is anathema to humanistic thought, antipathetic to its aims and values."[29] Interpretation, she says, is the basis of the humanities, and interpretation is "performative rather than declarative." In this way, "each instance or reading constructs a text; discourses create their objects; texts . . . are not static objects but encoded provocations for reading" (86, 88). It's a useful reminder that contrasting methods still obtain across the disciplines, and that, for example, probability is "not the same as ambiguity or multivalent possibility," as Drucker says (90). The latter are central to the humanities and have to be taken into account in digital humanities work. "Flexible metrics, variable, discontinuous, and *multidimensional* will be necessary" for sophisticated graphical analysis of texts from a humanities perspective (in the case of her own research, she has shown a particular interest in temporal relations) (94; my emphasis).

Probabilities are not the same as ambiguities. But, on the other hand, methods such as probabilistic topic modeling might well be able to point to, or expose for interpretation, the kinds of ambiguity humanists are interested in. Drucker is not arguing against all quantitative approaches, at any rate, but for more self-conscious and more critical uses of text mining, data analysis, and data visualization in humanities research, perhaps even for more visualizations of qualitative evidence, instead of only what is readily amenable to quantizing. But, in the process of making the argument, she gives perhaps too little credit to both scientific and digital humanities practitioners. Certainly, computer-science specialists working with data understand that graphs and other sophisticated forms of visualization make arguments (rather than transparently present positive facts). Likewise, most digital humanists who are seriously engaged with quantitative methods have no illusions about the tendentious and constructed knowledge such procedures afford. For example, Matthew Jockers, of the Center for Digital Research in the Humanities at the University of Nebraska, speaking specifically of Google's Ngrams, cautions that, "we must not be seduced by the graphs or by the notion that this data is quantitative and therefore accurate, precise, objective, representative, etc."[30] In fact, most serious practitioners see quantitative analysis as working in conjunction with more qualitative interpretation. Rather than naively opposing the supposed objective facts provided by quantitative methods to the subjective interpretations of qualitative approaches, DH scholars analyzing large corpora of texts tend to talk about differences in *scale*. This is a crucial distinction. Ted Underwood, of the University of Illinois, has begun to apply probabilistic topic modeling—via the technique known as Latent Dirichlet Allocation (LDA)—to available large corpora of texts, for example, the eighteenth- and nineteenth-century collection digitized by the HathiTrust project. He was trained as a literary critic, however, and he invariably argues that such analyses merely open our eyes to patterns not otherwise apparent, and that a feedback loop akin to the hermeneutic circle obtains in such work: You zoom out to look at the big data (or relatively big, in a humanities context), then you (or others) zoom in to interpret individual texts or authors in relation to the hypotheses opened up by the quantitative analysis, and so on.

Likewise, Matthew Jockers says that it's "the exact interplay between the macro and the micro scale that promises a new, enhanced, and perhaps even better understanding of the literary record. The two approaches work in tandem and inform each other."[31] He prefers the term "macroanalysis" to Franco Moretti's famous phrase "distant reading," in part because it emphasizes this dual approach. Moretti has unfortunately contributed to the confusion by claiming that "quantitative data are useful" precisely because "they are independent of interpretation" —although he also adds that such data "are challenging because they often demand an interpretation that transcends the quantitative realm"—and can work to falsify existing theoretical explanations of literary history (30). This sounds like the kind of implicit positivism Drucker is criticizing. Nonetheless, Moretti too has suggested that it's the shift in scale afforded by distant reading that really matters, not the supposed objectivity of the data. Quantitative analysis is, for him, only part of an overall approach that continues to require close reading, as well. Using terms from the discipline of history, he argues that "event, cycle, *longue durée*" are "three time frames which have fared very unevenly in literary studies" (14). Literary critics are comfortable with the first, the detailed event, up close, the individual text, line, or word. Literary theorists are comfortable with the last, "the very long span of nearly unchanging structures." But the middle term, "cycles," has been relatively neglected. This is a scale of attention that might reveal patterns at the level of genres, for example, "*temporary structures within the historical flow*" (14; emphasis in original). He uses graphs to plot a particular "life-cycle" in literary history, the rise and fall of certain genres of novel, which he speculates may reveal a more common pattern—"a sort of hidden pendulum of literary history" (18), genres that in effect, at any historical moment, "seem to arise and disappear together according to some hidden rhythm" (20)—and he later refers to "the cycle as the hidden thread of literary history" (26). He goes on to posit the changing of generations—and thus reading audiences and markets—as behind this (21).

It's not only the shifts in scale—from close to distant, and theoretically back again—that offer the overall critical insights. Quantitative methods and the graphs that display their results are useful for revealing hidden dimensions of texts and of literary history as a whole. The new views opened up by data analysis of text-based archives have been compared to adjusting a magnifying lens to reveal, at different levels of granularity, what was there all along, but hidden to the human eye. I've borrowed this metaphor from the report of the first researchers who responded to the NEH's Digging Into Data Challenge,[32] but it's important not to think strictly in terms of differences of scale or size. Grasping the hidden, data-rich dimensions of texts and of the physical world in general is also like shining lights of different wavelengths, infrared say, to reveal the invisible but present objects and features of what we normally experience only in the quotidian light of day. Quotidian experience (to extend *that* metaphor) is increasingly a multispectrum, multilevel experience. At least, it's increasingly possible to toggle between different views, different dimensions of the everyday world. And this is, I think, central to the mandate of the new digital humanities: to make such perceptions possible and to provide a framework and tools with which such multidimensionality can be experienced, interpreted, and incorporated into humanistic discourse.

Popular writer Steven Johnson (who, incidentally, briefly studied with Franco Moretti) argues that our era's "defining view" or way of seeing the world could be defined as "the long zoom,"

> the Google maps in which a few clicks take you from a view of an entire region to the roof of your house; the opening shot in *Fight Club* that pulls out from Edward Norton's synapses all the way to his quivering face as he stares into the muzzle of a revolver; the fractal geometry of chaos theory in which each new scale reveals endless complexity. And this is not just a way of seeing but also a way of thinking: moving conceptually from the scale of DNA to the scale of personality all the way up to social movements and politics—and back again.[33]

Johnson cites the famous 1977 educational film by Eames Studios, *The Powers of 10*, as an early embodiment of this dynamic. But his primary focus in the essay, what for Johnson is "the work that will fix the long zoom in the popular imagination," is a video game just then being released, an ambitious sandbox game by Sims-creator Will Wright, *Spore*. (The game was released 2008, but was heavily demoed for several years prior to that.) The game's levels step up from Cell to Creature to Tribal to Civilization to Space, each time, as in *The Powers of 10*, allowing players to zoom out and radically expand their perspective. The opening level is a kind of 2D platformer, not unlike various indie games of the same era with *Pac Man* cultural DNA (such as *flOw*, for example), where you play as a single-celled creature navigating the primordial soup. When you eat enough and avoid being eaten long enough to grow and "evolve," the camera zooms out and adds a dimension as you shift from a 2D to 3D game world; then, an animated cutscene shows your creature climbing out onto land.

Spore uses procedural animation for its user-generated content (creatures at various stages of "evolution," as well as vehicles, buildings, spaceships, etc.)— hence the "sandbox" nature of gameplay. Even in advance of its release, developers (and Wright himself) called *Spore* a "massively *single*-player online game," a system of asynchronous content creation and sharing, much like what happens on Facebook and other social-media platforms that have grown up since *Spore* was first announced. (YouTube was directly integrated into the game on release, so that users' own videos of their newly designed creatures and objects could be shared via that channel.) Players make and edit creatures (and their implements and tools); then the game engine animates them procedurally, according to their in-built features. Once you've finished editing a creature (from existing primitives), the game's algorithms take over and make a birdlike creature hop like a bird, or a three-legged lizard-like creature hobble around appropriately. Because the game's programming animates the creatures, wherever they're plugged into the game, the actual data files generated by users for each creature can be extremely small, highly compressed for easy uploading and downloading over the network. Each player plays locally but can share globally. User-generated content can be downloaded into any local game, and the outcome of a battle, say, can be recorded publicly on the game's network. *Spore* was conceived—clearly in imitation of then-emerging social-network platforms such as Facebook—as a platform for asynchronous sharing and management of *data*. It's essentially a CMS and social-network platform, with the game as its content. In some ways, it's very much like the classic game of collecting creatures and managing their statistics, Nintendo's *Pokémon*. Creature files are like the details printed on *Pokémon* cards (there are even digital images in *Spore* made to look like paper cards), but with the key data encoded. I play *Spore* by editing data files (though, thanks to the WYSIWYG graphical editor, it looks as though I'm poking and stretching and shaping little creature–avatars) and then "publishing" my files to a server-hub, where they can be downloaded, shared, and used by you in various cooperative or competitive scenarios. My peaceful creatures may populate your Tribal level as decorative NPCs, or they may serve as prey for your more aggressive creatures. The results of all these massively single-player interactions—the data generated— are then made available to me. According to Wikipedia, Maxi released *Spore*'s API as a series of RESTful Web services primarily in the form of XML files— which, in terms of system architecture, could also describe any number of new digital humanities projects. The idea is to give other developers or hardcore users access to player and game data. *Spore* appears to be a multi-tiered universe of animated worlds in which funny or scary cartoon creatures engage in mating, eating, fighting, building, and exploring in a wide variety of environments. But behind that brightly colored, visible game universe is a "hidden" digital universe (hidden to most players, anyway)—the code that makes up the procedural core of the game, a system for the generation and editing of encoded files that are then recombined, aggregated, collected, and traded in shifting constellations and nodes across a wide network. Each highly compressed creature file (in a loose, metaphorical sense, its DNA) is brought to life, given visible dimensions in the (game) world, but your interactions—along with countless similar interactions— are collected, as with any such video-game property, as encoded digital data, to be decoded, analyzed, recombined, and downloaded, to irrupt into an infinite number of other worlds, overlapping across the network of networks. (In other words, it's a lot like everyday life today.)

Minecraft (2009) is a game that appears very different from *Spore* graphically, but is also a massive sandbox, with a procedurally generated world and focused (even more) on the user-generated content. You play *Minecraft* by building things—almost any kind of thing you can imagine—out of voxel-looking primitives, 3D blocks. You mine them as raw materials of various kinds and then stack or connect them to make buildings, vehicles, objects, and structures. It's reminiscent of playing with Lego blocks, as part of the challenge is to make something that looks organic or realistically rounded out of the blocky materials. Aesthetically, the results look decidedly retro-styled, pixelated in a 16-bit way, which adds to the appeal. Even more than in *Spore*, eschewing realistic graphics for stylized forms allows for a resource-efficient massive game world. You can travel very far in the virtual world of *Minecraft*. It's technically not an infinite sandbox terrain, but it will feel that way to most players, as the game procedurally generates the part of the world you travel to on the fly, rendering it in successive "chunks" of data consisting of 16 × 16-pixel blocks as you get to them. Often, you can see this happening as you navigate and the world forms out in front of you. (I'll have more to say about *Minecraft* and making things in Chapter 5.)

Again, even more than in *Spore*, *Minecraft* allows for a sandbox style of play in which you just build and explore. When playing in Survival mode, however, you are prey to creatures that spawn at night, and you must build adequate shelter to protect yourself from them, or you'll be attacked, lose health, and die. In this mode, the game can be won, in terms that resonate with the traditions of science fiction and fantasy—by navigating through portals among parallel dimensions. You "win" *Minecraft* (in so far as anyone tries to do that) by defeating a dragon who lives in another dimension, accessed via underground, dungeon-like ruins. When you succeed in battle, you are allowed to exit that dimension and return to the main world. As in most video games (just exaggerated in *Minecraft*'s stylized way), the transparently metaphorical fantasy elements of ruins, dragon to defeat, a race of Endermen, etc., join the metaphors of *portals*, alternative *dimensions*, and, for that matter, the game *world* itself. These metaphors descend from the conventional genres and conventions of video games since *Adventure* and *Zork* (and, before them, from board games and *Dungeons and Dragons*-style RPGs), but they turn out to be surprisingly apt, among the images that are particularly useful for thinking with in this era, when the master metaphor of cyberspace has given way.

On Metaphorical Thinking

Games and science fiction have, from their inception, imagined counterfactual situations, layered, multidimensional realities among them. And, likewise, cyberspace was part high-tech start-up hype, part cultural metaphor. There never really was another dimension apart from the material world, never really was a cyberspace. If it was always a consensual hallucination, does the eversion amount to a collective sobering up? If, as Nathan Jurgenson has argued, cyberspace was an "untenable" and delusional "collective fiction," and if the "digital dualism" on which it was based is really no more than "ridiculous," a "common (mis)understanding," then does the eversion represent simply a final debunking, the stripping away of illusion?[34] In that case, is the New Aesthetic actually just a series of satires, more or less conscious, aimed at debunking digital dualism, and are New Aesthetic irruptions of the digital into the physical cited as signs of an already-exploded notion of the digital realm as somewhere other?

I don't think so, not quite. I don't think the New Aesthetic, even, much less the larger phenomenon of the eversion, is anything so simple. Ambivalence is at the heart of both the New Aesthetic and the larger eversion. For me, the metaphors of glitch and irruption and eldritch extrusion from another dimension that the New Aesthetic has been collecting, and that are showing up everywhere in the world at large, are meaningful. These metaphors of interdimensional transit are signs of something real—real attitudes, ambivalences, conceptual struggles in response to specific technological changes. For this reason, I think the metaphors offer useful ways to think about our current situation. Jurgenson himself, in responding to New Aesthetic irruptions, asks: "How do we understand these objects? What do we call them? Why do they exist? What do these objects say about the complex relationship between information and material, digitality and physicality, atoms and bits?" ("We Need a Word"). Precisely. These questions are the point of these metaphors, I believe, though not always consciously or intentionally so. How do we understand this complex relationship as it's in the midst of shifting? Although it's true, of course, that cyberspace was never *really* another dimension, it's also true that it was widely figured that way for almost two decades. Our experience of digital networks has, during that time, often *felt as if* it were interdimensional. In what many consider the first fictional representation of cyberspace (but not yet with that name), Vernor Vinge's novella *True Names*, the protagonist, Roger Pollack (aka Mr. Slippery), describes his perception of his digital life from the perspective of his physical life, once he can no longer go online, no longer visit the Other Plane: "What he had become since the spring was a fuzzy dream to him when he was down in the physical world. Sometimes he felt like a fish trying to imagine what a man in an airplane might be feeling."[35] Pollack's comic metaphor privileges the high-flying digital realm over the physical world, but it also captures the surreal feelings that can still, at this late date, characterize the border exchanges between the two. Dreams and metaphors, fictions and hallucinations, are ways for the culture to reimagine its relationship to the network. In the past decade, we have experienced (and continue to experience) "a rearrangement," and we may well "need new terminology that makes reference to the enmeshed, imploded, overlapping, interpenetrating nature of the physical and digital," as Jurgenson says ("We Need a Word"). But this isn't a matter of simply discarding fiction for reality; there's no point in trading a digital dualism for another kind of dualism—or a monism that devalues the power, even if it's a negative power, of collectively accepted metaphors. Deconstruction is not debunking: It reveals the rifts and contradictions of a relational construction by putting into play the relationality and difference (as *différance*). The whole point is that such constructions are difficult (or impossible) to see, much less escape. It's true that we now "live in an AR that exists at the intersection of materiality and information, physicality and digitality, bodies and technology, atoms and bits, the off and the online" ("IRL Fetish"). But for now, living in this AR still sometimes *feels* like living at the confluence of overlapping dimensions of existence. That changing experience is worth understanding.

To invoke another metaphor from speculative fiction, it's like inhabiting the urban landscape of China Miéville's noir alternative-history detective novel, *The City & The City* (2009), in which two fictional European cities, Besźel and Ul Qoma, occupy the same geographic space but maintain separate identities, as if they existed in parallel universes or adjacent dimensions.[36] Residents are raised to inhabit their cities without acknowledging the overlap, to "observe borders" that are invisible, to "see and unsee only what [they] should" (36). They must *unsee* the civic others passing by on the street, actively *not* perceive the architecture, city parks, vehicles from the opposing city that are right there all along in the same physical place—or, as the residents of both cities say when they mean crudely, physically adjacent, "grosstopically" close (80). To cross over without papers or even to see that your house is standing right beside a building from the other city, or that your street is literally, physically coextensive with its mirror from the other city (its "topolganger" [132]), is to commit "breach," an ominously serious category of crime, like a state of sin (one is said to be "in breach"), to be punished by unseen forces (known simply as Breach). When breach happens unexpectedly, say when a bus from one city crashes in such a way that it cannot be ignored, the Besźel term for it is "protub"—short for a "protuberance" from the other city (a term that now invokes the New Aesthetic's "irruptions" and the eversion more generally) (65). *The City & the City* is about political and social constructions, a way of representing ideology and institutional interpellation of the subjects of those constructions. On some level, therefore, it's clearly about Jerusalem, Beirut, Berlin, and the partitioning of every major city in invisible ways, along lines of power and money, so that one must learn to unsee the homeless sleeping in the subways, for example. I wouldn't want to obscure those political interpretations. But even Miéville has said that, although he rejects allegorical decodings of the book, he wishes to differentiate those from legitimate metaphorical readings, not because allegory "reads too much into a story, but because it reads too little into it" (320). Metaphor, he says, is "fractally fecund" (321), and, in that spirit, I find that the novel's controlling metaphor works as a figure not just for ideology but for technology, for how collective metaphors shape experience—and what it feels like to live in the midst of a shift from one dominant metaphor for technology to another, to live in (the) breach, as it were. The frisson of this experience, the chill of recognizing once-hidden data manifest as a series of protuberances into everyday life, is like living in those overlapping cities, straddling two alternative worlds or two dimensions of existence.

Dimensionality is a metaphor that allows us to think in meaningful ways about the layerings, and the degrees of invisibility, of the data and connections and objects that surround us. Such metaphors help us to grasp the process we are still undergoing in order to continue to work through what it means. We are still experiencing the eversion of cyberspace, and the "new" dimensions of existence opened up by the eversion are still in the process of being revealed. One of the roles of the new digital humanities in our present moment might be to help us all learn new ways to see some of these hitherto unseen (but always-present) dimensions of mixed-reality existence, the people, places, and things opened up by the conjunctions of the digital and the physical.

★

Notes

1. James Bridle, "We Fell in Love in a Coded Space," Liftconference, April 6, 2012, http://youtube.com/watch?v=tuin-6DIRG8.
2. For this book, it seems appropriate to cite H. P. Lovecraft's fiction in a digital edition (Kindle, in my case) compiled from public-domain texts by "a library worker and library student (Master's in Library and Information Science, specializing in archives), a crafter, a reader, and a geek" who goes by the handle, Cthulhu Chick. Her edition is based on Project Gutenberg texts. Cthulhu Chick, ed., *The Complete Works of H. P. Lovecraft* (2010), http://cthulhuchick.com/free-complete-lovecraft-ebook-nook-kindle/, "From Beyond" (loc. 1935).
3. My thanks to Nicholas Hayward and his students in Digital Humanities 400 (fall 2012) for reminding me of some of these advantages of QR codes.
4. Maura Judkis, "QR Code Tattoo Signals End of the QR Code?" *Washington Post* The Style Blog, December 19, 2011, http://washingtonpost.com/blogs/arts-post/post/qr-code-tattoo-signals-end-of-the-qr-code/2011/12/19/gIQAJW7y4O_blog.html.
5. Sander Veenhof, QR of Life, http://exvirtual.com/qr.
6. "Russia's Futuristic QR Code Covered Pavilion," My Modern Met blog, http://mymodernmet.com/profiles/blogs/russia-pavilion-venice-architecture-biennale. Extra credit for this one goes to the collective English 415 Tumblr, The Network Everts, http://networkeverts.tumblr.com.
7. Conceptual preview video, "Google Glass: One Day . . . ," spring 2012, https://http://youtube.com/watch?v=9c6W4CCU9M4&feature=player_embedded, now archived at official site: https://plus.google.com/+projectglass/posts. Since that video appeared, beta-test versions of Glass have been distributed, and, as I write, Google is hoping to release a commercial product by the end of 2013. See Joshua Topolsky, "I Used Google Glass: The Future, With Monthly Updates," *The Verge*, February 22, 2013, http://theverge.com/2013/2/22/4013406/i-used-google-glass-its-the-future-with-monthly-updates.
8. Bruce Sterling, "An Essay on the New Aesthetic," Beyond The Beyond blog, April 22, 2012, http://wired.com/beyond_the_beyond/2012/04/an-essay-on-the-new-aesthetic.
9. James Bridle, "Waving At the Machines," Web Directions South 2011, http://webdirections.org/resources/james-bridle-waving-at-the-machines.
10. James Bridle, "#sxaesthetic," BookTwo blog, March 15, 2012, http://booktwo.org/notebook/sxaesthetic.
11. Kelly Goeller, *Pixel Pour*, April 2008, http://kellotron.com. My thanks to her for permission to reproduce the photo used in the illustration and for her explanation of her materials and methods.

12. Julian Bleeker, Flickr, "Pixel Spout" [sic], April 18, 2008, http://flickr.com/photos/julianbleeker/2434362687.
13. "Wreck-It Ralph 8-Bit Lane, Truman Brewery, Brick Lane, London, January 11–13, 2013," http://youtube.com/watch?feature=player_embedded&v=wQkE3VPUPuM#!.
14. Ray Zone, *Stereoscopic Cinema & the Origins of 3-D Film, 1838–1952* (Lexington: The University Press of Kentucky, 2007), 141–43.
15. "Mario is Too Mainstream," Dorkly, http://dorkly.com/video/30941/dorkly-bits-mario-is-too-mainstream.
16. Patrick Jagoda has produced the best close reading I know of this aspect of *Braid*, in which he argues that the game's "secretiveness about the atom bomb does not exist for the sake of some empty Hollywood-style plot twist," but that the "game's surreptitiousness comes formally to figure the epic concealment of the Manhattan Project itself," in "Fabulously Procedural: *Braid*, History, and the Videogame Sensorium," *American Literature* (forthcoming, 2013), e.g., 12–13.
17. L. Pajot and J. Swirsky, producers, directors, *Indie Game: The Movie* (2012), Canada: Flutter Media.
18. Sal Cangeloso, "*Fez* soundtrack is Full of Secrets," April 20, 2012, http://geek.com/articles/games/fez-soundtrack-contains-hidden-information-20120420.
19. Elijah Meeks, "TVTropes Pt. 1: The Weird Geometry of the Internet," Stanford University Libraries & Academic Information Resources, Digital Humanities Specialist blog, December 21, 2011, https://dhs.stanford.edu/social-media-literacy/tvtropes-pt-1-the-weird-geometry-of-the-internet.
20. Patrick LeMieux and Stephanie Boluk, "Eccentric Spaces and Filmic Traces: Portals in Aperture Laboratories and New York City," *Proceedings of the 8th Digital Arts and Culture Conference, After Media: Embodiment and Context* (Irvine, CA: University of California Press, 2009), http://escholarship.org/uc/item/95b6t1cm.
21. Willard McCarty (willard.mccarty@mccarty.org) and Elijah Meeks (emeeks@stanford.edu]), "proof," Humanist List Archives, January 13–14, 2012, http://dhhumanist.org/Archives/Current/Humanist.vol25.txt.
22. See Jerome J. McGann, *Radiant Textuality: Literature After the World Wide Web* (New York: Palgrave, 2001), 167–91.
23. Stephen Ramsay, *Reading Machines: Toward an Algorithmic Criticism* (Champaign: University of Illinois Press, 2011).
24. For born-digital texts, the issues are somewhat different, but there is always some physical dimension involved in these, as well, if only at a microscopic level.
25. McGann, "Marking Texts of Many Dimensions," in *Companion*, eds. Schreibman et al., http://digitalhumanities.org/companion.
26. McGann, *Radiant Textuality*, 164.
27. Franco Moretti, *Graphs, Maps, Trees: Abstract Models for a Literary History* (London and New York: Verso, 2005), 1.
28. Willard McCarty, "Modeling: A Study in Words and Meanings," in *Companion*, eds. Schreibman et al., http://digitalhumanities.org/companion.
29. Johanna Drucker, "Humanistic Theory and Digital Scholarship," in *Debates*, ed. Gold, 85–95 (86).
30. Matthew L. Jockers, "Unigrams, and Bigrams, and Trigrams, Oh My," author's blog, December 22, 2010, http://matthewjockers.net/2010/12/22/unigrams-and-bigrams-and-trigrams-oh-my.
31. Matthew L. Jockers, "On Distant Reading and Macroanalysis," author's blog, July 1, 2011, http://matthewjockers.net/2011/07/01/on-distant-reading-and-macroanalysis. And see *Macroanalysis: Digital Methods and Literary History* (Champaign: University of Illinois Press, 2013).
32. Christa Williford and Charles Henry, *One Culture: Computationally Intensive Research in the Humanities and Social Sciences: A Report on the Experiences of First Respondents to the*

Digging Into Data Challenge (Washington, DC: Council on Library and Information Resources, 2012), 1.

33. Steven Johnson, "The Long Zoom," *The New York Times Magazine*, October 8, 2006, http://nytimes.com/2006/10/08/magazine/08games.html?pagewanted=all&_r=0.

34. Nathan Jurgenson, "We Need a Word for That Thing Where a Digital Thing Appears in the Physical World," *The Atlantic*, July 9, 2012, http://theatlantic.com/technology/archive/2012/07/we-need-a-word-for-that-thing-where-a-digital-thing-appears-in-the-physical-world/259570/; and compare "Digital Dualism versus Augmented Reality," Cyborgology blog, February 24, 2011, http://thesocietypages.org/cyborgology/2011/02/24/digital-dualism-versus-augmented-reality/, and "The IRL Fetish," *The New Inquiry*, June 28, 2012, http://thenewinquiry.com/essays/the-irl-fetish.

35. Vernor Vinge, *True Names*, http://ny.iadicicco.com/Finished/20,000%20Ebooks/Vernor%20Vinge/Vernor%20Vinge%20-%20True%20Names.pdf, 44.

36. China Miéville, *The City & The City* (New York: Random House Digital, 2011; copyright 2009), Kindle edition.

3
PEOPLE

Cyberspace. A consensual hallucination experienced daily by billions of legitimate operators, in every nation, by children being taught mathematical concepts . . . A graphic representation of data abstracted from the banks of every computer in the human system. Unthinkable complexity. Lines of light ranged in the nonspace of the mind, clusters and constellations of data. Like city lights, receding.[1]

In William Gibson's famous descriptive definition from *Neuromancer* (1984), although the hallucination of cyberspace was massively distributed, "consensual," shared by billions, the imagined space itself was eerily empty. A graphic representation of data as lines of light, like city lights, but barely any avatars, very little or no communication among the billions of users, legitimate or not. Partly inspired by the outer-space settings of earlier science fiction (Gibson has said he needed a place to set the story that would replace the rocketship), this network as Gibson pictured it was sublime, inhuman, a vast and empty nonspace. This is one of the more striking discrepancies between cyberspace as Gibson and others first imagined it and the network as it's now actually experienced daily by perhaps over two billion "operators." Especially since the changes described at the time as Web 2.0, around 2004–2006—which used modest technology developments to promote a shift in emphasis from what the network had been, but were accompanied by many small shifts in software, services, platform, and architecture—there has been an increasing focus on the fact that the network is peopled, and, in a fundamental sense, is people. Sometimes the people are merely harvested for their data, or as data, it's true, but often at the same time they contribute in various ways as curators, and even sometimes as producers. Their very awareness of one another's presence as the basis for being online has changed overall expectations for the network. In that difference is a context, and arguably a calling, for the digital humanities.

The new emphasis on the social nature of the network is, of course, often just a marketing line, a way for Facebook to gather and re-leverage your online interactions as data. Nonetheless, I think there's something significant about viewing the network in this way, as fundamentally dependent on billions (or millions) of "operators," openly and socially present within the system and, simultaneously, out in the world—rather than all taking consensual hallucinogenic trips at the same time from the jacked-in privacy of their consoles. This goes beyond the clichés of so-called net populism. I mean something more precise: I mean to call attention to the extent to which the mundane human role in constructing and managing the Internet, while being in or moving through the world, was obscured by the 1990s ideology of cyberspace, so that the rise of the so-called social networks in the early 2000s looks, now, in retrospect, like a shift away from that ideology. Now, "Web 2.0" and "the cloud" and "social" (as a standalone term) have sometimes replaced a cyberspace ideology with other different forms of euphemism, obscurity, and trivialization ("liking" things is a weak form of curation, certainly). I don't want to celebrate and perpetuate new clichés, and I don't mean to imply that the eversion has been an epiphany, a return to some transparent truth. However, the shift in emphasis toward mundane social networking has, I think, contributed to the restoration of a sense of two-way complexity—a certain reflexivity—in the way people imagine the network with which they're so closely involved. In a very real, mundane sense, the Internetwork is now assumed by most people who use it every day (with a kind of shrug) to be a social phenomenon. For good and ill, the network is people.

The Significance of CAPTCHAs

The roles played by large numbers of human users in making the network what it is can best be glimpsed in the many small details of everyday online life. Consider something as ubiquitous as CAPTCHAs. You see them all the time when you sign on to commerce Websites—those little boxes with odd-looking words in them that you are asked to read and then type out in a simple form. The idea is to get you to prove you're human, not an automated script or bot designed to log in to Websites for nefarious purposes. It's a reverse Turing test: Instead of questioning a machine in order to ascertain whether it's an artificial intelligence, CAPTCHAs question humans in order to prove they're non-artificial intelligence.

As I mentioned in Chapter 2, James Bridle has cited CAPTCHAs as among the features of the New Aesthetic. For him, they're evidence of how we're learning to cooperate with machines, learning how machines see the world. To me, they're more like QR codes, two-way portals between digital data and the physical world, computer and human, triggers for repeated, quotidian acts of translation in today's mixed-reality environment. Whereas QR codes are designed to be read by a computer (via your phone app), CAPTCHAs, developed by Carnegie Mellon University professor Luis von Ahn around 2000, are designed so machines *can't* read them.[2] They distort text samples to the very boundary of legibility—and sometimes beyond it. That's why you often have to reload and get another sample if one's too wavy or marked-through or scrunched up to read. Thus you prove you are not a robot. The point of CAPTCHAs (which stands for "completely automated public Turing test to tell computers and humans apart") is to link analog and digital directly, to put them into dialogue with one another, in order to clarify the difference between the two, but with the ultimate purpose of securely *getting people onto the network*. About 200 million CAPTCHAs are reportedly solved by humans every day.[3]

This larger purpose was made clear with the introduction in 2007 of reCAPTCHA, a repurposing of CAPTCHA by one of the inventors, Luis von Ahn himself, in order to channel all that human labor, all those micro-efforts, into the work of digitizing texts. Like a hydroelectric generator or the brake system in a hybrid car, reCAPTCHA captures the energy generated daily by other activities, in this case all the tiny login transactions that happen all the time on the Web. Instead of just gaining access to online data, human users can help to produce online data in a 10-second act of micro-digitization. The original CAPTCHAs made use of random strings of characters. The wavy words in reCAPTCHAs are taken from failed OCR (optical character recognition) transcriptions produced by scanners reading printed texts. When you read a reCAPTCHA, you are correcting a glitch in a Google Books text, for example (Google acquired reCAPTCHA in 2009), or a passage in a back issue of the *New York Times*. So, what a machine tried but failed to translate from physical book to digital text is reread, retranslated by a human attempting to log in to a site selling shoes, say. The distorted look of the reCAPTCHA is a deliberate glitch meant to trip up bots, but it also reflects the real vagaries of machine reading in the process of digitization, the whole reason for reCAPTCHAs in the first place. A control word is included in order to prove the human can read what the machine has already successfully read, so that it can be determined with some degree of probability whether that human has likely also deciphered what the machine could not read. Each reader becomes part of a vast crowd of anonymous proofreaders, if not quite "billions of legitimate operators." As I write, over 100,000 Websites reportedly include reCAPTCHAs, allowing users to transcribe more than 40 million words a day. The digital world, from the point of view of reCAPTCHA, is crowded with humans, just waiting (whether they know it or not) to contribute to creating and improving the network through what von Ahn called "human computation" and what has since become widely known as crowdsourcing. Amazon's Web service, Mechanical Turk, introduced in 2005 and named after a famous eighteenth-century automaton, likewise crowdsources various network tasks, from commenting music CDs to choosing higher-quality photographs, better performed (at least at present) by humans than by machines. The automation of

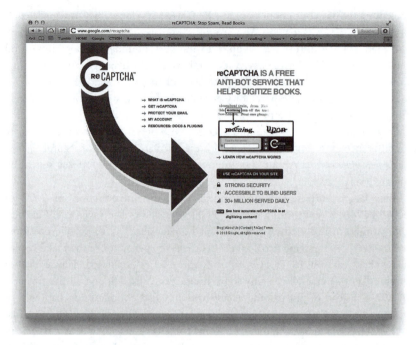

FIGURE 3.1 reCaptcha

the Internet has been greatly exaggerated, at any rate, and there has been a trend, even among AI and search-algorithm developers, to look to human–machine cooperation as the key, rather than striving for autonomous intelligence for the machines. "Increasingly, behind the curtain" when it comes to the most AI-like interactions with networked technology, from Siri to Google search, "there is a decidedly retro helper—a human being."[4]

Agrippa and the Illusion of Cyberspace

It's important to see how different from early visions of cyberspace is this view of the Internet as *crowded* (think of that descriptor in the active sense, as meaning "run by crowds"). The fact is, the actual network was radically less populated in its early days than it later became. Network use has mushroomed over the past 25 years or so. In 1985, the year after *Neuromancer* was published with its first mention of cyberspace, there were only 2,000 computers connected to the Internet; two years later, it was 30,000 computers; by 1989, it was 159,000. In 2011, there were 2 billion users on the Internet, from every country on Earth.[5] The network is teeming with people, now, on a scale that makes that fact obvious to everyone. Of course, the actual practices of adept early users of the Internet, though their numbers were much smaller than today, were always highly social.

They involved bulletin board systems (BBSs), MUDs, and Usenet groups populated by many others, and one of the signature experiences of being online was the sense that the winking cursor could come to life at any moment with the text-based voice of someone very far away. Chatting or exchanging files with someone on another continent was itself thrilling, especially accompanied with the sense that it was happening for free over the connections established by governments and universities and early ISPs. Actual Internet use has always been social in nature, if less massive in scale than it later became. But the notion of cyberspace as an abstract idea was anything but social. Quite the contrary: It was the austere territory of loners, cold architectural models of data, menacing AIs flickering on the verge of visualization, all green and amber in the darkness, an immaterial realm, the ether. This conceptual space lay behind much of the development and design of the 1990s, including some academic ideas about the role of technology in education and scholarship, whatever the social truth on the boards or in IRC (Internet Relay Chat).

One very useful historical example of both that early vision of immateriality and its own insubstantiality is a work of art that, when viewed in its cultural context, illustrates the early ideology of cyberspace and reveals it *as* ideology. The experimental multimedia work, Agrippa, appeared in 1992, at an important moment of transition just a couple of years before the Internet was to become, for most people, synonymous with the World Wide Web (starting with the release of the Mosaic HTTP browser in 1994). Agrippa the work included at its center a poem, "Agrippa," by William Gibson himself, and was published 10 years after he had first coined the term cyberspace and helped to establish the contours of the idea of the network in the popular imagination. Because Agrippa was also the focus of important foundational work in the digital humanities, as I'll show, it provides a context for understanding how the more recent emergence of DH as a set of interdisciplinary practices was connected to these shifting views of the network.

Agrippa was a mixed-media collaboration among author William Gibson, visual artist Dennis Ashbaugh, and publisher Kevin Begos Jr. The object at its center, or that became its vessel, was something like an analog-and-digital version of an artist's book, a tradition in which the book is treated as a physical object, with print text, drawings, handwriting, inserts, popups, or constructions, working to deconstruct or explode conventional ideas of the book, or print as a medium, by treating both as the objects of art. In the case of Agrippa, one component is the text of a poem about discovering an old photo album (whose brand name is the source of the title), embedded in an artifact by Ashbaugh that signifies "The Book," with graphical illustrations, etchings of DNA images, the whole wrapped in a gauze shroud.[6] The poem wasn't printed in the book; it was recorded on a floppy disk physically embedded in a cutout in the pages.

The most memorable feature of the poem is that the text encrypted itself as it was opened on a personal computer and read, disappearing as it scrolled down the screen for the first and last time. Except, the text of the poem was somehow very quickly (the next day) released onto the Internet, where it still remains available in various versions as I write. I remember scrolling through the text for the first time in a mailing from a discussion list. The phosphoric images on the screen and the dot-matrix letters of the copy I printed out helped to generate a sense that the text had floated free from its original "body" in the book by Ashbaugh—made of paper, boards, prints of etchings, gauze fabric—had been unlocked from its encryption (which was falsely rumored to be military grade) by a lone hacker and released into the wild to be distributed as if in literary imitation of samizdat or cultural contraband. Information wants to be free, and this was clearly a postmodern prank on the book collectors who would decide not to read the text in order to preserve the value of the limited-edition object. The work focused pertinent questions for literary and cultural studies, from Walter Benjamin's aura of the work of art in the age of mechanical reproduction, to the semiotics of the book after the death of the author, to Derridean *différance* and the deconstruction of presence. But most of all (as I recall it), when it first appeared, Agrippa seemed to many to represent the *immaterial*, disembodied nature of the digital—a text that was conjured by a kind of technical alchemy out of the analog, produced dynamically in the ether as it dissolved into thin air.

It turns out that the history of Agrippa was at once simpler and more complicated than that. It was certainly more mundane, as thoroughly documented and analyzed by Matthew Kirschenbaum in his groundbreaking digital humanities book, *Mechanisms* (the title of which is taken from Gibson's poem), as well as an essay he contributed to The Agrippa Files Website—a networked archive on the work as a whole—on which he collaborated with Doug Reside and Alan Liu.[7] It took a materialist digital humanities approach to reveal that Agrippa, rather than being a demonstration of the immateriality of cyberspace, was actually a prime example of the multiply material nature of texts in the digital age. As a work— digital poem, physical book, including Ashbaugh's artwork in multiple media, performance of the public "Transmission," afterlife on the Internet—Agrippa *is* the far-flung network it spawned, a conceptual work or happening made up of what happened, or, better yet, something like a distributed, crowdsourced *game* of meaning, a view that would seem to be supported by remarks made by Kevin Begos Jr., the publisher behind Agrippa, in a spring 2012 interview by Courtney Traub in *The Oxonian Review*.[8]

> *Begos:* I doubt that there would be any publisher ready to experiment with such innovation, which tends to be driven by artists and designers rather than the companies themselves.
>
> I would contrast this to the enormous investment that online game makers have made. It's come out of virtually nowhere to become this multibillion-dollar world market. Hypercompetitive but constantly evolving—there's this incredible competition to make games more realistic and more experimental, and it's attracting a lot of creative people.

Traub: I think many people might argue that much of the true narrative experimentation is taking place in the games realm. The experimentation people thought would be happening with books is going on more in gaming.

Begos: I think that's completely true. That's where the real developments are taking place and legitimate breakthroughs in terms of how people interact with artwork and with each other. They've built platforms that will evolve.

After this interview appeared, Kirschenbaum suggested on Twitter (November 26, 2012) that Agrippa anticipated the New Aesthetic. I agree, but, more precisely, it was an early harbinger by the inventor of cyberspace of what he later called the eversion of the network, its transformation outward into mixed reality. One medium in which this mixed reality is today experienced widely and embodied effectively is that of games. That is, I think, what Kevin Begos is getting at when he imagines games as the medium in which the kind of experiment he created in 1992 would take place today. I'll come back to games. For now, just to review: Gibson published Agrippa in 1992, 10 years after he introduced the term cyberspace and at a crucial moment in the history of the Internet, just before the Mosaic Web browser was introduced. Over a decade later, in 2005, The Agrippa Files Website (ed. Liu et al.) went online. I see this site, along with Kirschenbaum's *Mechanisms* (2008), as a crucial early example of the new-model (everted) DH in practice. As the Website appeared, Gibson was just on the verge of saying in print that the cyberspace he had named back in 1982 was everting.

The key event in the history of Agrippa, as Kirschenbaum established, was the performance on December 9, 1992, known as the Transmission. In front of a live audience at the Americas Society on the Upper West Side of New York, the poem was "played" from a diskette in Begos's Macintosh laptop and projected onto a screen, accompanied by a prerecorded reading by magician Penn Jillette. It scrolled by once on the screen and, in effect, self-destructed, encrypting itself so that it could never be opened again. It will be difficult for those raised doing PowerPoint presentations in school to believe, but the projection—especially from a Mac—was not easy to arrange in 1992, and so a few NYU students were recruited to make it happen. They solved the problem, significantly, with a kluge, by pointing a Hi8 video camera at the laptop screen and projecting from the camera. As Kirschenbaum first reported (both in *Mechanisms* and in "No Round Trip"), while they were at it, the students surreptitiously recorded the scrolling text on a tape loaded in the video camera, supposedly without Begos and the organizers knowing what they were doing. The next day, mysterious hackers known as Templar and Rosehammer released the text of Gibson's art-book poem on the Internet, a plain-text ASCII file that enabled the poem to "propagate rapidly across bulletin boards, listservs, newsgroups, and FTP sites" ("No Round Trip"). Those of us who downloaded the text, once the story got out, had the impression we had received the poetry from cyberspace. It felt a little like the later experience of having access to a bit-torrent version of an unreleased album, and it was widely assumed that the hackers had risen to the challenge of the reported "NSA encryption," cracked it, and released the text from the proprietary format in which it had been bundled to be sold to collectors and libraries—in other words, like the "Straylight run" raid on space-based property engineered by console cowboys in Gibson's own cyberpunk novel, *Neuromancer*. The poem had been liberated, it seemed, moved from a locked-up, expensive diskette to cyberspace, like a disembodied AI construct being uploaded to the fictional matrix in Gibson's story. The whole thing seemed a perfect illustration of the immateriality of information in cyberspace that was an ideological given at the time. Information wants to be free and thus tends toward radical fluidity and disembodiment. It was as if the text on the diskette was the soul of Gibson's poem, which the hackers had freed from the coffin of Ashbaugh's paper-and-cloth "book of the dead" and released into the ether.

It was too good to be true. As Kirschenbaum established through his media-forensics approach, which included interviews with the anonymous hackers who pulled it off, the release of "Agrippa" was a clever but relatively lo-fi hack, more social engineering than code breaking, as much punk as cyber, notably mundane, the result of exploiting mixed media (*Mechanisms*, 226, 225). The secret videotape of the Transmission was later that night transcribed as plaintext, typed into a computer by hand, and in that way actually transmitted to the world at large (or at least the subset of it on the net in 1992), posted first to the MindVox BBS, and from there it spread:

> the brilliant act of low-tech, manual, and analog transcription through which Rosehammer and Templar accomplished their "hack" of Agrippa (analog video copied by hand as text) ineluctably dates Agrippa as the product of a certain technological moment at the cusp between old and new media.
>
> ("No Round Trip")

In 2004–2005, a team that included computer forensics specialists was able to gain access to a collected diskette and image it, making an exact copy of its data so that the poem "Agrippa" could be emulated in a software environment on the Web, which mimicked the Macintosh computer like the one from which the Transmission took place. This emulation is still available on The Agrippa Files Website, allowing users to view Gibson's poem playing as it did during the Transmission, over and over again, "thereby eliding the foundational premise of the original work: its read-once-only evanescence." Every time it plays, however, the data are indeed encrypted as originally intended. "Each individual instance of the disk image is only useable once" (The Agrippa Files).

The moral of the story (in this retelling) is that the poem "Agrippa," a self-consuming artifact with a deliberately created aura, was never the example it was taken to be of the immateriality of the digital. But many *did* take it that way in the 1990s, under the influence of what Kirschenbaum calls the "medial ideology that leapt to embrace the conceit of a disappearing book and a vanishing poem" (*Mechanisms*, 239)—and what I see as an effect of the larger ideology of cyberspace.

One strength of Kirschenbaum's approach is that it refocused attention on the elided materialities of digital media operating at different levels: forensic materiality (physical, silicon and wire, magnetic impulses inscribing hard drives) and formal materiality (symbols, code, and the logical and procedural structures that symbols and code express, for example). This may sound like dualism, but it's not. Formal materialities are not the "mind" or "soul" of the machine, supported by the "body" of forensic materialities. It's not a question of information floating free of its substrate, in Katherine Hayles' terms.[9] Electrical impulses, formal structures, logic gates, transistors, machine language, user interface, it's all inscribed in order to be experienced, none of it *truly* ethereal (that's just an effect of the limits of human perception). A good deal of displacement and slippage, and what Katherine Hayles calls the effect of the "flickering signifier," (xiv) may indeed shape our experience with digital media and the Internet over which much of it now reaches us, but that's very different from having recourse to the metaphysics of digital immateriality. Instead, Kirschenbaum's distinctions offer a way to account for the layers of any digital media object as a system, with components and features connected to one another across those layers. Because they *are* connected, because they're the product of human design—to paraphrase the old joke—it's materialities all the way down.

It only took that shift in perspective to see the publication history of Agrippa in a new light, as a vivid illustration of the opposite of the cyberspace clichés with which it was at first associated. What had once seemed to many to be a parable of the immateriality of cyberspace appears now as a complex story about the inevitable materialities of the network—and the central role still played by human agents in executing those materialities. Kirschenbaum sees Agrippa as a prime example of "the capacity of the digital object to take on and accumulate a material, indexical layer of associations" (*Mechanisms*, 231), and also as a vivid example of the social nature of texts, as "it owes its transmission and continuing availability to a complex network of individuals, communities, ideologies, markets, technologies, and motivations" (*Mechanisms*, 240). Posting to the Humanist listserv on January 8, 2013, Kirschenbaum summarized the argument of *Mechanisms* in social terms, reminding us that, "computers, like all technologies, are the artifacts of human endeavor. Because we live in a fallen world, these artifacts are inevitably and invariably material." Agrippa was, of course, a product of its mixed-media moment. But its *ongoing and changing reception*—from being the exemplar of the immateriality of cyberspace, to (thanks to the initial efforts of Liu, Kirschenbaum, et al.) revealing the sociology of even digital texts—also tells a story of changing views of the network on which its meaning depends. In other words, in retrospect, Agrippa looks very much like a harbinger of the eversion.

The transcendent immateriality of the digital as an illusion, is in fact what Gibson said cyberspace was: a consensual hallucination, a collective trip that now appears to be winding down (or at least entering a major phase shift). It's interesting in this regard that Penn Jillette was literally the voice of the Transmission, because, as part of Penn and Teller, he has for years demonstrated the way illusions work, despite their very material, even geeky, technical underpinnings: by suspending collective disbelief. The audience wants to believe. It's a small thing, partly a linguistic coincidence, a matter of probabilities in a single author's lexicon, but it nevertheless seems significant that the poem "Agrippa," which is about the material record of technologically aided memories (photography) and mechanisms that divide time (cameras, guns), ends with an image of the author in Tokyo, "walking through Chiyoda-ku"

> in a typhoon
> the fine rain horizontal
> umbrella everted in the storm's Pacific breath
> tonight red lanterns are battered,
> laughing,
> in the mechanism.[10]

There's that slightly odd word, *everted*, which this same author would use 15 years later to describe the feeling of what by then had happened to cyberspace. The social and physical aspects of the Internet, and of our interactions with it, have come to the fore in dramatic ways since 1992. The social dimension of the network has a history, and the culture's willingness to repress or acknowledge that dimension for a time has a history as well.

Looking at the basic timeline makes it clear that there is a significant contrast between the reception of Agrippa ca. 1992 and the reinterpretation of it produced in 2004–2005. Especially now, looking back at the social-media boom that was taking place at the precise moment as that reinterpretation, Agrippa seems to demonstrate three features of the network, even back in 1992:

1. It's *material*, ineluctably based in wires, optical fibers, trenches, and server rooms, if also electrical impulses, and the formal, procedural logics of algorithms encoded in software or machine code.
2. It's *located* (if multiply-located, distributed), not an invisible dimension apart from the world, not even a vague global mesh, but a way of connecting and navigating among specific objects in the world, including data in the world, *and including people as points of presence in both the physical world and on the network* (see no. 3).
3. It's *social*. People and their relations, institutional, personal, and technical, however much in cooperation with machines, *are* what we mean by the network, in the end.

One additional point follows from these three: New media on this network, understood in this way, are all about translation, navigation, switches, ports. As the editors say on The Agrippa Files Website, "the 'hack' wasn't only about transcribing a single instance of the text; it was about enacting a modal shift in its semiotic nature, thereby allowing it to propagate endlessly and effortlessly."[11] That's what makes Agrippa and [re]CAPTCHAs related instances of human–computer interactions in the present moment, the era of the eversion.

Katherine Hayles has argued that human–machine systems such as the Internet are best understood as "dynamic heterarch[ies]," characterized by "intermediation" of human and machine in "recursive feedback and feedforward loops."[12] Like the New Aesthetic, her theory realizes that we are increasingly interoperating with machines, with computers, in various phased extensions of cybernetics. The study of such hybrid machine and human identity, a key part of cyberculture studies in the 1990s, owes much to Gibson's notions of cyberspace and the related fictions those notions influenced, as well as to radical theories of AI and transhuman or posthuman identity, including the "geek rapture," the supposedly coming Singularity. In the 1990s, largely for rhetorical reasons, such studies often downplayed the mundane human role in the network, and exaggerated the increasing dominance by the impersonal machine, as if total dominance of humanity were the end, the telos, toward which computing technology was headed. But the pendulum swung in the other direction around 2004. This was the moment of so-called Web 2.0 and the emergence of social media as what the Internet did best. Google's public offering took place in August 2004; Facebook had just moved to California on its way to dominance. And, at that same moment, digital humanities milestones can be added: *A Companion to Digital Humanities* was published in 2004, and The Agrippa Files Website went online in mid 2005. The eversion of the network can be seen in the reinterpretation of Gibson's own capstone work on the ethereal nature of cyberspace.

The Games Realm

> *Traub:* I think many people might argue that much of the true narrative experimentation is taking place in the games realm. The experimentation people thought would be happening with books is going on more in gaming.
>
> *Begos:* I think that's completely true. That's where the real developments are taking place and legitimate breakthroughs in terms of how people interact with artwork and with each other.

In these 2012 remarks about Agrippa, Kevin Begos Jr. seems to be contrasting the publication of artists' books, or books in general, with the production resources and vast commercial market for games, suggesting that some significant creativity in games is the result. He says it with apparent envy: The "real developments" and "legitimate breakthroughs" are happening in games, rather than in other forms of art. But his contrast, and his focus on what Traub calls "the games realm" in 2012, may divert attention from the degree to which Agrippa, with the theoretical and imaginative issues it embodies, was from the start connected to games and gamelike media.

As I said in Chapter 1, Gibson's vision of cyberspace in the early 1980s was inspired by arcade gamers—and the author's projections onto the gamers, which he watched from a distance, of desires for immersion and transcendence. It's an important fact to remember: Cyberspace was at its inception imagined as the world inside a game. The supposedly immersive, quasi-mystical symbiosis of player and arcade cabinet (actually descended from pinball machines) translated into the cyborg graft of cyberpunk hacker and his or her "console." Even the names of the machines for accessing cyberspace are reminiscent of 1980s games. And the space behind the screen—the graphical limitations of which in 1982 we must work to remember—was projected into the 2030s as the nonspace of cyberspace. But what about the games that were around as generic points of comparison when Agrippa was developed? Are there ways in which it was gamelike already in the context of games in 1992?

To start, the idea of books and other media combining in hybrid ways was in fact common in a number of games and gamelike computer-based media at the time. Take the tradition of IF (Interactive Fiction) games, which persist today in a kind of dedicated subculture but were popular in the 1980s. They're remembered for their command-line text-only interface, played on a PC and loaded from diskettes, with only some very basic graphics, starting with ASCII art, added later in the development of the genre. IF games, like all games, were also characterized by the dedication of the player community to co-constructing the game worlds—and the paratextual worlds surrounding the games. Rather than the mechanics or design of specific video games at the time, the most useful comparisons with Agrippa as a work of art might be found in the reception of IF games and other games, which was invariably social, collectively constructed, and which made creative use of the interrelation of digital text produced procedurally by the game programs and imagined, projected, or otherwise supplemental materials for building out the game world from a series of narrative prompts for player commands and descriptions of settings. Of course, there's no IF without a user's active imagination, as you are given descriptions, brief speeches, and prompts for action or navigation and must co-construct the game experience in collaboration with the game's program. But it's sometimes forgotten that games of this sort commonly offered in their boxes tangible aids to imagination, various paratextual objects, collectibles, or physical game tokens, from maps, fictional letters or postcards, documents, ID cards, plastic tokens such as a glow-in-the-dark "magick stone," and other found objects from within the diegetic game world, to supplemental collectibles or souvenirs. This sort of thing existed for non-digital games, as well, including *Dungeons and Dragons*, for example, where the game takes place as a kind of live performance prompted by books and rolled die and the interpretations of a gamemaster. In the case of IF, the objects were tellingly called "feelies" by the dominant publisher of IF in the 1980s, Infocom, and its player community at the time. Many of Infocom's "grey box" games (1984–1989) were released "in a book-like box" that included a tray containing feelies, as well as the game diskette and documentation.[13]

Tangibility, physical instantiation, it was implied, was in contrast to the more cerebral objects produced within the game itself. Nick Montfort has pointed out that the feelies in Infocom games in fact served as a kind of copy protection, as sometimes successful gameplay required the use of these objects, like the world descriptions in the printed manual for *Moonmist* or the elaborate decryption wheel for *A Mind Forever Voyaging*, which of course would not be included in a pirated digital copy, and without which gameplay would be impossible.[14]

It doesn't take much of a leap to see Agrippa as a similar kind of boxed set (though in a high-art register): a diskette with a program that played a core text, packaged in a boxlike book whose very essence is textured tangibility—and collectibility. Like the copy protection provided by clues in the IF feelies, Agrippa's self-encrypting text and prohibitively high price made it an ironic commentary on the very act of collecting versus consuming, and on the difference between intellectual property and physical property. Unlike the developers of the commercial games, the collaborators of Agrippa probably intended, or at least expected, some form of piracy to extend the reach of the work, like the very hack that actually did transcribe the poem onto the Internet.[15] But, in both cases, such communities of players were ready to see locked content as a challenge—trained to see it that way by the logic of games itself—were ready to rise to the challenge and beat the game, including the metagame of copy protection, even if it meant having recourse to a "cheat." And in each case, the design of the games and the design of Agrippa combine digital media with physical objects linked to those digital media, so obviously physical they're called feelies in the case of the IF games. The supposed untethered immateriality of the digital—a legal and commercial problem in the one case and an artistic theme in the other—motivates links to things you can touch. However inadvertently, that hybrid, the digital yoked to the physical, characterizes a good deal of games and gamelike media, besides Agrippa, in the 1980s and 1990s.

Kirschenbaum has already pointed out that Agrippa can be related to the genre of "artifactual fiction," and the larger work has a very important "artifactual dimension" (*Mechanisms*, 221, 218). Agrippa's fetish of the book and experimentation with mixed forms also characterized many other examples of media at the time, especially the CD-ROM hypertexts as published by the Voyager Company in the early 1990s. Like the 3.5-inch diskette in Agrippa, CD-ROMs are now becoming an increasingly obsolete physical medium for digital data, but were once everywhere. They were a dominant format for music from 1982, and, for a brief couple of years before the World Wide Web (and for a very brief time after its appearance), they were a major format for the publication of electronic books, as well, including many with multimedia content. CD-ROM e-book sales alone added up to almost $1 billion by 1994, with more than 8,000 titles published, and bookstores selling them. Sales dropped off radically after that, though some publishers continued to use them for reference works for a time.[16]

The Voyager Company eventually became known for publishing the Criterion Collection of films, but in the very early 1990s it was a major publisher of literary and artistic hypertexts. Voyager CD-ROMs came in a flat cardboard box, tastefully designed and including a labeled spine suitable for shelving, and they were to be played on a properly configured PC or Macintosh computer. They had text to read on the screen, illustrations, audio, video clips, slick layouts, and page-like visual designs, often filmic, even when the content was not strictly related to film, as with the company's edition of the Beatles' *A Hard Day's Night*, for example, which allowed, before DVDs, for searching and scene selection, outtakes, and images of related documentary materials. The *Poetry in Motion* CD-ROM published by Voyager in 1992—the same year as Agrippa—was essentially a re-edit of a documentary film by Ron Mann, with recut interview and performance video clips by contemporary poets, sometimes, as many were avant-garde or Beat poets, accompanied by music, and a table-of-contents menu that allowed for random access of the performances, and texts. Thumbnail windows down the margin showed the videos, each screen centered on "wallpaper" images behind the video windows, white-page layouts containing the text of each poem, beautifully typeset. Buttons at the footer allowed you to select versions of the text "as performed" or "as published," in itself a statement about the variant nature of texts, and a feature that made the CD-ROM useful for teaching literature. (I used it in my own Introduction to Poetry classes until changes in operating systems and CD-ROM drives made it impractical. As I write, a few of the individual video modules ripped from the CD-ROM survive out on YouTube.)

The late 1980s to early 1990s was a period of mixed-media, mixed-format electronic publishing. Earlier on, Eastgate Systems had published, mostly on diskettes, what it called "serious hypertexts," including the first "canonical" hypertext fiction, Michael Joyce's *Afternoon, A Story* (1987), with its compact Barthesian lexias. By the early 1990s, at the same time that Voyager Company was publishing its first CD-ROMS, Eastgate was still publishing works on diskette, such as Stuart Moulthrop's *Victory Garden* (1992), the navigation and structural organization of which was based on a hyperlinked image map. Indeed, as Kirschenbaum notes, an acclaimed Eastgate hypertext, *Uncle Buddy's Phantom Funhouse*, by John McDaid, was published on diskette in 1993 and came with "a boxful of faux documentary materials," not unlike the boxlike artist's book and "accompanying paraphernalia" of Agrippa (*Mechanisms*, 221n22). The Eastgate Website describes the experience of this "hyperfiction" in terms that sound exactly like playing a mixed-media game:

You'll have to pop the floppies into your Mac, drop the tapes into your boombox, and get ready to meet Buddy's friends, read his email, listen to his band, and sort out his (very strange) Tarot deck. Surreal and humorous, this is a world you will often return to and long remember.[17]

Much of game studies since the 1980s has understandably made a point of specifying what makes games unique, analyzing what sets them apart from film and literature. But it's important to remember that, historically, genre distinctions were often blurred, and often for interesting cultural reasons. Some critics in the late 1980s and early 1990s criticized multimedia hypertexts as merely adding superficial "bells and whistles" to the words that made up the poems or stories, and it was sometimes said that publishers such as Voyager and Eastgate were reducing literature to video games (as it was assumed by these critics that games were superficially about the sensory stimulation provided by the bells and whistles). Neo-Luddite critics such as Sven Birkerts would soon be publicly decrying the Death of the Book in the electronic age, at the same time that hypertext theory was being taught alongside cyberculture studies in some universities.[18]

The brief transitional time between wider adoption of the Internet (though still via dial-up connections, and in the form of email or Gopher searches, Usenet groups, or MUDs, say), and the exponential burst of interest brought about by the Mosaic browser and the Web around 1994, was the unstable moment in which Agrippa was published.[19] Physical storage and delivery media were in flux and overlapping, as well. In the context of Voyager's beautiful CD-ROMs and Eastgate's complex hypertexts at the same moment, the delivery of the poem "Agrippa" as a scrolling plaintext file on a 3.5-inch diskette was already something of a (cyber)punk gesture. Still, like those other hypertexts, Agrippa was about putting text into a media mix, as one component in an imagined world created by digital and physical (or, at least, somatic-feedback) components. In that sense, the neo-Luddite critics were precisely right: All of these experiments were about treating texts like games, or, more accurately, exploring the serious gamelike affordances of texts, broadly conceived.

One more juxtaposed example of a different kind of media on CD-ROM will help to further establish Agrippa's historical context. At the moment of Agrippa's Transmission at the end of 1992, brothers Rand and Robyn Miller were working on a game using Apple's hypertext authoring software, Hypercard, as a kind of flip-book-style animation platform. In development from 1991, *Myst* was released on CD-ROM for Macintosh in September 1993. It soon became, by some counts, the best-selling PC game of all time (until 2002, when *The Sims* displaced it). In the game, you explore a mysterious island from a first-person point of view, solving puzzles in order to unlock linked parallel worlds and to understand the backstory. You experience the game world as beautifully painted images, not photorealistic but aesthetically detailed, with occasional embedded video-clip cutscene speeches by live actors. And, like Agrippa, *Myst* is a multimedia work obsessed with books and the idea of the book.[20] Images of books show up everywhere in the game world, including especially magical books with people trapped in them, or that contain portals to other worlds. The in-game books are odd, hybrid objects. Some contain text and images that offer clues to the game. But some are old, large, leather-bound volumes on pedestals in niches that, when opened, turn out, oddly enough, to contain video screens in their cut-out pages, with live NPCs who address you directly, or bird's-eye-view flyovers of new worlds to which you are about to be transported. The self-conscious allegorical imagery couldn't be clearer at the meta-media level. *Myst*—like Agrippa, I'm arguing—is on one level about the transitional, mixed-media historical moment in which it was published, a moment when a portal to the digital realm was awkwardly embedded in the pages of a deliberately analog, antique codex book—or at least (in the case of *Myst*) in the digital image of that kind of iconic physical object.

Myst's backstory, or novelization, was published separately in 1995 as a physical hardcover book, complete with faux-leather binding, with fake water stains and scratches, and with its title made to look "stamped" or "burned" into the cover. It's a book that signifies "Book" in as many graphical ways as it can, just as the digital game's story and graphics are consistently, intensely bibliocentric. The published prequel novel, though it appeared soon after the CD-ROM game, is like the boxed feelies of earlier IF, contributing to the paratext of the game world, the threshold to actual gameplay that helps to prepare the player for the experience, a constellation of both digital and physical objects that make up the larger work called *Myst*. As a medium, games have developed sets of practical conventions for crossing and mixing media—digital and physical—in order to afford copy protection, create a deeper imaginative experience, and connect with and actively engage the fanbase that is crucial to any game's success. Both within the diegetic game world and in the surrounding paratext, the game happens in the social space, the grid of possibilities created by the conventions of the game, the platform and procedural, programmed structure of play, and the always somewhat unpredictable engagements of the players. The famed "magic circle" of gameplay actually marks a fluid and expansive social space. Agrippa is fascinating in part because, as Kirschenbaum says, it "sets in motion unintended, emergent, distributed events that transform the work in ways that were probably unanticipated but nonetheless clearly licensed by the original project ambitions" (*Mechanisms*, 244). This is, in fact, a pretty good definition of what makes any good game successful.

Digitization and the Crowd

What does "digitization" mean, really? Many seem to think of it metaphorically as a kind of vaporization, or perhaps like using the transporter on *Star Trek*, as the dematerializing and transporting of analog objects (books, say) as pure dis-embodied information, online, up to the cloud, over into the adjacent but invisible digital dimension: atoms "blown to bits."[21] This metaphor is only reinforced when libraries or other digitizers really do unbind and discard, or put into deep storage out of sight, the paper or vellum originals that have been scanned or photographed or had their texts keyed into digital files. But for many, digitization is imagined as a "one-way trip," like the bullets and camera shutters in "Agrippa." Books are sucked into the scanners and transformed into data, then whisked off to cyberspace, where they lead very different lives.

Of course, the digital humanities is in a position to challenge this metaphor, to educate the public according to a very different model, as DH practitioners know firsthand that the process is, in fact, highly recursive; is usually designed for two-way exchanges between analog and digital objects, from physical to digital and back again, designed with preservation of, and access to, archival originals built in; and, finally, that digitization has, in recent years, grown increasingly *more*, not less, dependent on readers collaborating with machine at every stage.

The digitization of our cultural heritage, archives and artifacts of various kinds, not only books and manuscripts, has been one of the imperatives behind the rise of the new digital humanities, one way it has remained associated with the longer-lived practices of humanities computing. The process of digitization has been underway for decades, driven by both not-for-profit and commercial agents. Michael Hart founded Project Gutenberg in 1971 at the University of Illinois, hand-keying in a copy of the U.S. Declaration of Independence on an ARPANET-connected mainframe.[22] The history of Western media is often summarized as running from Gutenberg to Google,[23] but we might think in this case of the gap, not of five and a half-plus centuries but of three-plus decades, between Project Gutenberg and Google Books (begun as Google Print and Google Library Project) in 2004. The new DH emerged in part in response to an exponentially accelerated push to digitize the archives in the era of better, inexpensive scanners and OCR software, distributed, more powerful desktop and mobile computers, and massively increased network bandwidth. But the earlier digitization project, begun by Michael Hart and named for the pioneer of the press, had (for all the flaws of its often hastily digitized texts) been based on crowdsourcing, and this basis remained crucial in response to the challenge posed by Google's massive digitization project, often using scanners with automated robotic page turners (but, of course, also relying on human operators at every stage, as ghostly images of people's hands in the scans remind us from time to time).

An influential article by Gregory Crane, published in 2006 (in the midst of the eversion), posed the question in response to what Google was doing: "What Do You Do with a Million Books?"[24] In 2009, the then-new NEH ODH, led by Brett Bobley, responded to this call, in part, and to the discussion to which it contributed with its Digging Into Data Challenge. Already, the controversial

Google Books and its competitor counter-projects—the Open Content Alliance (2005) and the HathiTrust initiative (2008)—were busy scanning, offering to DH practitioners the tantalizing prospect of large corpora of texts on which to experiment with mining, analysis, and visualization. Works such as Moretti's *Graphs, Maps, Trees* (2005) had paved the way theoretically. But, as Crane noted, many existing commercial digital collections, of the kind to which university libraries were subscribing, were creating a new kind of problem:

> Vast collections based on image books—raw digital pictures of books with searchable but uncorrected text from OCR—could arguably retard our long-term progress, reinforcing the hegemony of structures that evolved to minimize the challenges of a world where paper was the only medium of distribution and where humans alone could read.
>
> (Crane)

A world in which humans alone could read was, by 2006, already being supplanted by a world in which humans and machines both read in various kinds of feedback and feedforward loop (anticipating in this commonplace way the New Aesthetic's interest in understanding how the machines see the world): "Already the books in a digital library are beginning to read one another and to confer among themselves before creating a new synthetic document for review by their human readers." But the existing OCR was sometimes unreadable by the scanners and computers, starting with the obvious problems of older typefaces that the software could not recognize, most obviously the so-called long 's', widely used before the late eighteenth century, that many modern scanners rendered as an 'f,' and ligatures that connected one letter to another. The gap between printed materials and digitized product didn't much affect human reading of the photographic page images in these collections, but research, even in literature and even using paper-based materials, often proceeds by way of "reading" of very different kinds, more or less "distant," from index searching to comparative scanning. Bad OCR posed a serious problem for search and, more deeply, for *re*search, including digital humanities efforts to treat corpora of texts with a wider lens, as (relatively) big data.

Efforts to train computers to see the printed texts with greater accuracy have improved the scanning process a great deal, but some years back it became clear to many of those involved in digitizing texts that a solution that leveraged human intelligence might be much more effective, much sooner, than relying strictly on existing scanners and the limited AI available for character recognition. Laura Mandell, Director of the Initiative for Digital Humanities, Media and Culture at Texas A&M University and creator of 18thConnect, has said, "the way forward may not be through machines alone but through determining optimum machine–human interaction."[25] Her own work has started with existing OCR, produced early on by the large commercial databases by Gale/Cengage Learning, such as ECCO (Eighteenth Century Collections Online), for example. The publisher shared the OCR freely and allowed Mandell's teams to run through new scanning processes, then turn over to human correctors, potentially all registered users of 18thConnect.org, using a software tool designed for the purpose called TypeWright, inspired by the Australian Newspaper Digitisation Project. This crowdsourcing of OCR correction is based on the same fundamental principle behind reCAPTCHA—distributing the work of digitizing among machines and humans according to the strengths of each, with the goal of producing more accurately searchable texts that are amendable to the manipulations of various data-analysis and text-mining tools. (The corrected OCR is gradually returned to ECCO as it accumulates, thus improving the commercial database for future research.) In this way, a series of interconnected loops of human and machine reading are built cumulatively, as flaws in earlier machine reading are corrected by human rereaders and fed back into the database that will be searched and processed by machines. This is a truer, more complex, way to define digitization: not at all a one-way process of atomization, a system by which paper-based archives are blown to bits, but an intricately negotiated series of human and machine translations, back and forth from analog to digital and back again, as layers of data are added to existing physical materials, then refined over time by interactions with both machines and humans.

The digital humanities scholar and literature Professor at Northwestern University, Martin Mueller, names this process "collaborative curation" and deliberately refers to the text-correction "workflow" as a "mass-production environment."[26] This curation, he says, "occurs in a social and technical space" and relies on the work of "many hands." He argues, however, that this process is actually only a speeded-up version (though by orders of magnitude) of what happens in the "print world," as texts are produced, corrected, refined, annotated, and otherwise enriched by collaboration. The goal is to create software that encourages and supports collaborative curation *en passant*, as Mueller says, which implies an environment in which the larger process of digitization always includes in its scope multi-staged collaborative curation.

In this view, the problem with all those early plaintext Project Gutenberg e-texts, say, is that they are often hastily produced digital surrogates of what were in the first place problematic, error-filled editions (whatever is in the public domain or to hand), and that they usually remain frozen in rough, scanned form, that they are not part of a dynamic and open ecosystem for ongoing correction and augmentation. In other words, if such texts are unreliable, it's because they're *not properly* crowdsourced but are the products of lone "digitizers" with a copy of a book and a flatbed scanner (or time to key in whole texts). Of course such texts are full of errors. Errors are not the real problem—uncorrected errors are, and the absence of any collaborative curation. And, as Mueller argues, this is where the crowd comes in—a diverse range of participants, from high-school students who can solve micro-problems (along the lines of a reCAPTCHA) to experts in ancient Greek paleography. "Collaborative curation allows for a division of labor that matches tasks with the skills of curators," but also—and this is a crucial point—a "more radical division of labor divides tasks between man and machine" (6). Collaboration takes place between humans and computers as well: a view of the network's potential—and specifically its social potential—based on the general rejection over the past decade of the austere ideology of cyberspace.

At University College London, with the support of the college's Centre for Digital Humanities, the Transcribe Bentham project is crowdsourcing the transcription of 40,000 papers handwritten by eighteenth-century utilitarian philosopher Jeremy Bentham.[27] Transcribing these papers is, of course, the first step toward digitizing them, making them accessible for reading and study, but also making them amenable to machine reading and processing, including text and data mining and analysis. Paleography is a complicated area of study. Anyone who has edited manuscripts from earlier centuries knows that, even in the relatively more modern eras, reading manuscripts involves complicated questions about chain lines and watermarks and texture of paper, the vagaries of different inks, quills, and pencils, layerings and chronological sequence in which passages, insertions, cancelations, or corrections were written, rough drafts versus fair copies meant for press or safekeeping, identifying the author's hand versus those of family members or editors (or censors)—all of this before or while you "simply" transcribe what is written on a sheet of paper or in a pocket notebook. But, if we're honest, all of us who have done this kind of work also know that sometimes you just need another pair of eyes, and there are times when an amateur or outsider's perspective is actually better. In a commonsense way, it would seem good practice to enlist many pairs of eyes to translate from manuscript to typed digital text. This is the premise behind Transcribe Bentham, which is using the network as a whole to enlist interested amateurs in helping to prepare a 70-volume scholarly edition of the *Collected Works of Jeremy Bentham* (which has been underway since the 1950s). Users create accounts and access the online interface called the Transcription Desk, based on a tool developed from open-source software, where a digital image of a manuscript page appears, which people can transcribe by typing in an adjacent text editor. If the transcription is used in the *Collected Works*, the user is credited for her or his contribution to the edition.

There are, of course, a set of easy ironies, ripe for the taking, about an online, mass-produced edition of the works of a thinker who famously (or infamously) articulated the calculus of the greatest good for the greatest number, and whose name is associated, thanks largely to Michel Foucault, with his design for a modern prison built with machinery for total surveillance, the Panopticon. But the fact is such calls for public involvement are traditional in the preparation of scholarly editions. Formerly, the "public" might have meant the very small world of subscribers to *Notes & Queries*, and they might have been asked to identify a reference in a text, rather than helping to transcribe thousands of the author's manuscripts. The network just makes possible the mass distribution of such small acts of collaboration in order to get things done. The key point is that a project such as Transcribe Bentham is not turning over an important, skilled, scholarly task to just anyone out there among the "general public" (as the UCL publicity refers to its user base). It's first of all set up for self-selection by people willing to establish accounts, log in, and manage the interface, but, more importantly, it aims to turn over the work to very *many* users among the general public. As Bentham would have appreciated, actually, the odds of accurately transcribing the work—or at least of having a sufficient number of attempts to make interpretation more convincing—may increase as the number of transcribers increases. The software is designed to handle massively multi-user transcription, as it were, and to concatenate the results in order to allow the expert editors to arrive at the best readings. The general motto of crowdsourcing applies in this case: The wisdom of crowds means that no one knows everything, but everyone knows some thing. What I might not see, you may be able to. The hive mind can collectively achieve what individual bees can't.

Co-op Mode

That last sentence was a reference to the genre of ARGs, and I want to use it to shift the subject for a moment to games. One of the earliest and best known ARGS was *I Love Bees*, a viral marketing game in 2004 to promote Microsoft's *Halo 2* that took on a life of its own. The game's creator, Jane McGonigal, is the best-known theorist of ARGs and the key inventor and developer of the genre.

People from all over the country played the game, a kind of networked descendant of the geeky live-action role-playing games (LARPs) college students had played for decades, or like a scavenger hunt played out across the real-world map, with the support of the online data provided over the Internet and phone lines, as well as in more concrete forms of media. For at least a certain period for some players, it was difficult to tell where the game left off and reality began—a kind of deliberate recreation of the legendary reported effect of Orson Welles' 1938 radio play, *War of the Worlds* (which, like *Halo*, was also about alien warfare, you'll recall). In the end, the storyline of the *I Love Bees* ARG intersected in interesting ways with the story of the video game it was created to market. But, for many players, the ARG had a life of its own quite apart from the ostensible purpose of marketing *Halo*. It demonstrated the pleasures and practical benefits of harnessing what came to be called the wisdom of crowds—a more optimistic version of what some dark science fiction called the hive mind (one source for the game's bees motif). In this case, they played along with and collectively helped to solve puzzles, complete quests, and produce a distributed work of fiction in which they were all actively engaged in real time, a very real, if temporary and opportunistic, networked community that was not virtual, that deliberately crossed digital media objects with physical objects and places.

McGonigal has created a number of ARGs, pervasive games, and so-called serious games, for example, *Find the Future* (2011), designed to coincide with the 100th anniversary of the New York Public Library. For the kickoff event, a team of 500 gamers were selected to spend the night in the main branch on 42nd Street, documenting key works and artifacts in the archives, including Dickens' letter opener and Kerouac's glasses, as well as an original copy, in Jefferson's hand, of the *Declaration of Independence*. As players completed a series of quests based on finding the artifacts and scanning QR codes using a mobile iOS app, they wrote short essays that were collected, printed, and made into a bound paper book on the spot, there in the library (an artisan bookbinder was onsite), which was then accessioned, added to the stacks as part of the permanent collection. The reports were also added to the Website, where an online game with quests for users continues. Special power-ups are associated with the artifacts—Thinking Lion, Conjuring Hand, Hero's Compass—that are like the motivating "badges" that have been so controversial in the educational arena, fairly arbitrary achievements attached to finding and documenting the artifacts that wrap an experience of basic library research and browsing in a game structure. The game continues online and in New York Public Library branches. ARGs make a design feature of the necessity for even digital games to take place in a mixed-reality space that includes physical controllers, the player's body, the space in which you play, arcade cabinetry, tokens, booklets, guides, and feelies—or their modern equivalents: collectible plastic replica weapons or miniature action figures.

Digitization games, such as reCAPTCHAs, harness human intelligence and skilled activity to augment or aid in the process of moving analog artifacts online, or, to put it more precisely, to aid in the process of attaching data and metadata to those objects so that the users can do things with them—or their data and digital surrogates—online. In other areas of science and scholarship, similar games have been employed. *Foldit*, for example (2008), developed by the University of Washington, has crowdsourced the folding of proteins, getting players to arrange 3D models of proteins in ways that translate to actual molecular science. *Type Attack* is a game for transcribing text from digital images in which players compete to see how fast they can transcribe a given text. The creator of reCAPTCHA, Luis von Ahn, also designed *The ESP Game* to escalate the creation of metadata tags for images on the Web, partly in order to make image searches more effective. (It was, for a time, made use of by Google image search.) Once again, a limitation in traditional AI, something the machine can't do very well—recognize graphical images—is sourced to humans working in symbiotic cooperation with machines. His term for this, again, is "human computation," a construction not coincidentally close to "humanities computing" or "digital humanities." Pairs of users are shown an image and then independently come up with keywords to describe it. When their words match, that word is applied as an image label, and they're given another. Note that it takes a large number of players, however—a crowd—for this game to really contribute to image metadata in any meaningful way. One human tagging images won't do: hence the basic structure in which pairs of taggers symmetrically validate (or not) each other's tags. For today's casual mobile gamers, this should sound very familiar. Indeed, playing *Draw Something* on Facebook works the same way.

The cooperative competition to complete a task is the most important gamelike feature adopted by these "games with a purpose." It's what they have in common with games in general: the particular form of their social nature. It's not just that you can trash talk players in online play; even single-player games are structured around the social potential implied by their very algorithmic structure. You play versus other players, live or asynchronously, in separate moves, but also—and this is a crucial point—you play versus NPCs, essentially software robots of varying degrees of sophistication. Or, you play versus the game as a whole, which is to say versus the design, including algorithmic constraints and affordances of the programming and rules and story, which is always also, to some degree, playing versus the designers' intelligence. In a classic console game such as *Mario Kart*, which may seem trivial to outside observers and non-gamers, I am frequently playing across all these modes of interaction: with live players from around the world (the opening setup uses an animated globe to indicate the location of each), with NPCs of various kinds, with the designed features of each level—track shape, hazards, power-ups—and, ultimately, with the software programs running all of this (on Nintendo servers, across the Internet's protocols, and on my console as accessed from an optical disk), on top of the software and hardware platform of my Wii console with all its components, and across the digital and physical infrastructure of the Internet itself—including, ultimately, fiber-optic cables under the oceans that make possible the multiplayer interactions of our cartoon avatars and their racing vehicles. People often focus on the highly competitive nature of video games, but think for a moment about the level of *cooperation*, of *collaboration*, really, involved in a bout of *Mario Kart* (or *Call of Duty*). The very idea of playing *versus* all these kinds of others—other players, AI, the game, and the designers—is based on a profound and subtle notion of cooperative competition. As I have argued elsewhere, it's as much like improvisational theater as it is an actual physical or verbal fight. It can be nasty or combative, yes, sometimes toxically so, depending on the game and the player community (and the level of anonymity, for example).[28] But, ultimately, video-game gameplay amounts to a joining (within or at the circumference of the famous magic circle) of human and machine intelligences in a combined effort—what Katherine Hayles calls a "dynamic heterarchy"—to make a game happen, to make meaning. That's the reason games are important for the digital humanities: Both are based on, and can help us learn to make good use of, this kind of fundamental human–machine dynamic. This dynamic is fundamental to our interactions with the network as a whole, as we see in miniature every time we solve a CAPTCHA. Digital humanities crowdsourcing is just a more pronounced way of leveraging the more profoundly gamelike features of the digital network (rather than the superficial features targeted by so-called gamification) for the purpose of making something meaningful, making meaning. That's already what digital games afford: collaborative modes of harnessing together human and machine intelligence, across the perceived boundary of the physical and the digital. That, in fact, could serve as a pretty good definition of the digital humanities.

Coda re: Agrippa Again

On July 22, 2012, it was announced on the Internet that the Agrippa code had been broken. (I saw it on Twitter as I was working on this chapter.) The legendary encryption that had seemed such a challenge to the hackers in 1992 was cracked by participants in an open cryptanalysis competition, making use of materials recovered and curated by The Agrippa Files Website. The winning submission was by Robert Xiao, but the whole effort was reported in a collaborative open-source mode. All the submissions and implementations of code were published online under a Creative Commons License (Attribution-Noncommerical 3.0 Unported). The contest sponsors implemented the decryption/re-encryption in Javascript, so that anyone who was curious could run the process in a Web browser. Quinn Dupont, at the University of Toronto, summed up the key historical revelation: "The contest proved that Agrippa does use encryption, although the cryptographic algorithm is very insecure, even for its release in 1992." So the rumored "military-grade" encryption—which led to debates at the time about censorship and national security—was yet another fiction spun from ideology, like the notion of cyberspace itself. More significantly for the purposes of this chapter, the gamelike cooperative competition of the contest vividly demonstrates both the true nature of the original artifact/event that was Agrippa (though this was obscured by the ideology of cyberspace in the 1990s), and something essential about the digital humanities in action. Matthew Kirschenbaum himself, praising the contestants for making a valuable contribution to scholarship, summed it up on Twitter (July 22, 2012): "Like AGRIPPA itself, the whole 'contest' was an exercise in collaboration and crowdsourcing."

★

Notes

1. William Gibson, *Neuromancer* (New York: Ace Books, 1984), 51.
2. See Wikipedia on the history of CAPTCHA and reCAPTCHA, http://en.wikipedia.org/wiki/Capcha and http://en.wikipedia.org/wiki/Recaptcha; as well as on Luis von Ahn, http://en.wikipedia.org/wiki/Luis_von_Ahn.
3. The reCAPTCHA Website, http://google.com/recaptcha/learnmore.
4. Steve Lohr, "Algorithms Get a Human Hand in Steering Web," *New York Times* (March 10, 2013), http://nytimes.com/2013/03/11/technology/computer-algorithms-rely-increasingly-on-human-helpers.html?hp&_r=0.
5. Andrew Blum, *Tubes: A Journey to the Center of the Internet* (New York: Ecco/Harper Collins, 2012), Kindle edition.

6. Editions and copies vary in significant ways, but those differences are not my focus here. For the bibliographic and archival details, see Matthew G. Kirschenbaum, *Mechanisms: New Media and the Forensic Imagination* (Cambridge, MA: MIT Press, 2008), 213–48; and the scholarly Website produced at the University of California Santa Barbara, The Agrippa Files, ed. Alan Liu, Paxton Hehmeyer, James J. Hodge, Kimberly Knight, David Roh, Elizabeth Swanstrom, and Matthew G. Kirschenbaum, http://agrippa.english.ucsb.edu/.

7. Matthew G. Kirschenbaum, Doug Reside, and Alan Liu, "No Round Trip: Two New Primary Sources for Agrippa," The Agrippa Files (posted 2008), http://agrippa.english.ucsb.edu/kirschenbaum-matthew-g-with-doug-reside-and-alan-liu-no-round-trip-two-new-primary-sources-for-agrippa.

8. Courtney Traub, interview with Kevin Begos, Jr., *The Oxonian Review*, 19.1 (April 23, 2012), http://oxonianreview.org/wp/an-interview-with-kevin-begos-jr.

9. N. Katherine Hayles, *How We Became Posthuman: Virtual Bodies in Cybernetics, Literature, and Informatics* (Chicago: University of Chicago Press, 1999), e.g., 2.

10. William Gibson, "Agrippa," author's Website, http://williamgibsonbooks.com/source/agrippa.asp.

11. Kirschenbaum et al., "No Round Trip."

12. N. Katherine Hayles, *Electronic Literature: New Horizons for the Literary* (Notre Dame: Notre Dame University Press, 2008), 45, 48.

13. The Infocom Gallery, http://infocom.elsewhere.org/gallery/.

14. Nick Montfort, *Twisty Little Passages: An Approach to Interactive Fiction* (Cambridge, MA: MIT Press, 2003), 158–59.

15. Following the Transmission, there were even reports that Gibson, or Gibson through an intermediary, had confirmed that the release of the poem into the wild was part of the overall plan. See The Agrippa Files, http://agrippa.english.ucsb.edu.

16. Eileen Gardiner and Ronald G. Musto, "The Electronic Book," in *The Oxford Companion to the Book*, eds. Michael F. Suarez and H. R. Woudhuysen (Oxford: Oxford University Press, 2010), 164–71 (166).

17. Eastgate Systems, *Uncle Buddy's Phantom Funhouse*, http://eastgate.com/catalog/Funhouse.html.

18. Sven Birkerts, *The Gutenberg Elegies: The Fate of Reading in an Electronic Age* (London: Faber & Faber, 1994).

19. Kirschenbaum, *Mechanisms*, 219.

20. Steven E. Jones, "MYST and the Late Age of Print," *Post Modern Culture* 7.2 (1997), copy available http://pmc.iath.virginia.edu/text-only/issue.197/jones.197.

21. I take the phrase from a book on the digitization of everyday life: Hal Abelson, Ken Ledeen, and Harry Lewis, *Blown to Bits: Your Life, Liberty, and Happiness After the Digital Explosion* (New York: Addison-Wesley Professional, 2008).

22. "Project Gutenberg," Wikipedia, http://en.wikipedia.org/wiki/Project_Gutenberg.

23. Peter Shillingsburg, *From Gutenberg to Google: Electronic Representations of Literary Texts* (Cambridge, UK: Cambridge University Press, 2006).

24. Gregory Crane, "What Do You Do with a Million Books?," *D-Lib Magazine* 12.3 (March 2006), http://dlib.org/dlib/march06/crane/03crane.html.

25. Laura Mandell, "OCR Workshop Proposal," Initiative for Digital Humanities, Media, and Culture, IDHMC CommentPress, 2012, http://idhmc.tamu.edu/commentpress/ocr-workshop.

26. Martin Mueller, "Collaboratively Curating Early Modern English Texts," Project Bamboo wiki draft, August, 9, 2011, https://wiki.projectbamboo.org/plugins/viewsource/viewpagesrc.action?pageId=24648795.

27. "Transcribe Bentham: A Participatory Initiative," http://ucl.ac.uk/transcribe-bentham/.

28. Steven E. Jones, *The Meaning of Video Games* (New York: Routledge, 2008), 108–10.

4

PLACES

It's hard to imagine the Internet today without maps, flags, pins, directions, check-ins, and, in general, data tied to location. If cyberspace is leaking out into and colonizing the world, as William Gibson has said, one of the preconditions for this—in material terms—was the exploitation of GPS (the global positioning system), made possible after the previously established "selective availability" was turned off in May 2000. Though the immediate result for average users was more accurate navigation systems in their cars, in relatively short order we had Google Maps. Gibson himself once cited Google in general as "a central and evolving structural unit not only of the architecture of cyberspace, but of the world" now that we have entered the era of the eversion.[1] Along with the 3D Google Earth, Google Maps became a crucial piece of the search giant's Web services just after its initial public offering in August 2004, and—along with the competing free and open-access OpenStreetMap, as well as persisting commercial services (some of which predate Google's)—the Google Maps API has led to countless applications, including digital humanities projects. Because of a series of related developments, maps and linked data have been at the heart of recent changes in our understanding of the network that surrounds us, the shift implied in Gibson's relocation of Google's influence from "cyberspace" to "the world." The dominance of mobile platforms has meant that, for many users, maps + data are inseparable from what they think of as accessing the Internet. The eversion of cyberspace is intertwined with the rise of networked mapping services, and the metaphor of eversion provides a broader cultural context for the so-called spatial turn in the humanities during this same period. The more general metaphorical turn—from the notional nonspace of cyberspace to the world as a dynamically mapped series of overlapping, data-rich places—has stimulated new kinds of digital humanities research and, more generally, pointed to a shift in the orientation of the humanities outward, toward the complex terrain of the physical world.

Network in Space

GPS still seems mysterious to many, though it's a kind of banal mystery increasingly taken for granted. Especially when they access it on their phones, many people may have trouble separating GPS from the Internet and the cell-phone network as a whole. Apps-based interfaces for mobile devices have made it easier to treat maps, like other apps, as modular functions of a mysteriously remote set of data sources. On the face of it, nothing would seem closer to a cyberspatial idea of the network than such remote services from on high—in the case of GPS, literally from space, data beamed from orbiting vessels that are invisible, or only visible as slowly moving stars across the night sky. The GPS system is more complicated than that romantic orbital vision, even as most people actually experience it daily. Even a cursory review of the material realities of the system shines a light on the mixed-reality nature of the network on which so many of us now depend every day for countless tiny data transactions.

Everyone knows that the satellites in orbit around the Earth provide us with locational data that translate into walking or driving directions via detailed maps. People see the little glowing pin or arrow icons on handheld maps pulsate with what they take to be their signal, a source of data from space. Some have used dedicated devices in their cars or on their boats for even longer, and many have had the data personified as turn-by-turn directions read aloud. The movies, and a general paranoia about what this essentially military technology is capable of seeing on the ground, have given all of us a sense, more or less accurate, that a constellation of satellites is always looking down on us and can see our devices and tell us where we are, provide pictures, even, of places around the globe. Google, with some other services, has now attached some of those pictures to maps, so that you can see the Great Wall or a hurricane from space, or zoom in on your own backyard and see the shed you tore down last summer still standing in the slightly dated photo. We are beginning to take for granted the ability to gain an orbital view.

The GPS system is, of course, more complicated than that, both messier and literally more down to earth. It's true that civilians (and the businesses that market services to them) do have a relatively new ability to connect to satellite data in a much more accurate way than just over a decade ago. Just to focus on the U.S. satellite system for the purposes of explanation: At midnight on May 1, 2000, the government turned off selective availability to the GPS (which had been created in 1973), unscrambling the signals of the existing 24 plus satellites so they could be received by commercial and individual users, instantly increasing the accuracy and strength of GPS applications of all kinds.[2] Of course, the military retained an even more precise, exclusive capability than was provided by this standard service, but the descrambling in 2000 improved standard GPS precision from about 100 meters to about 20 meters. A series of steps followed, including a more dispersed oversight of the system, beyond the Department of Defense, with the establishment in 2004 of the National Space-Based Positioning Executive Committee, and successive waves of system upgrades and modernization. Meanwhile, that same year, Google acquired a small company, Where 2 Technologies, and its mapping application became Google Maps (2005). Over the next few years, as features were added and the program evolved, it led to a mobile application (2006) and to cross-integrations of various features with the company's other mapping and GIS application, the one with the visually impressive 3D animated globe interface that spins and allows you to zoom in from space, Google Earth. The basic core technology of Google Earth, a CIA-funded program called EarthViewer 3D, developed by Keyhole, Inc., was acquired by Google in 2004, at the same time as Google Maps. Google Earth was originally a standalone program for the PC; you had to download it and run it locally on your computer. Later, it was made available to run in a Web browser. 3D and 2D mapping services have different potential users and applications, but there is a good deal of overlap in the underlying technology of the parallel systems. Nevertheless—thanks in large part to the introduction of smartphones in 2006–2007—2D Google Maps have probably had the more pervasive impact on more people's everyday lives and on the wider culture.

The Maps API, introduced in 2005, allowed developers to create custom mashups of Websites and programs with Google Maps, and this was crucial for digital humanities applications, as we'll see below. (A year later, the OpenStreet-Map Foundation was established to produce the same kinds of service for free in a distributed, collaborative, open-access form.) In order to understand what's at stake in those humanities applications, to understand how Google Maps and Google Earth, GPS and GIS helped the new DH to emerge, I want to disentangle for a moment the threads of the systems involved, to rehearse in simple language the basics of using something as ubiquitous as Google Maps. What are you doing when you access GPS in Google Maps on your mobile phone or tablet?

At the time I'm writing, the Google Maps app has continued successfully to compete with Apple's own proprietary mapping software for iOS 6—which was released hastily to negative reviews. Glitches abounded in Apple's maps, creating distorted images and misdirections (a Tumblr blog was created just to collect them[3]), illustrating the importance of deep data, built up over time and frequently updated, over well-designed user interfaces when it comes to geolocative applications—or, arguably, any applications that connect Internet data to the physical world. At any rate, the Google Maps app for iOS (which is like Apple's own app in many of the general characteristics I'll be summarizing) allows you to see a map view, a "satellite" version, or a hybrid of both versions overlaid. But, in fact, all the maps are hybrids, in the sense that the satellite version is actually composed predominantly of high-altitude aerial photography, though some satellite imagery may be used for very long zooms. The maps are loaded in graphical segments or "tiles," as needed, using a combined Web services technique known as AJAX (asynchronous Javascript + XML). That's why you see the edge of the map building itself out in front of you as you scroll. GPS is invoked when you touch the small blue compass arrow icon, which drops a blue pin on your location. Radiating blue circles actually indicate that Location Services are turned on for your phone and that your location has been determined, though some mistakenly take the animation as a direct indicator of a GPS signal being received, by analogy with the familiar bars indicating cell-phone signal strength.

In general, any time actual GPS satellite data are invoked, a minimum of three orbiting satellite signals are received and interpreted, through a process known as trilateration. That means that radio-wave messages, containing precise time (based on onboard atomic clocks), identifying information and current location from three satellites, are received and decoded by your device in order to gauge your distance from each. The overlapping spheres thus determined, each containing a satellite at its center and you on its outer circumference, provide your approximate 3D location on Earth, to within 10 meters, expressed as latitude, longitude, and elevation. A fourth satellite is used to confirm the timing of the atomic clocks in the satellites, further pinpointing the location of the receiving device.

But an iPhone or Android phone, for example, is designed to combine this kind of trilateration using its GPS radio receiver with additional available data about nearby WiFi networks and cell towers, which help the device estimate satellite locations before they're transmitted via live signals, or when transmission temporarily fails. That's Assisted GPS (AGPS).[4] The Location Service on your phone is relying on more than GPS, a system of various signals and data sources, processed locally on the phone as well as (in the case of the iPhone) on Apple's servers (and potentially preprocessed at a number of points along the way, from satellites, to monitoring stations, to cell towers). The device passes along nearby WiFi networks and cell towers to a server, where approximate coordinates are calculated and sent back. Apple has said it keeps these location data about WiFi and cell towers cached on its servers. One technology writer has speculated, then, that the little blue pin and radiating circle is a telling indicator of this process in action.

> Typically, you see a large blue circle appear nearly instantly, a result of what must be a consultation of the local database. The circle becomes smaller as more information is used, still from cellular and Wi-Fi sources, to create a better trilateration. This data is also used to provide more clues into decoding the best GPS satellite information, allowing the use of quite small fragments of data or even raw signals to get a better lock. Finally, the circle becomes a single dot when iOS is confident it has a solid GPS lock.
>
> (Fleishman)

Determining location on your mobile device is the result of a complicated set of engagements with many networks, interwoven or alternating sets of data from different sources all around us, using different protocols and transmission channels to beam signals from buildings, towers, and, yes, devices orbiting the Earth. The geolocation databases of network and signal locations that Apple and others are creating and keeping, and which may also, of course, be valuable for marketing (both Apple and Google have run into challenges to this set of practices in recent years, for different reasons), are in part crowdsourced—built up from data gathered over time from very many anonymous sources, including mobile phones. As of 2011, Google Maps Map Maker allowed users on the ground (the saying is apt in this case) to make corrections to the maps online, which are then vetted by Google or local experts before being posted to the public maps.

Even in this most literal instance of the network's being located in space, using devices that surround the globe in an orbiting mesh, the GPS system is in significant ways Earthbound: It's monitored, informed, and controlled by a corresponding mesh of terrestrial stations and antennae, and is actually employed on our mobile devices in alternating cooperation with the grid of cell towers or WiFi routers scattered across the map. The data of the whole system are very much two-way, or multichannel, actually, and they are dependent on very many users whose devices are participating in the data gathering all the time. Even a rudimentary understanding of how this system of systems works, the kind of basic summary of the material platforms involved that I've just rehearsed, serves to remind us that the GPS is tethered to the terrestrial map, positioned on the Earth we inhabit, contrary to conventional mystifications of what satellites can do from on high. GPS is no more cyberspatial than the Internet itself.

Fictions of the Locative

There were precursors to Google Maps, of course, including navigation systems for commercial and private use in vehicle systems in the 1980s, though they were necessarily less accurate than they became after selective availability was turned off in 2000. Long before that, futurists and science-fiction authors had imagined such applications, and fiction and reality, as mediated by real precursor technologies, are actually much closer than many people realize. On the other hand, the emerging technologies have been re-formed by the contingencies of real-world conditions, by the collective desires and experiences of the people who use them, so it's sometimes the swerves from imagined precursors that matter the most. The gaps between imagination and reality, the distance between fictional versions and realized technologies, often prove the most instructive.

Neal Stephenson's *Snow Crash* (1992) famously imagined an online VR more populated and gamelike than Gibson's cyberspace had been: the Metaverse. It's a fictional, virtual place, still recognizable in part because the best-known virtual world that was actually developed, Linden Lab's Second Life, was deliberately modeled on it, with its customizable avatars, spaces for social interaction, games, businesses, classrooms, constructible objects in a 3D VR in which real estate, islands, buildings, and geological features make up the experience. Second Life was introduced in 2003 and was the center of intense publicity, even hype, in the two to three years that followed, but experienced a possible decline in residents—and certainly experienced a decline in public attention—thereafter (for a number of reasons, this is hard to determine, as some bots may have been counted along with some people who are inactive but whose avatars are left "camping" in the world), a decline noticeable by around 2009.[5] In many respects, it represents the high-water mark for cyberspatial, immersive, 3D virtual worlds as a model of the future of the Internet.

In *Snow Crash*, as any user of Second Life—or, for that matter, any user of a MUD from an earlier era—might do, Hiro Protagonist returns to his personal home space, his office, in the Metaverse, only to find a new (virtual) object placed there:

> A globe about the size of a grapefruit, a perfectly detailed rendition of Planet Earth, hanging in space at arm's length in front of his eyes . . . a piece of CIC software called, simply, Earth. It is the user interface that CIC uses to keep track of every bit of spatial information that it owns—all the maps, weather data, architectural plans, and satellite surveillance stuff.[6]

The CIC is a fictional version of the CIA, and the navigation object is understood to be advanced technology made available for early-adopter civilian use. The globe-shaped model includes detailed graphics representing weather systems, and even satellites orbiting the globe, like the ones that provide the data for building the model (Hiro thinks at first that one of these tiny images of an orbiting satellite is a gnat in his field of vision). When you concentrate and zoom in, the view changes with a single, rapid, swooping sensation, "like a space-walking astronaut who has just fallen out of his orbital groove" (109–10), an animation feature that found its way into the real Google Earth—though that may also have been inspired by the Eames Studios' film, *The Powers of 10*, with its vertiginous zooms out into space and back into Earth.

This fictional navigational software, Earth, was a direct inspiration to the coders at Keyhole Inc. who created the program mentioned above, EarthView 3D, which, again, was the precursor to Google Earth and was indeed developed with CIA funds. Google Earth still makes use of the Keyhole Markup Language (KML) for its globe-based 3D modeling and mapping software. Layers and features are always being added by developers. As with Google Maps, the API is available, so that independent developers can incorporate Google Earth in different Websites and programs. It's remarkable in many ways how close to the science-fiction technology imagined in 1992 is the real technology released 13 years later.

But pause for a moment to notice one very important difference between Stephenson's imagined Earth and Google Earth (or even its precursor, EarthView 3D), one that makes all the difference between 1992 and today, Stephenson's

Metaverse and the actual network as it has evolved: In the novel, Hiro Protagonist—through his avatar, actually—is using the Earth application *inside* the immersive VR world of the Metaverse. He's logged in when he uses the spinning grapefruit-sized globe. Nowadays, almost all people use Google Maps and Google Earth out in the real world. That's the whole point. Now, like almost anything else you can think of, Google Earth has been instantiated virtually inside Second Life. Back in 2007, developers Josh Knauer and Stephane Desnault created what they called GeoGlobe, a virtual version of Google Earth accessed from within the (actual) virtual world.[7] Although it included a (blank) globe icon, it was more like Google Maps in terms of the user experience than like Stephenson's floating small globe. In the version now shown only in video (the SURL, or Second Life URL, now seems to be linked to a region inside SL that no longer exists), your Second Life avatar was located *inside* an inverted virtual globe, built using SL's VR room, so it's as if you were standing in a giant round room like an IMAX movie theater, surrounded by the world map. You could zoom in and click on markers created using KML to pop up labels and URLs from which you could access Websites. But this is an exception to the rule. Although it has certainly been possible in limited ways to access Google Maps or Google Earth from within virtual worlds, in general, this has proved much less compelling than the myriad uses of these programs, online, yes, but not immersed in VR—usually on a mobile handheld device, navigating the physical world. Most people just assume that the whole point of Google Earth and Google Maps is to use them in conjunction with the actual topography of the physical world, either while navigating places or with direct reference to data taken from, or pointing to, physical places.

This shift, from imagined virtual Earth to today's Google Earth, provides a context for Stephenson's 2011 novel, *Reamde*, as a revisionist account by the author of *Snow Crash* of the relation of online worlds to the real world, of the Metaverse to the physical universe.[8] In terms of genre, it's more techno-thriller than science fiction, the story of a tech mogul who created an MMORPG clearly inspired by *World of Warcraft*, but with some features that resemble Second Life (or *Minecraft*) as well. The action of the book plays out in both the traditional fantasy world of the game—where a virus is released that's like a more realistic version of the titular Snow Crash software from Stephenson's earlier book—and the real world, ranging from the Pacific Northwest and the woods along the Canadian border to Asia and back. The geographic theme runs throughout the story—routes and maps and shortcuts and portals are everywhere—and it runs back and forth across the porous boundary between the two worlds, suggesting that it's just part of mundane reality nowadays to move in and out of game worlds and the real world, that points of contact or portals in and out are part of the fabric of everyday life.

And yet, this is not a novel about the world becoming a video game, or not exactly. That is the case, more or less, with Ernest Cline's novel, *Ready Player One* (2011), in which a dystopian future world ca. 2044 is besotted with 1980s pop culture and has (as in *The Matrix*) flipped the relationship: The online world has become the preferable destination for most of the world's population, a refuge from a depleted and overcrowded urban landscape. In one passage about the real world, we see crowds of homeless people in tent cities standing around barrel fires or waiting in line at free solar-power recharging stations, "wearing bulky, outdated visors and haptic gloves. Their hands made small, ghostly gestures as they interacted with the far more pleasant reality of the OASIS ('Ontologically Anthropocentric Sensory Immersive Simulation') via one of GSS's free wireless access points."[9] The OASIS is a globally ubiquitous, online virtual world. It's a kind of MMORPG, like *World of Warcraft*, and contains countless actual games, but it's also the alternative world in which the majority of the world's population conduct their business and otherwise live out their daily lives. In other words, it's a fictional realization of the hype that once surrounded Second Life and cyberspace as a whole. The novel's protagonist, Wade Watts (or Parzival, his online avatar), lives physically in "the stacks," a literal stack of mobile homes outside Oklahoma City. But the point is that it might as well be almost anywhere. (Only proximity to servers to avoid lag really matters.) Wade spends as much time as possible hiding out in an abandoned van (which he describes in fanboy style as his "refuge," "Batcave," and "Fortress of Solitude"), where he logs on to attend school virtually and to play games in the OASIS. He has a true second life online, which is really more like his first life, as his rare forays out into physical reality are harsh and dangerous experiences (at least until the very end of the story).

The novel is massively nostalgic ("massively" seems the more precise term in this case, rather than the more idiomatic "deeply"). Not only is it overloaded with references to 1980s pop culture, it also feels oddly like a kind of wistful celebration, one last full-on representation of the old ideal of cyberspace or the Metaverse—the lawless frontier where people access the 3D online world using goggles and haptic gloves and suits, living through their avatars in a kind of posthuman virtuality that seems better than the degraded real world. Explicitly, the book intends a critique of this vision, of course, as its scenes in the dystopian physical world make clear, as well as moments when the protagonist realizes the emptiness of his online existence—"the world I spent my days in was not, in fact, the real one" (195)—and sees his immersion rig for what it is: "an elaborate contraption for deceiving my senses, to allow me to live in a world that didn't exist . . . [a] cell where I had willingly imprisoned myself" (197–98). At one point near the end, he is told, baldly, "reality is *real*" and "don't hide in here forever" (364). And the Hollywood ending is about as simple as it gets: The alienated hero finally kisses the girl In Real Life (experiencing "the strange new sensation of actually touching one another") and suddenly loses his addictive desire to go online (372). Nevertheless, the logic of this critique implies the inevitable triumph and universal appeal of total immersion, as well as assuming a functioning binary opposition between online life and real life, what, as I discussed in Chapter 1, Nathan Jurgenson calls "digital dualism." The most telling indicator of the nature of this fictional vision of the future is found in a small detail: The wearable interface suits popular with gamers are known as "dichotomy wear" because they're "wired for OASIS use."

> They didn't have haptics, but the pants and shirt could link up with my portable immersion rig, letting it know what I was doing with my torso, arms, and legs, making it easier to control my avatar than with a gloves-only interface.
>
> (300)

The wearables are "dichotomy wear" rather than, say, "augmented-reality wear" or "mixed-reality wear"; their purpose is total immersion, based on the assumption that the two worlds are ineluctably divided.

By contrast, Stephenson's *Reamde* takes a somewhat jaded look at the limitations of immersive online experiences and is set in the present (or very recent past). Its protagonist founded a company that built a highly successful MMORPG, but he raised his funds as a drug smuggler hiking across the US–Canada border in a remote territory, and the story, which involves, as I've said, a virus unleashed in the virtual world, also focuses on the real-world persons in their localized, seedy Internet cafes and shared apartments doing the "gold farming" inside the game, as well as various modes of transportation, rooms and buildings, coastlines, cities—and the modes of communication and navigation by which people traverse them all, from "obstreperous" GPS units to notes written by an abductee on paper towels and hidden in the plumbing. Significantly, the MMORPG in which half of the action takes place is called *T'Rain*, which began with the desire to model the geology of the virtual world as finely detailed *terrain*—and to do so more realistically than in any previous game. *Reamde* may be a techno-thriller but it's definitely *not* a cyber-thriller, to use another term sometimes seen in publishers' marketing. If anything, it's an Earthbound *infrastructure*-thriller, a book about cables and power supplies and sources of clean water, about "war-driving," cruising around looking for signals from wireless networks in foreign cities, about the uses and uselessness of cell phones of various kinds in various situations (including their linking of photos to GPS coordinates), the hazards of ubiquitous surveillance video cameras, rickshaws and boats and private jets (and the security they can evade), and about weapons, pointedly used for good and ill as the narrative unfolds.

In fact, in 1996, Stephenson wrote for *Wired* magazine one of the best accounts ever published of the physical infrastructure of the Internet, "Mother Earth Mother Board."[10] The mocking steampunk summary at its beginning reads: "In which the hacker tourist ventures forth across the wide and wondrous meatspace of three continents," using the console cowboy's term in Gibson's *Neuromancer* for physical space, the limiting space of the body, but in this case in an article that's about installing manholes, laying the FLAG transoceanic fiber-optic cable, and the people and businesses and institutions who do all of this. The piece is clearly date-stamped as a product of its time by the use of terms such as "meatspace," and by the following passage on the technological deconstruction of the global, which sounds at first as if it could have been taken straight out of 1990s cybertheory by Paul Virilio, say,[11] or, for that matter, out of the pages of *Wired* or *Mondo 2000*:

> Wires warp cyberspace in the same way wormholes warp physical space: the two points at opposite ends of a wire are, for informational purposes, the same point, even if they are on opposite sides of the planet. The cyberspace-warping power of wires, therefore, changes the geometry of the world of commerce and politics and ideas that we live in.
>
> (loc. 1790)

Consider for a moment what we English teachers call the rhetorical situation of this passage. The story was written for the readers of *Wired*, in its heyday, by an insider whose fictions contributed to the new cyberspace zeitgeist. Heard in this context, the opening sounds more ironic, even mocking in its references to cyberspace, not to mention "wormholes" and "meatspace." Notice how Stephenson reverses the expected direction of the relationship for his *Wired* audience: It's not cyberspace that dematerializes the world, it's "wires" that remind us of the materiality of cyberspace. The *effect* of the loss of distance in global communications, the apparent changes in the geometry of the world, are qualified in engineering terms as "for informational purposes." And then, of course, a truly massive magazine article follows, taking up almost 50 pages in the print version, with detailed, concrete descriptions of the very material and sometimes fragile physical infrastructure that makes that informational effect possible in the first place.

Stephenson's article is itself mapped, plotted in relation to actual places around the globe. In fact, he makes a point of taking a GPS receiver with him (this was before smartphones, remember) and beginning each section with the exact coordinates of the site about which (and often in which) it was written, "in case other hacker tourists would like to leap over the same rustic gates or get rained on at the same beaches" (loc. 1856). The real point is to increase location awareness in himself and his 1996 readers, because, simply put, "we all depend heavily on wires, but we hardly ever think about them," about how many wires there are, "how they got there, who controlled them, or how many bits they could carry" (loc. 1827–1837).

In both its choice of subject and its approach, Stephenson's long article paved the way for the more recent account of the infrastructure of the Internet by Andrew Blum, *Tubes* (2012), in which the author also travels the globe in search of the physical cables and wires and routers and data centers that make up the "physical Internet."[12] But Blum frames the problem in a new way that resonates for our own moment, in the wake of the eversion. His quest takes place explicitly along an ambiguous boundary, what he calls "the interstices of the physical and electronic worlds" (20). He admits at one point that this is a difficult division to navigate, that, despite visiting sites and handling yellow fiber-optic cables, it's hard to "grasp the narrow seam between the physical and logical" dimensions of the Internet, between infrastructure and information. This is, he suggests, still a "rarely acknowledged chasm in our own understanding of the world—a sort of twenty-first-century original sin. The Internet is everywhere; the Internet is nowhere" (20). However, in the end he repudiates the latter "sin" for himself and asserts that, in fact, "the Internet is always *somewhere*" (241; my emphasis). And that somewhere is by definition located, is locatable, on the terrestrial globe: "Contrary to its ostensible fluidity, the geography of the Internet reflects the geography of the earth; it adheres to the borders of nations and the edges of continents" (27). As Stephenson was already suggesting in his *Wired* article and as Blum continues to explore in his book, the opposite of the "nonspace" of cyberspace—or, really, its ineluctable material limit—is not really "meatspace," it's some place on Earth, however data-saturated a place it becomes. To use Blum's terms, today an increasing number of us live along the "seam" between physical topography and digital data. So a sense of place has come back into visions of the Internet with a vengeance, and it's important, in part, because it directs attention to the human agents and human costs behind our newer metaphors for the network (e.g., the cloud). As Stephenson said in 1996, "It behooves wired people to know a few things about wires—how they work, where they lie, who owns them, and what sorts of business deals and political machinations bring them into being" (loc. 1846). To varying (and still unevenly distributed) degrees, and in the most banal of ways, most of us (at least in the developed world) are all wired people now.

Maps in Games, Gamelike Maps

Neal Stephenson's 2011 novel is about the interweaving of virtual worlds and the physical world, and so it focuses on geography and the digital systems we now have for capturing, marking, and analyzing geographic data, as well as on detailed descriptions of the game world, the terrain of *T'Rain*. Video games conventionally include their own in-game maps, especially RPGs or games with extensive worlds in which navigation is central to gameplay, but also other genres. Sometimes these maps are to scale; often they are interactive and navigable: You can move around on them as a way to traverse the larger game world. Some-times they just allow you to click on locations to jump to them. Sometimes, as in racing games, a small-scale abstract map of the level or world in which you're racing shows up in the corner of your screen and is animated live, with tokens showing your progress during the race. Some maps are accessed by calling them up in menus; others are achieved as special items you can have in your inventory, giving you an advantage; some are available as mini-maps in the corner of the screen via a HUD or that you have access to at any time from within the game, sometimes with dynamic updates showing your location or the location of your destination, or that of resources or enemies. Because of their genre family resemblance, many video-game maps owe something to maps in earlier books of fantasy, often found on the flyleaf inside the covers or as illustrations—think of Tolkien's Middle Earth, or even A. A. Milne's Hundred Acre Wood—or as a tipped in, fold-out print. Traditional board games, too, relied heavily on elaborate maps, and early text-based adventures often expected players to construct their own maps as they explored the game world. And many early games provided among their boxed paraphernalia (like IF feelies) a game journal meant in part for the purpose of drawing or filling in maps. A large part of gameplay across many mainstream genres involves navigating and keeping track of locations via such maps, a set of skills we might call "orienteering," after the real-world competitive sport using map and compass to find one's way in unfamiliar terrain, for which there's even a Boy Scout merit badge.[13]

One open-world RPG, *Elder Scrolls V: Skyrim*, has attracted a good deal of critical attention, in part for its extensive and beautifully rendered game world. As critic Tom Bissell explains in an influential review, the 1996 *Elder Scrolls* game, *Daggerfall*, already had a game world "reputedly the size of Great Britain," and the 2006 game, *Oblivion*, was extremely capacious.[14] Instead of the usual game convention of a backdrop beyond which you really never could go, in this open world, "if you can see something . . . chances are you can visit it." Most of Bissell's review of *Skyrim* is spent on the problem of dialogue with NPCs as a narrative vehicle, but the keynote is his opening praise of the game's vast interactive open world, which he compares to his childhood experience with *The Legend of Zelda*, a celebrated franchise that helped to establish conventions for orienteering and exploring very large game worlds. Zelda's Hyrule, like the Province of Skyrim, is huge and mostly open—you can go almost anywhere you like, up to a point—and it contains entrances to numerous dungeons in which the hero avatar pursues quests through tunnels and labyrinths of ingenious design, solves puzzles, and engages in battles with bosses and lesser enemies. In Zelda games, the larger world is viewable on an in-game mini-map, but the dungeon maps must be found and acquired separately. In Zelda games before 2011's *Skyward Sword*, you can also find a compass that points you to treasure and other objects of your quest. (The HUD compass in *Skyrim* is a kind of slider along the top of the screen, less like the earlier Zelda games' inventory item and more like a built-in game-world navigational feature.) In the later Zelda game, interestingly, the dungeon map resembles modern GPS maps, in the sense that the compass function is built in, showing you the location of treasure chests, say, as interactive icons on the navigable map. But it's schematic, abstract and line-drawn, with cartoon symbols. *Skyrim*'s in-game map, by contrast, is a realistically rendered, high-altitude, wide-zoom overview that, anachronistically enough, looks a lot like a Google Earth satellite view.

In fact, a number of fan-based Websites have created interactive online *Skyrim* maps using the Google Maps API and, in some cases, an image of the rustic-looking paper map that shipped with the game as a collectible object (see figure 4.1). The map's data and topography are, of course, all fictional, but they respond to the user in exactly the way a real Google Map would. In spring 2012, an interactive iOS map app for *Skyrim* was released by the makers of the official *Game Guide*, so you could use your iPhone or iPad as a mobile interactive map during gameplay (see Figure 4.2). Some users complained online that it wasn't made available for Android, and some complained that it only offered what could be found in the game or on the Web for free, but its real significance may be to serve as just one more marker of the penetration of Google Map-like digital cartography into gaming, along with the rest of everyday life. And, remember, this is technology that was based in part on fictional and gamelike technologies in the first place. It's less that the physical world has become a video game and more that video games have become like the Google-mapped version of the world we now inhabit.

Maps and games go together, as games are always, in part, world-simulations that require orienteering skills. One of the fun things people have always done with GPS is a kind of orienteering gamelike activity called geocaching, in which you use GPS coordinates and mobile maps, and sometimes paper maps and notebooks, to locate hidden caches of significant objects or texts out in the world, the goal being the collecting of the experience of finding them. One company has created a system arguably intended to monetize the DIY activity of geocaching, called Munzee.[15] It uses QR codes or near-field connection (NFC)

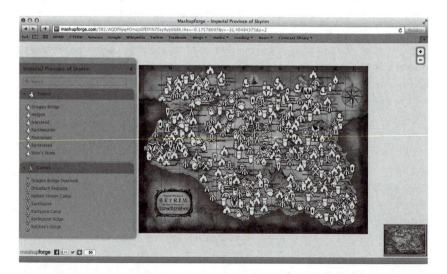

FIGURE 4.1 *Skyrim* map mashup

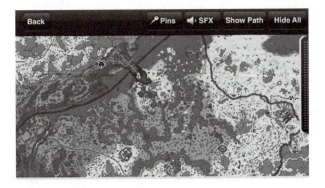

FIGURE 4.2 *Skyrim* Map iOS App

codes on stickers or plastic tokens to be distributed on physical objects out in the world, to be captured by other players. You get points and level up for captures, but also when others capture what you've cached. The company Website contains a custom map, with pins showing all Munzees (the word stands for the tokens as well as the game itself), leaderboards, help files, and images, as well as a trailer presentation unabashedly pitching the system as "a three-headed monster that blends geolocation with socialization, gamification, and marketing"—for use in business-loyalty programs, for example (the video points out that, unlike other social media check-ins, Munzee requires customers to actually come inside the business to capture their scanned QR codes), as well as team-building at corporate retreats, etc. The site also links to a store where you can buy QR-code stickers and tags, T-shirts, and other merchandise.

ARGs and AR artworks have obvious roots in the practice of geocaching, a kind of media-enhanced scavenger hunt. Wayfinding of this kind is gameplay boiled down to its orienteering essence, as both games and maps are world-simulations with data layered onto them. The world-simulation can take the form of a grid painted on a board, a series of scrolling platforms, or a cinematic 3D VR, and the data can be cards, tokens, numbers generated by rolling dice or some other counter, or statistics, items in inventory, character history, and level. Data layered on a world-simulation form a fundamental duality at the heart of games.

There's another kind of duality involved in playing video games, as this normally produces in the player what Katie Salen and Eric Zimmerman call a "double consciousness," a simultaneous sense of both the immediate, embodied physical environment and the virtual game world.[16] Gameplay takes place at the boundary between the embodied physical world and the game—along the circumference, really, of Huizinga's famous (or notorious) magic circle.[17] Inside the game, the structure of play mirrors this fundamental duality: a (virtual) bodily awareness of (virtual) physical reality combined with mental and sensory experience of an imagined world. Even within a game, gameplay consists of successful layering of a *world map* and *data* about the (game) world represented in the map. We see this at work in the conventional HUD—with its meters or indicators of health, inventory, or ammunition, as well as targeting reticules, or compasses, arrows, maps, and other navigational aids—superimposed on the player's view of the game world, as if on your screen, whether from a first- or third-person point of view. And Nick Montfort is getting at the same fundamental dual structure when he argues that gamelike IFs can be understood as consisting of two basic features: a world model (which can be mapped) and a parser (a script that processes the player's input in a meaningful way).[18] Although Montfort is careful to distinguish IF from video games per se, they are clearly parts of the same media family and share cultural DNA (conventions, structures, assumptions, gameplay mechanics), along with many of today's RPGs, action games, and puzzle adventures. That basic duality—Montfort's world model + interactive parser, or, to put it more generally, world + data about the world—remains a defining feature of all video games. In fact, a stripped-down schematic version of this duality is the definition of a map, which is a visual, graphic representation of data, like any "graph," but in this case a representation in *geo*graphic form that includes the data of spatial coordinates, a world model. Maps are about the relationship of world representations and layers of data of various kinds. This relationship is rendered more dynamic, and made mobile, networked, by today's digital-platform maps.

DH Data, Located

In his study of mobile technology and its effect on human subjectivity, Jason Farman rightly says that the long history of maps shows that "our traversal of space has long been understood as the correspondence between the material world and the ways we represent that world."[19] But it's important to see that those mapped ways of representing the world have, for centuries, included not just mimetic images but also data. As influential information designer Edward Tufte explains, it was in the seventeenth century that, "the combination of cartographic and statistical skills required to construct" the data map came together, "fully 5,000 years after the first geographic maps were drawn on clay tablets."[20] It's that combined form—mimetic-scale map plus (historically, usually statistical) data— that leads directly to today's digital maps and GISs. Maps are among the most traditional and powerful tools of the humanities. But GIS maps in particular have been, in the past decade, powerful platforms for the new digital humanities. The advent of digital maps, based on satellite and other networked data, available off the shelf, via APIs, and capable of combination with any source of data in mashups, is the particular form of mapping that has fueled much new humanities work in the past decade. In literary studies, Franco Moretti's *Graphs, Maps, Trees* helped to establish distant reading, the long view on literary and cultural history, as key to using computers in research. As visual modes of representing data, maps thus can reveal to humanities researchers patterns that might not otherwise be apparent (just through the reading of a very many novels, for example). Close reading, as important as it remains in literary studies, provides insufficient data, too slowly, for patterns to emerge at the higher level of abstraction that comprehends the sweep of literary history. For the pattern of a collection of narratives in *Our Village*, for example, to emerge, Moretti says, "we must first extract it from the narrative flow, and the only way to do that is with a map."[21] As with graphs, the map is a deliberate abstraction, a reduction of the objects of attention; it doesn't itself stand in the place of an interpretation or explanation, "but at least it shows us that there is something *that needs to be explained*" (39; emphasis in original). What he proceeds to find is a *series* of maps, layered representations of the relations of culture to physical place: "a map of ideology emerging from a map of *mentalité*, emerging from the material substratum of the physical territory" (42). The patterns that emerge from such mapping amount to organized data, represented as layers laid over the cartographic representation of physical space, itself one of the layers.

That last clause in Moretti's assessment raises a question crucial for the digital humanities: "the material substratum of . . . physical territory." Even in those literary studies in which the world being mapped is fictional, that world is treated in terms of data as if it were a material territory. Indeed, this is one of the insights literary studies has to offer: how every model of the world, including those that model its materialities, is constructed, a representation, open to interpretation, rather than the given "substratum" to the data. But that does not mean that every representation dissolves into mere metaphor. It makes a difference what's being modeled, makes a difference when material realities—economic, geographic, climatic, etc.—are deliberately modeled. In the past decade, as historian Karen Halttunen observes, "space and place have never been more analytically important than they have recently become in the humanities and social sciences, demonstrating that globalization—with its acceleration of border crossings—has actually made place more important, not less."[22] This is more than the adoption of a new set of tropes. The methods opened up by the use of GIS, she goes on to argue, have led to an increased emphasis on the material conditions of place.

> Initially, for many of us, spatial analysis tended to the metaphorical, as we adopted the idiom of borders and boundaries, frontiers and crossroads, centers and margins. But increasingly, scholars in a wide range of disciplines beyond geography have begun to address spatial issues more materially. Another way to understand this material emphasis within the spatial turn is simply as an increased focus on the always-being-made connections between place and data, data and place.
>
> (Halttunen)

The importance of this increased focus on place-linked data—dynamic data from multiple sources, different kinds of source, which can be applied to visual representations of various kinds, including maps—can be illustrated in the story of two digital projects about the history of Harlem. The first, the Virtual Harlem project, was begun by Bryan Carter of Central Missouri State University in 1997–1998, as an immersive VR representation of 10 square blocks of the New York neighborhood during the Harlem Renaissance period of the 1920s–1930s. As you walked the virtual streets, you saw landmark nightclubs, theaters, and buildings associated with writers such as Langston Hughes and Zora Neal Hurston, and you could hear audio tracks and sometimes view films of in situ performances at the Cotton Club, for example, by musicians such as Cab Calloway. It was primarily a learning space, a way for students to become immersed in the historical context of that important school of literature and the arts, although, as it developed, it also aimed to support humanities research. Between 1999 and 2001, funded in part by an NSF grant, Virtual Harlem was ported, with the help of the Electronic Visualization Laboratory (EVL) at the University of Illinois, Chicago (UIC), to the fully immersive 3D VR environment, the CAVE (Cave Automatic Virtual Environment), in which users stand surrounded by walls made up of giant projection screens, and use stereoscopic glasses with a location tracker that adjusts the projections to match head movement, and sometimes a haptic glove or other controller, in order to access and navigate the virtual city streets from a first-person perspective, while standing and moving in a limited way within the space. The CAVE technology was at the center of VR experiments in the 1990s, across a variety of disciplines, the sciences as well as humanities. A number of related VR technologies, some networked, were developed by the EVL, with Virtual Harlem as one test case. In about 1999–2000, the UIC Website declared that researchers were "beginning to convert the Virtual Harlem project from a compelling demonstration to a dynamic visual history database," with the addition of

> a set of analytic tools that parallel Geographical Information Systems (GIS) by visualizing the full history of the neighborhood, incorporating census data, real estate data, investment/reinvestment data, and crime and health data, in addition to the cultural information that helps to give the data meaning.[23]

This stage was never completed. By 2005, Bryan Carter had instantiated a version of Virtual Harlem inside Linden Lab's Second Life, where it took on some of the customs and conventions of that larger metaverse, including being built on three separate islands (two builds of Harlem "sims" and one Virtual Montmartre) and, more radically, deliberately becoming a "community made up of residents of Second Life interested in this historic period."[24] There are still traces of that community's involvement, but, when I visited in the summer of 2012 while working on this chapter, I found it typical of many Second Life locations these days in that the streets were eerily deserted.

FIGURE 4.3 Virtual Harlem in Second Life

The cultural heritage notes on key locations were often interesting (though they were read aloud by slightly robotic-sounding synthesized voices), and the impressive architectural builds and sometimes effective historical layerings of texts or music tracks were my rewards for exploring what otherwise felt a lot like a ghost town. This is not at all a criticism of Virtual Harlem in its Second Life phase; it just reflects conventional limitations of Second Life as a platform—and, before that, of MUDs and MOOs. Such spaces were designed as VR spaces for social networking or gameplay. They're at their best when they combine the live interaction of multiple avatars with environmental cues, manipulable objects, and navigable spaces.

A very different kind of project, Digital Harlem, can serve as a useful contrast of different approaches in different eras to digital models of place. I hasten to add, again, that Virtual Harlem was designed primarily as an immersive learning environment, whereas Digital Harlem was designed for online, data-centric historical research. But I think those different aims are also partly products of their eras in humanities computing, including real issues concerning funding and institutional support for different kinds of digital work in the two eras. In general, they help to illustrate the shift in focus over the past decade from the elusive ideal of fully immersive virtual worlds, to recombinatory uses of existing networked platforms, tools, and services, in order to represent competing data models of the world. Digital Harlem makes no attempt at realistic mimetic representation of the historical neighborhood. Its relatively mundane interface is a series of maps, data overlays, and a digital archive of documents of different kinds. It was part of a larger research project on the everyday lives of ordinary African Americans living in Harlem in the 1920s. It began in the archives of legal records and newspapers and resulted in a database that was intended, ca. 2002, to be linked to maps using the widely adopted ArcGIS software. By 2006, however, the project had decided to use Google Maps (which, remember, had just become available the previous year) as what the researchers originally thought of as a temporary fix. It soon became clear, however, that "this simplified, Web-based form of GIS would serve the purposes of the project, and Digital Harlem became one of the first scholarly sites to employ what has become known as the geospatial Web."[25] As Stephen Robertson points out, using GIS led directly to the granular focus of the project on individual street addresses, using a real-estate atlas from 1930 to build overlays. Robertson connects this detailed level of attention to Karen Halttunen's materialist methods, methods which in turn are part of the larger spatial turn in humanities research. Robertson adds that Digital Harlem's attention to material realities was made possible by digital tools, as the scalability of the maps, for example, would not be feasible in print. "Layers of different data, and hence large quantities of data, can be combined on a single map, providing an image of the complexity of the past."

In some ways, these two Harlem projects are apples and oranges, serving different audiences and different purposes at different times. The earlier project

FIGURE 4.4 Digital Harlem

was a pioneering experiment that reflected advanced ideas, just a different paradigm for the use of computing in humanities research. I was myself involved in modeling "immersive" learning environments in the late 1990s, one version of which was supported by a grant from the NEH.[26] My comparison of the two digital Harlems isn't meant to be invidious, just to illustrate two different platforms and sets of technologies for approaching a similar humanities topic. The different user interfaces and expected user experiences help to illustrate what has happened to digital humanities research in the past decade. The ports and migrations that Virtual Harlem underwent tell part of the story, including the difficulties of access and usability posed by truly immersive VR in a networked environment. The practical decisions made by the later project, Digital Harlem, tell another part of the story. As networked services, off-the-shelf, free, and open-source mapping software, GPS availability, and more accessible GIS came together around 2005 as existing (and mostly free) technologies, epitomizing the inside–out eversion of cyberspace into geographic space, the 2D model, rich with data, seemed to many researchers to afford new ways to pursue historical and cultural questions in a digital environment. The new-model digital humanities emerged along with, and, in part, in response to, those new affordances. Harlem remains a place in the real world, of course. I used to live on the edge of it and walked every day some of the streets that are recreated in Virtual Harlem in the partly imagined historical moment of the Harlem Renaissance. It's easy for me to imagine a new project that would apply the layered data and historical media of both projects, but in an AR application that could be accessed while actually walking down 125th Street (using something like Google Glass). At any rate, this kind of digital humanities project, even if it is to be accessed only on the Internet, seems likely to explore AR as well as locative possibilities.

There are any number of GIS-based digital humanities projects I could cite as illustrations, but they almost all have in common the use of off-the-shelf solutions in combination with existing networked CMSs and database software (even established proprietary software such as ArcGIS has become easier to use since the 1990s, as expectations have changed in response to networked products). And they share the aim of addressing a wider audience on the Web, sometimes to enlist users in crowdsourcing, and sometimes to publish their data for downloading and reuse. For example, Neatline, developed by Bethany Nowviskie and Adam Soroka through the Scholars' Lab at the University of Virginia, is designed as a suite of software tools that can be added to the open-source Omeka CMS—which was itself developed at the digital humanities center at George Mason University (the CHNM). The idea of Neatline is to make it easy for scholars, students, and curators to build "geotemporal" exhibits for the Web, to make available so-called slippy maps, with Google Maps as the best-known example, which load dynamically as the user pans or zooms, loading just the image tiles as called for making possible the live responsiveness to user manipulations we now associate with Google Maps and similar applications. Like a good deal of the resources built by

DH researchers, Neatline was based on another Web 2.0 concept, the mashup. It combines responsive slippy-map services with annotation and dynamic timelines, so the scholar can "tell stories." In contrast to the usual analytic goals of big data, the goal of this project is more qualitative: historical interpretation of smaller sets of materials using maps in conjunction with timelines, and the maps and timelines are themselves potential objects of interpretation. One of the available plugin tools is Neatline Maps. For those who can install the software, this allows you to use open-source Java-based GeoServer as a repository and server for historical "georeferenced" maps you create to reference in your exhibits. The plugin integrates these maps with the Omeka CMS, but also works in conjunction with Google Maps, Google Earth, and other map services. The name of the product, Neatline, is taken from cartography and refers to the enclosing border that contains a map and its data augmentations—legend, scale, keys, etc. It's a self-conscious reference to the digital humanities' combinatory methods.

This same use of off-the-shelf, often open-source software in new combinations, thanks to available APIs, is the reason Google Maps and Google Earth have been so amenable to digital humanities experiments. They're generally compatible with the DH support for open-source software and with the hacker ethos that many practitioners share. Many among the current leaders in the field were young programmers, graduate students, or what later came to be called alt-ac workers (people in alternative academic positions, whether non-tenure track or non-faculty, or, sometimes, working outside the academy in related areas), designers working on grant-supported digital humanities projects in the Web 2.0 years of 2004–2008—the moment of the eversion. They were often responsible for bringing developments in the vernacular Web—social networks and the geospatial Web among them—into scholarly projects. It's hard to overestimate the importance of this model, a programmers' model, really, for doing humanities computing, and it can be hard for traditional humanists to appreciate its power. The shift of Virtual Harlem into the existing platform of Second Life is one mark of it, but the shift by Digital Harlem from using expensive proprietary ArcGIS software to Google Maps as its infrastructure is an even more significant mark—especially because the relatively non-flashy vernacular interface, those ubiquitous maps with pins that so many of us take for granted on our phones, was the basis of its scholarly innovation. This is true of many of the most intellectually significant projects in the geospatial digital humanities. They look at first like any number of map-based apps with which we're familiar, for finding restaurants or checking into locations so our friends can find us (or just follow us from afar): maps with pins and teardrop-shaped flags, attached annotations, meticulously prepared but straightforward to use layers and visualizations of data that you can toggle on and off.

English professor and digital humanities scholar Ryan Cordell is working on a digital edition of the publication history of Nathaniel Hawthorne's short story, "The Celestial Railroad," in the 1840s and 1850s, a project that has involved mapping print culture in antebellum America.[27] He has experimented with GIS for tracking over 50 reprints of Hawthorne's satirical story, based on *Pilgrim's Progress*, after its initial publication in 1843, as an instance of the larger question of "how spatial data might help situate histories of textual transmission and reception" in wider contexts. He sees the maps he constructs as "extra-textual," a way of telling the story of how a text makes its way through the world—in the literal, geographic sense. He uses historical maps and census data in the mix, as well as the publication history, and then manipulates the data in various ways to highlight different contexts to see what patterns might emerge—including demographic shifts among different Protestant denominations, for example, and the role played by the railroad in the material transmission of the story regionally, via its successive reprints.

These modest initial findings are just the beginning of the research in a DH project such as this one. As Franco Moretti and others have argued, maps are analytical tools in the sense that they shed light on patterns in data that might otherwise remain hidden. "A good map is worth a thousand words, cartographers say, and they are right because it *produces* a thousand words: it raises new questions, and forces you to look for new answers."[28] These DH practitioners, just as Moretti suggests, are using maps, not as illustrations, but in ongoing experiments, altering variables, tweaking models, manipulating layers, working with data. As Moretti readily admits, this involves engaging in intellectual processes that have traditionally been considered uncongenial to the humanities: "abstraction and quantification" (5). Especially that last quantification is often what distinguishes digital humanities applications that use maps from earlier humanities mapping. The 'I' in GIS stands for information, after all, and in fact for information structured as data. The practice of digital humanities GIS involves watching for signs of meaning, in the form of abstract patterns, to emerge from the layers of data that can be attached to, and that include, representations of place, the geographical, physical world.

The deliberately ad hoc and experimental nature of this kind of work can be seen in dramatic form in Professor of Literature and New Media Mark Sample's project, *Haunts*, which grew out of a THATCamp session on geolocation in 2010.[29] Both Cordell and Nowviskie have spoken and written about the ludic, playful aspect of the kinds of experiment they are doing with GIS. Sample, whose own research includes game studies, explicitly frames *Haunts* as a gamelike project, an experiment in playful historical thinking—the exercise of freedom within constraints posed by structure—that uses existing platforms associated with gamelike social interactions in relation to place, geolocative social software applications such as Foursquare and Gowalla. Normally, in these applications, you check in to a bar or restaurant or city park, and your friends see where you are with a GPS-pinned map interface. If you check in to the same location early and often enough in Foursquare, you become "mayor" of that site. It's a kind of gamification of public social life, especially when it involves consumption, and

Sample has compared it to "gimmicky entertainment coupon books" (and this was before Groupon had joined the ranks of such platforms). The *Haunts* project uses these platforms for its own experimental and pedagogical purposes, as ready-made and available geotagging tools. As the platforms already make it possible for users, instead of posting tips on the best cocktails in a neighborhood, say, to "define their own places and add tips that range from lewd to absurd," Sample has experimented with having his students at George Mason University use Foursquare to "add new venues to the app's database," but these must be "Foucauldian 'Other Spaces'—parking decks, overpasses, bus depots, etc.—that stand in stark contrast to the officially sanctioned places on Foursquare (coffee shops, restaurants, bars, etc.)." One point this makes is just how much of our everyday lives we spend, without noticing it, in these "nether-places, that are neither here nor there" when it comes to commercial and social power. In other words, this exercise in repurposing—or, in a loose sense, hacking—Foursquare can help teach humanities students to see what they have learned to unsee, to track their own movements through all of these mundane, "unglamorous unplaces," and, as Sample suggests, *that* could prove to be "one of the best uses of geolocation—to defamiliarize our daily surroundings." In *Haunts*, teams of students go out into the world to tag public places with fragments of a larger narrative, a real or imagined story of trauma. In effect, they create a collective AR story, tied to specific geographic locations, to be experienced not only by the rest of the class but anyone thereafter who, via the app on their cell phone, happens upon a data-rich site of collaborative educational creativity (the data just happen to be date-stamped, student-composed narratives). Thanks to the vast hardware and software and communication infrastructure of orbiting satellites, monitoring stations, fiber-optic cables, cell towers, networked servers, and portable devices, a fictional world can be made to augment or haunt the real physical world. It's significant that Neatline and other scholarly GIS projects so often present themselves as being engaged in storytelling and play. In its own gamelike way, *Haunts* dramatizes the enriching role a geolocative digital humanities might play out in the world.

Layering and Haunting

I'll have a good deal more to say about AR or mixed-reality applications in the next chapter, but I want to point out here, much as Brian Croxall did in the comments to Mark Sample's June 1, 2010 blog entry on *Haunts*, how close Sample's DH media experiment was to the spirit and themes of William Gibson's *Spook Country* (2007), which, as I said in the Introduction, was the first novel in which he articulated the eversion of cyberspace.[30] For the heroine of that novel, Hollis Henry, the signs of the eversion, the New Aesthetic irruptions before the fact as it were, begin with locative art. The cyberspatial has turned into the geospatial, and artists are building installations you experiences out on the street but wearing goggles, so that a data layer is added to what you experience. Those data, however, are anything but a free-flowing realm transcending time and space. On the contrary, by design, they're mostly images of historical events and are pinned via GPS to specific locations in the real world. These works allow you to see the unseen by combining the invisible grid of GPS data, via the Internet, with physical settings. The first installation Hollis experiences is on the street in LA where the young actor River Phoenix died of an overdose in 1993. The artist Alberto has used GPS data and 3D computer graphics to "install" a stylized image of the corpse at that location, so that the digital ghost of River Phoenix haunts the spot for anyone in the know—and with the right visor attached to a laptop, or a cell phone duct-taped onto a portable GPS device (though Gibson was not yet able to imagine the iPhone with its GPS radio, he anticipated Google Glass). "I guess you could say it started on the first of May, 2000," the artist explains: "Geohacking. Or the potential thereof" (22). A curator explains it as revealing "cartographic attributes of the invisible" through a form of "spatially tagged hypermedia" (22). Out on the street, Hollis dons the translucent visor while the artist taps on the keyboard, then she looks down the street toward the corner of Clark and Sunset Boulevard, sees the Viper Room bar and, on the sidewalk in front of it, sees the dead actor's body shiver into her field of vision, like glimpsing a ghost: "The boy seemed birdlike, in death, the arch of his cheekbone, as she bent forward, casting its own small shadow" (7–8).

Haunted, like everted, is just a metaphor for the experience of living in a spatially tagged mixed reality. But it's a metaphor about glimpsing what had been for some time invisible because unseen, and still often remains invisible until invoked—the digital "realm"—as it manifests itself in everyday life. Gibson's metaphor of haunting, like Mark Sample's, is no medium's illusion. It's clearly meant to reveal the hidden wires, as it were, because we're aware (though with varying degrees of specific understanding) that the machinery is creating a hybrid experience we're still learning to navigate, a liminal or boundary experience— literally, materially, at the border where digital reality crosses over to physical reality. The awkward visor, the duct tape, the flicker (or shivering) are all signs of this experience. But the most obvious sign—the clue to what we might choose to call the *interdisciplinary* nature of this haunting—is that Gibson's imagined artist does not work alone. Alberto is a designer, a visionary, and a graphic artist. What he does, he says, is "not that different from designing figures for games" (41). His partner in making locative art is Bobby Chombo, a gifted programmer and system-level hacker (the fictional descendant of Gibson's earlier cyberpunk geeks and console cowboys). Without Bobby, Alberto confesses, he "couldn't get his stuff up on the grid" (50). As all the DH scholars I've cited here would likely testify, Alberto's avant-garde art in this regard resembles the collaborative nature of the digital humanities at the present moment, which is also usually a team effort, combining computing with cultural analysis, scholarship, and creativity— another form of hybridity, another kind of mixed reality.

★

Notes

1. William Gibson, "Google's Earth," *New York Times*, August 31, 2010, http://nytimes.com/2010/09/01/opinion/01gibson.html.

2. For this summary I've used Wikipedia, "GPS," http://en.wikipedia.org/wiki/GPS, as well as materials on the official U.S. Government site, http://gps.gov.

3. "The Amazing iOS 6 Maps," http://theamazingios6maps.tumblr.com.

4. Glenn Fleishman, "How the iPhone Knows Where You Are," *Macworld*, April 28, 2011, http://macworld.com/article/1159528/how_iphone_location_works.html.

5. On the decline of occupancy and activity in Second Life after 2007, see Heath and Heath, *The Myth of the Garage*. Wikipedia suggests that the "perceived decline in concurrent users," 2009–2010, "correlates precisely with new policies implemented by Linden Lab reducing the number of bots and campers," http://en.wikipedia.org/wiki/Second_life. In other words, there never were as many actual, active human users as were reported.

6. Neal Stephenson *Snow Crash* (New York: Bantam, 1992), 106.

7. "Google Earth Inside Second Life: GeoGlobe," Google Earth Blog, March 28, 2007, http://gearthblog.com/blog/archives/2007/03/google_earth_in_seco.html.

8. Neal Stephenson, *Reamde* (New York: Harper Collins, 2011). Kindle edition.

9. Ernest Cline, *Ready Player One* (New York: Crown, 2011), Kindle edition, 276.

10. Neal Stephenson, "Mother Earth Mother Board," *Wired* 4.12, (December 1996): 97–160; reprinted in *Some Remarks: Essays and Other Writing* (New York: William Morrow/Harper Collins, 2012), Kindle edition, loc. 1783–3616.

11. Paul Virilio, *The Lost Dimension*, trans. Daniel Moshenberg (New York: Semiotext(e), 1991), e.g., "With the interfacing of computer terminals and video monitors, distinctions of *here* and *there* no longer mean anything" (13).

12. Andrew Blum, *Tubes: A Journey to the Center of the Internet* (New York: Ecco/Harper Collins, 2012), Kindle edition.

13. This connection between video gameplay and competitive orienteering was suggested by Will Farina in a paper he wrote for English 415, spring 2012, "Orienteering and *Skyrim*," which also developed many of the connections to *Skyrim* that I build on below.

14. Tom Bissell, "One Night in *Skyrim* Makes a Strong Man Crumble," *Grantland*, November 29, 2011, http://grantland.com/story/_/id/7290527/one-night-in-skyrim-makes-strong-man-crumble.

15. http://munzee.com.

16. Katie Salen and Eric Zimmerman, *Rules of Play: Game Design Fundamentals* (Cambridge, MA: MIT Press, 2004), 455.

17. Johan Huizinga, *Homo Ludens: A Study of the Play Element in Culture* (Boston: The Beacon Press, 1950). The concept of the magic circle has been central to, and controversial within, game studies. For one critical perspective on the metaphor, based on locating play at the perimeter instead of within the circle, see Jones, *The Meaning of Video Games*, 14–15.

18. Nick Montfort, *Twisty Little Passages: An Approach to Interactive Fiction* (Cambridge, MA: MIT Press, 2003), viii–ix.

19. Jason Farman, *Mobile Interface Theory: Embodied Space and Locative Media* (New York and London: Routledge, 2011), 45.

20. Edward R. Tufte, *The Visual Display of Quantitative Information* (Cheshire, CT: Graphics Press, 1983), 20.

21. Franco Moretti, *Graphs, Maps, Trees: Abstract Models for A Literary History* (London and New York: Verso, 2005), 39.

22. Karen Halttunen, "Groundwork: American Studies in Place—Presidential Address to the American Studies Association, November 4, 2005," *American Quarterly* 58.1 (March 2006): 2.
23. Electronic Visualization Laboratory, http://evl.uic.edu/core.php?mod=4&type=1&indi=168.
24. Introduction by Bryan Carter's avatar from within Second Life: http://mediacommons.futureofthebook.org/imr/2009/04/14/building-community-virtual-harlem-and-evolving-role-modern-educator-new-digitals.
25. Stephen Robertson, "Putting Harlem on the Map," in *Writing History in the Digital Age*, ed. Jack Dougherty and Kristen Nawrotzki, spring 2012, http://writinghistory.trincoll.edu/evidence/robertson-2012-spring.
26. With Neil Fraistat and Carl Stahmer, in the Romantic Circles MOO. See Neil Fraistat and Steven E. Jones, "Immersive Textuality," TEXT 15 (2003): 69–82. Though the model was of a navigable space, following the conventions of MUDs and the adventure-style games from which they were derived, the MOO had a necessarily lo-fi interface, and was designed for networked interaction on the existing Web rather than anything approaching self-contained, realistic total immersion.
27. Ryan Cordell, "Mapping the Antebellum Culture of Reprinting," presentation, MLA 2012, Seattle, January 7, 2012.
28. Franco Moretti, *Atlas of the European Novel, 1800–1900* (New York: Verso, 1999), 3.
29. Mark Sample, "Haunts: Place, Play, and Trauma," Sample Reality blog, June 1, 2010, http://samplereality.com/2010/06/01/haunts-place-play-and-trauma.
30. Brian Croxall comment on Mark Sample, "Haunts," Sample Reality blog, June 1, 2010, http://samplereality.com/2010/06/01/haunts-place-play-and-trauma/; Gibson, *Spook Country*.

5

THINGS

If, as William Gibson says, cyberspace, having everted, has now "colonized the physical," one thing that means in practice, in terms of everyday experience, is that the objects around us are increasingly data objects, in one sense or another.[1] Sometimes they are "live" with transponders, such as RFID tags, beaming signals about their identity, location, ownership, and history. Sometimes they are tagged with barcodes or QR codes meant to be read by machines. But even if objects are tagged in more conventional print form, with strings of characters or serial numbers, these can be read using OCR and then incorporated into, or verified as part of, larger data collections. One way or another, an increasing percentage of things in our environment—human-made things, but not only human-made things—are being made into what author (and friend of Gibson's) Bruce Sterling has named "spimes," objects + data, things that are tagged so that their data, their history, can be accessed, aggregated, and mined or processed, and so the objects are physically trackable over their lifecycle.[2] The logical result is really the eversion looked at from another perspective: not only an Internet of Things but a revelation of the material nature of the Internet. Given such a world, the long experience of the humanities, on the one hand, in dealing with the artifacts of human culture as primary objects (manuscripts, books, pictures, paintings, sculptures, collages, installations, performances, recordings, films and videos, software programs, etc.), and, on the other hand, in addressing the theoretical problems of objects and things, realism and materialism, would seem to amount to a calling. The idea of the Internet of Things, and ubiquitous computing in general, stands as a challenge, an exhortation to the humanities to, as Ian Bogost says, turn "toward the world at large, toward things of all kinds and at all scales."[3] For the *digital* humanities, such a turn seems imperative. At any rate, the Internet of Things and ubiquitous computing helped to form the context out of which DH itself emerged.

A Network Made of Things

These days, signs of connectivity—and literal connectors—are attached to things of all kinds. UPC barcodes, around since the 1970s, began to be joined in the 1980s and 1990s by RFIDs—radio frequency identification tags (often pronounced "arphids"). These are essentially chips with radio-wave antennae that beam their identity for readers to pick up. No human operator has to manually apply an optical scanner to RFIDs—no machine either, for that matter. The scanner that picks up the signal just has to be in the immediate vicinity of its radio signal. The use of RFIDs spread quickly as their price came down, in sync with the growth of widespread (if not quite ubiquitous) wireless access to the Internet in the new millennium. That combination suggested the possibility of a world of tagged and connected things. In an article published in the *RFID Journal*, Kevin Ashton claims to have originated the term Internet of Things in a corporate presentation 10 years earlier, in 1999.[4] Ten years later, Ashton observes, the idea was everywhere. In the article, he points to the limitations of human input and processing of Internet data; there's only so much that can be done in terms of accuracy and volume when it comes to scanning, typing, photographing, pressing buttons to create data "about things in the real world." These literally mundane data about material objects would seem to be of obvious importance. But it's interesting that Ashton still felt, in 2009, that he had to oppose the given, the glorification of the immateriality of cyberspace: "You can't eat bits, burn them to stay warm or put them in your gas tank. Ideas and information are important, but things matter much more." The subtitle of the article was "In the real world, things matter more than ideas." Never mind that ideas *are* things, in their own way, on a different scale; this is a piece in an RFID industry publication, not an ontological argument in a philosophical journal. But we hear in Ashton's language an intense aversion to the 1990s apotheosis of the digital, a pushing back (perhaps belatedly in 2009) against the ideology of cyberspace. Things matter, he argues, oddly enough (I mean that it's odd he has to argue this). And the Internet should pay better attention to things, both *as* things and in terms of the data they generate.

RFID tags are themselves things, of course, little computing things attached to other things. It's that attachment, the tagging—a rich term in today's technical environment, including in the digital humanities—that matters most. This tagging is all about adding data to the physical things, an act that in itself makes them networked objects, potentially spimes. Interestingly enough (when viewed against the backdrop of the timeline of the eversion), Bruce Sterling dates "the dawn of spimes to 2004," when the U.S. Department of Defense began to require RFIDs be attached to all supplies for the military; writing in 2005, Sterling predicts that, if this networked inventory system catches on in industry, as well, "then a major transition will likely be at hand" (*Shaping Things*, 12). Though a mixture of various systems is now being used, it's fair to say that the intervening years have begun to bear out this prediction. Nowadays, increasingly, every kind of thing is being tagged. The reason is not just simple inventory control, but a more comprehensive goal of data management. Sterling differentiates what he calls "gizmos"—most of our current tech-based devices—from spimes proper, which remain just over the horizon, for the most part. Gizmos can be linked to services on the network and allow for frequent updates of their features, but they are primarily portals to those services, such as the phones we carry. Spimes are simpler, in designer's terms. They're less computerized objects than they are individual nodes in a global digital network. Their lifecycles are designed to be trackable, to be "eminently data-mineable." Such objects are designed, Sterling says, to be "the protagonists of an historical process" (11). Their existence over time is their meaning. Tagged with the metadata they in part produce as they go through the world—both physically tagged with an RFID chip, say, and also tagged with their associated data on the network—spime objects are also nodes in social networks, points of exchange for varied "technosocial interactions that unite people and objects" (22). In fact, Sterling argues, when "properly understood, a thing is not merely a material object, but a frozen technosocial relationship" (68), the sum total of innumerable acts of materials-mining, design, production, marketing, use, recycling, or disuse.

Though they both depend on a version of so-called ubiquitous computing, this is not exactly the same thing as those "smart houses" people have been predicting for decades, now, with refrigerators that tell you when to buy milk, for example, or thermostats that regulate the heating system according to peak usage curves, or even floors that sense the cadences of your walk and adjust the lighting to suit you. Some of those technologies are available, now, but the idea of the smart house seems suddenly old fashioned. Such a house is more like a stage set, a fixed group of computing objects, than the more flexible Internet of Things model, in which you might have a number of small processors that plug into your wall outlets and communicate with one another, your own scanner system, with storage in the cloud, and a supply of cheap RFID tags to attach to whatever you like, from bananas to bicycles, making the things all around you into a configurable network of data objects. The Internet of Things model is the result of the shift in the past decade toward a more object-oriented modular design, a focus on the relationship between any material object and the data it might generate or that might be attached to it. Hence the emphasis on cheap sensors and tagging systems, and on how to network the data thus produced, rather than on complex computers statically embedded in the environment. A 2004 *Scientific American* article on the Internet of Things argued that it should be designed flexibly, according to the principles of the Internet as a whole: that is, according to the basic idea of packet switching, with its redundancies and open-ended routing, and using the existing Internet Protocol, with an "end-to-end" architecture that assumes that "the behavior of the network should be determined by what is connected to it rather than by its internal construction."[5] A very cheap sensor in a light bulb, sending and receiving data (about hours of use, for example) over the existing electrical wiring and WiFi network, is the ideal object in such a network—interrelated with many other objects tagged in other ways, but connected across a range of local area networks, or even personal area networks and NFCs, seamlessly making themselves part of the larger network of networks. Because it relies on existing network standards and, ideally, open-source code, off-the-shelf components used in a modular way are preferable—think tagged Lego blocks rather than elaborate "smart" (gizmo) refrigerators. The Internet of Things is as much about the integrity of the things as it is about the Internet, as much about atoms as bits. But the things in the Internet of Things are always potentially things + data, networked data objects.

What does this have to do with the humanities? Although academic humanities disciplines are a more recent invention that came along with the modern university system, the humanities as an area of research in the West has historically claimed as its origins the Renaissance study of classical texts in surviving Greek and Roman manuscripts. In this view, humanities research is ultimately based on significant material things: texts, works of art, cultural artifacts. The special category of things known as primary objects—manuscripts on paper or vellum, printed texts in books, cultural artifacts and works of art, electronic files—are the basis of almost all humanities scholarship, whether that means a classical manuscript or a medieval commentary on it; a first edition of a Victorian novel or print-shop records showing how the typesetting was done; a reprinted edition of a political tract that had a particular social influence, or a copy of a satirical cartoon from the same moment; a sketch in an artist's notebook, the oil painting based on it, or a financial ledger reporting the cost of canvases at the time. Even the most abstract philosophical or theological or literary–theoretical ideas take as sources, witnesses, occasions for debate, primary texts by thinkers from the past—or the recent past recorded in the published present. Subsequent research and critical analysis on authors, ideas, texts, or works of art, and the extended scholarly conversation through which research is published and vetted, can be traced back in almost every case to some primary objects. The status of the primary objects on which so much of scholarship is based—their preservation, modes of representation (texts in facsimile editions, say, or artifacts displayed in museum exhibits), provenance, reliability, stability, and variability—has been itself the subject of research, theory, and debate. This isn't a question of discovering the origin of discourse. It's about recognizing that discourse responds to prompts, and that it's prompted by things as much as ideas, that ideas are in fact among a universe of prompting things for humanities discourse, one that also includes a rich array of physical objects.

Self-conscious reflection about the primary objects on which research depends, along with the more general drive for historical knowledge, has meant that the humanities has remained focused on the things of material culture, even when these things seem to resist human understanding. But philosophical idealism has informed a good deal of critical theory, even arguably much of the cultural materialist or Marxist strains. So it was with a certain contrary attitude that the

English Professor Bill Brown proposed, in 2001, what he called Thing Theory, about "how inanimate objects enable human subjects . . . to form and transform themselves."[6] Thing Theory looks at the complexities of this process, at how some thing is turned into an object by and for the human subject that perceives it, grasps it. Responding in part to the terms and conceptual framework of Martin Heidegger, Brown suggests that thingness is the quality of material things that escapes our objectification of them, our turning them into objects for us. Things "lie both at hand and somewhere outside the theoretical field" (5). A thing is what we encounter before it becomes for us an object, or it is the sum total of the qualities of the object that we as subjects cannot capture in a subject–object relationship: "a recognizable yet illegible remainder" (5). Cultural-studies and literary scholars, historians, and anthropologists, and others working in humanities disciplines have become interested in recent years in *mere* things, everyday or mundane things. (Outside the academy, Henry Petroski's books on the pencil or the toothpick, for example, are further examples of this widespread interest.[7])

For some, this approach grows out of the traditions of Marxist theory in general, or the work of the Frankfurt school in particular, especially Walter Benjamin's struggles with materialist criticism in his speculative, unfinished Arcades Project, in which he wrote about the material culture of the arcades of Paris (the precursors to modern urban shopping malls): bicycles, fashion, iron construction, Chinese puzzles, caricatures, advertising posters, panoramas, books, plush upholstery, dolls, and daguerreotypes.[8] For many, paying critical attention to everyday material objects is a way to challenge the idealist premises of traditional history of ideas, to contribute to history "from below," even below the level of human actors per se. The ontology of things, their existence in the world, can complement or challenge the usual modes of abstract thought in humanities disciplines, and can extend the limiting focus of the humanities on the construction of the human subject. Bill Brown is primarily focused on how things construct human subjects, but it works both ways: Things can also stubbornly refuse to be objectified and in that way can complicate our theoretical assumptions about subjectivity.

Things are strange, once you look closely at them. Paying attention to the materiality of everyday things can work to defamiliarize our assumptions, including the assumption that the physical world is made up of raw material for the instrumental use of humans. In this way, Thing Theory makes a contribution to what has been called post-humanism. But historically, as Renaissance scholars confronted specific classical manuscripts, or eighteenth-century archaeologists unearthed ancient urns, the humanities has depended on the fundamental defamiliarizing act of encountering some strange thing. Mostly, the humanities have been concerned with human-made things, the artifacts and products of culture—but not exclusively, and especially not in recent decades, when interdisciplinary studies have introduced other kinds of things into the center of humanities research, things at the border of what humans make and what they find, such as breeds of cattle, or genetically modified laboratory mice, or large-scale weather patterns in relation to global climate change, as well as the history of shipping lanes or sea battles.

A number of recent philosophical discussions of objects, however, have systematically resisted the assimilation of things to humans and our cultures, in part reacting against Heidegger's idea that what matters most in examining *the thing* is how it's ready "to hand" and made to stand out against everything else when we put it to use, as opposed to a thing's tendency to always withhold its true identity, to "withdraw" itself, have an existence apart from its identity as an object for human use.[9]

That elusive, ultimate inaccessibility of things has recently been one focus of a branch of philosophical speculative realism known as object-oriented ontology (OOO). Philosopher Levi Bryant has characterized OOO as an "anthro-de-centric framework," and Ian Bogost has addressed OOO with what he calls "alien phenomenology."[10] Bryant suggests that alien phenomenology helps us to avoid the Ptolemaic assumption that we are the center of the universe, "opening us to a world of other beings such as the worlds of other animals, climates, ecosystems, technologies, etc., and how they experience or encounter the world" (Bryant, "Alien Phenomenology"). Bogost himself, a game designer and digital media studies scholar with a background in philosophy, likes to use "Latour litanies" (based on the writings of Bruno Latour), seemingly random lists of objects or things, as a rhetorical device, to make the point that every thing exists equally and to draw attention to the range of things that do exist, in the process contributing to an understanding of what Bryant calls "flat ontology." It's important to understand that, as Bogost says, for Bryant "the term object enjoys a wide berth":

> corporeal and incorporeal entities count, whether they be material objects, abstractions, objects of intention, or anything else whatsoever—quarks, Harry Potter, keynote speeches, single-malt scotch, Land Rovers, lychee fruit, love affairs, dereferenced pointers, Mike "The Situation" Sorrentino, bozons, horticulturalists, Mozambique, *Super Mario Bros.*, not one is "more real" than any other.
>
> (Bogost, *Alien Phenomenology*, loc. 292)

The subtitle of Bogost's book is "what it's like to be a thing," and the notion of the phenomenology of things, like the concept of the alien nature of things, counters the idealist assumptions of classical philosophy about the inevitable relation of objects to human subjects who give them meaning (and thus contributes to anti-correlationism).

On the other hand, as a game designer and programmer, Bogost is most interested in what he calls an "applied" version of speculative realism, "an object-oriented engineering to ontology's physics" (loc. 672). He calls for making things, "constructing artifacts as philosophical practice," and calls this practice (which is not necessarily limited to alien phenomenology) "carpentry" (loc. 1951), the act of "making things that explain how things make their world" (loc. 1963). Though this might seem a purely instrumental use of things—computer chips or lines of code—Bogost intends it in the engineering sense: to reveal constraints as well as affordances, the failures of human design as well as easy successes. Bogost's own acts of carpentry have usually involved making software objects, poetically expressive or parodic or persuasive video games, scripts for producing lists of things or images, and so on. But there is almost always something parodic, deconstructive, about Bogost's carpentry. The parody is explicit in his notorious anti-Facebook game, *Cow Clicker*, more an inside joke in *Guru Meditation*, and more subtle in *A Slow Year*, a collection of minimalist art games for the legacy Atari Video Computer System, based on the four seasons and requiring the player to watch carefully over time and perform basic inputs in response to the blocky images.[11] (One edition of the work was produced for the actual 2600 console, but others were made for emulation on modern computers.) The games are like "playable poems," the accompanying book says, "about the experience of observing things" (ix). These things include trees, falling leaves, a window, a cup of coffee, a stream, a floating twig, and to play you also have to interact with them in minimalist (and slow) ways. The book includes 1,024 poems (an allusion to the number of bytes in each of the four 1-kilobyte games), haikus generated algorithmically by a computer program, and is thus a mixed-media experimental

FIGURE 5.1 Ian Bogost, *A Slow Year*

publication that raises questions about genre (games, poems, artworks, code, books), platforms, and the nature of human–machine collaboration.

A Slow Year shares something with the New Aesthetic and its interest in seeing how machines see the world, as well as its attention to the porous borders between machine and human constructions of reality, the idea of an alien encounter as a productive if sometimes troubling exchange, in today's environment, between human and computer. But *A Slow Year* is also an example, by way of carpentered demonstration, of one aspect of the new digital humanities—a humanities about things, but in the era of the Internet of Things, which is to say the era of the eversion, when the digital is attaching itself to physical things in often unpredictable ways.

Note the terms used to describe a 2012 class on "Born Digital Materials" at the University of Virginia's Rare Book School:

> Archivists and scholars who work with computer-created content need to think about how "the thingness of things" translates to the digital realm, according to Matthew G. Kirschenbaum, one of the course's two instructors. "Computers are material objects engineered and built to sustain the illusion—or working model—of immateriality," he told us. "That is what makes computers different." If you want to understand, study, and preserve the things they create, not to mention the people doing the creating, it helps to appreciate the machines too—not just as objects but as artifacts.[12]

That could serve as a useful summary of the agenda of the digital humanities in general when it comes to things: to think about how thingness translates into the digital realm, and to understand, study, and preserve digitized objects. The *how* of the process of translation is a vast topic for investigation; the class described in this article involves hands-on work with legacy computers and software media, for example. The precise fate of thingness in the face of such translations is another crucial topic. The process itself is already well underway, and humanists can contribute a critical perspective by returning to the other part of the dialectic that defines our moment: by curating, editing, tagging, working with material objects, even when those material objects are parts of digital systems (hard drives or floppy disks, game controllers or ROM cartridges). Note, in particular, Kirschenbaum's hint at the fundamental problem that has defined our moment of eversion: the fall from the formerly presumed immateriality of the digital. Computers create the *illusion* of immateriality. It's incumbent upon digital humanists, not just to reveal that illusion for what it is, to reveal the thingness of the digital, but to interpret the effects of the illusion in a cultural context. DH scholars work at the interface, the place of translation and transit, between, on the one hand, material objects in the collective archive and, on the other hand, the increasingly ubiquitous, physically distributed, digital network. Humanities scholars today, we might say, have a calling to explore the materialities of the digital, even as they explore (and participate in) the data-enrichment of physical objects, in and out of the archives. Kirschenbaum's remarks emphasize the translation of things into the digital realm. But one might just as easily say that, especially in the past decade, the digital has penetrated the realm of physical things, has colonized the physical, as Gibson says. What *that* has done to things—including new kinds of hybrid thing with data attached to them (Sterling's spimes)—is a topic of equally pressing importance for the digital humanities, given its historical legacy as well as its newer orientations.

Making (DH) Things

Humanities computing at its inception in the mid twentieth century involved programming, using a variety of languages and punch-card input, for linguistic analysis and concordance building. Later on, at first mostly using the ur-markup language developed at IBM, SGML, it afforded text encoding, collation, and the creation of scholarly editions and archives, sometimes with multiple media. By the 1990s, with the advent of the World Wide Web, many humanities projects created Websites using HTML and then XML, in theory ideally encoded according to the TEI standard (a standard honored perhaps more in the breach than in the practice). The new DH has maintained this emphasis on the importance of coding and making things, but the nature of those things and the process of making them have changed, or been augmented. At least part of DH making, now, when it's at its most speculative and theoretically aware, is akin to Bogost's carpentry, or to prototyped design fictions. Digital humanities scholars don't only write articles and books (though they do that, too): They contribute to research and to theory by writing code, digitizing archival materials (both in the sense of properly scanning or photographing them and in the more complex sense of encoding them with metadata or in-line structural markup, using appropriate platforms and protocols for publication and access), building or porting and massaging large-corpora databases, creating new software tools for analysis and visualization, customizing or creating new versions of publishing or teaching platforms, new CMSs, all of which means getting their hands dirty digitizing, archiving, designing, coding, analyzing, and publishing digital objects of diverse kinds. For the past decade, DH making has also taken inspiration from the wider so-called Maker movement outside the walls of the academy. This has meant building not only software but hardware things, and, despite the suspicion of many that DH is instrumentalist, these things have been more often than not created in the spirit of investigation and creativity rather than utility.

The liveliest arena for such experimentation has been the network of THATCamps, founded at the Center for History and New Media at George Mason University but spreading to dozens of "unconferences" at different locations. Inexpensive collaborative workshop sessions are proposed on the spot, or with just an email exchange in advance. Though they can be about any aspect of technology and humanities that the participants propose, an important feature of the movement is its emphasis on building and creative hacking, involving programming and design of digital tools and Websites, yes, but also a significant amount of soldering and wiring, and some sewing. Inexpensive, DIY, open-source Arduino circuit boards—with a basic processor and other components that allow it to be simply programmed and integrated with other systems—and arrays of LED lights have been especially useful for such hack sessions. Arduino was developed in 2005 in Italy out of the open-source Wiring project as a student-project and prototyping platform. There have been other, similar products, such as the Raspberry Pi single-board Linux computer, created in 2006.

These small, DIY circuit boards and components are part of the Maker movement in general, represented in the magazine *MAKE* (launched 2005) and part of an open-source hardware movement in particular, which is itself another manifestation of the eversion around 2005, a shift of attention back to physical components, wires and chips and lights and actuators, electrical engineering as well as software engineering. The best-known practitioner and advocate for this movement is probably Limor Fried, who graduated from MIT with an MS in 2005 and immediately formed a business, Adafruit Industries, named for Lord Byron's daughter, Ada Byron, later Countess of Lovelace, a historical icon often said to be the first computer programmer, as she wrote documentation, or mathematical explanations, for the working of Charles Babbage's early machine, the Analytical Engine, in the 1840s. (Fried's nickname or handle online is Ladyada.) Adafruit sells kits for DIY projects in computing hardware—Arduino boards, small LED or LCD displays, and Raspberry Pis for example. The educational goal of such devices is important to the company, which was originally founded "to create the best place online for learning electronics and making the best designed products for makers of all ages and skill levels."[13] Fried has remained active in the public open-source and Maker movements. When asked by *Wired* magazine how "the DIY revolution" might change the world, she sounds a lot like a digital humanities scholar talking about the excitement of interdisciplinarity:

> Well, first, people are becoming more and more comfortable with the idea of making and hacking their own stuff, even though they don't identify as makers. When we did the Microsoft Kinect hack, where we published how to connect the Kinect sensor to a PC, we thought we'd see maybe one or two people doing really geeky robotic stuff with it. But it turned out that even though roboticists were really interested in it, it was actually artists who were the most excited. This goes beyond electrical engineering and computer science geeks. In five to [ten] years, I would be surprised if every public school doesn't have a required class in robotics mechatronics. You'll have a return of wood shop, but it will be metal/robotics/electronics shop, and kids are going to have to learn sensors and technology.[14]

Mechatronics, combined with coding, wiring your own boards to make some-thing move or flash or process or display, out on the table or on a screen, is one way to insist that the data are physically embodied: just look at what they're doing. And Fried's own MS thesis at MIT could stand as an example of interdisciplinary intervention in social space, in its own way a kind of performative DH, located on the scientific edge of the field, but with obvious humanities and social-science motivations and implications.[15] It theorizes and documents two devices she actually built—hacks or acts of performance art as much as engineering: a remote that turns off public TVs in bars or airports (or, in one notorious case, giant screens at a large technology conference), and a kind of personal Faraday cage that blocks cellular and WiFi signals in the space immediately surrounding you. These are, in effect, neo-Luddite devices, leveraging small-scale personal technology against the intrusiveness of big technology. Like most performance art, they are provocative, symbolic actions, a kind of practical manifesto: Program or be pro-grammed, as Douglas Rushkoff says.[16] But, more precisely, Fried's thesis projects involved awareness of the contested and crowded space today's public spaces have become, not in purely ideological terms, but in real, physical terms, as radio waves, for example, permeate vast segments of our environment today, and even penetrate our bodies.

Fried cites Interactive Design Professor Anthony Dunne in this regard, who wrote presciently, back in 1999, of the importance of what he called Hertzian space—the "complex soup of electromagnetic radiation" that now pervades and forms the spaces we move through every day.[17] Significantly, Dunne's book was reissued in 2005, because, as his new preface says, real technology had by that time caught up to his earlier assessment: "Bluetooth, 3G phones, and wi-fi are all now part of everyday life" (xi). But what he calls the "extrasensory nature of electromagnetic radiation," its invisibility and intangibility, "often leads to its treatment as something conceptual—which easily becomes confused with the notional, although of course it is physical and exists in space" (102). The design experiments Dunne documents or anticipates now appear to be part of the general eversion, the push to manifest that invisible materiality in the world. When Dunne first wrote, in the late 1990s, radio—a portion of the overall electromagnetic spectrum associated with early-twentieth-century communications—seemed like a strange subject, he says, tellingly, as all the talk was of "cyberspace, virtual reality, networks, smart materials and other electronic technologies" (101). Radio was interesting to Dunne in terms that were precisely aligned with what would appear, by the time the second edition was published, as the eversion of cyberspace. Ambient radio is a crucial piece of today's experience of the network, and it reminds us of the *process* of eversion we're in the very midst of now. As Dunne points out, when he was writing in the 1990s, objects were commonly said to "dematerialize," to be replaced with software and to appear to disappear "in response to miniaturization and replacement by services." But they also "literally dematerialize into radiation," he says, as electronic objects are "hybrids of radiation and matter" (101). His design theory explores, therefore, "the links between the material and immaterial," and, "whereas cyberspace is a metaphor that spatializes what happens in computers distributed around the world, radio space is actual and physical, even though our senses detect only a tiny part of it" (101). This takes Dunne to a logical conclusion that nicely anticipates my own thesis about our transitional moment: "We are experiencing a new kind of connection to our artifactual environment. The electronic object is spread over many frequencies of the electromagnetic spectrum, partly visible, partly not. Sense organs function as transducers, converting environmental energy into neural signals" (107).

Transducers, gateways for transformation, portals between realms—this gets at precisely what's most important in the era of the eversion. And it does so with a useful reminder of the dependence of our current hybrid network on radio waves as invisible but part of what are not finally *immaterial* (or merely notional) channels of communication—a crucial part, along with optical and other electrical segments of the spectrum, of what the network *is* for us, the "net" that makes it a network.

Evidently, many of us continue to need this kind of demystification, to require this kind of reminder of materialities below our usual sensory threshold, both in culture at large and within the academy. This process and these reminders are, I believe, crucial to the mandate of the new digital humanities. The impulse toward what might be called re-materialization is everywhere in self-identified DH research. Take THATCamp participant and History Professor William Turkel, for example, and a participant in the University of Toronto's ThingTank Lab:

> a place where the exploration, experimentation, and exchange of ideas are developed toward the building of internet enabled "things." The Lab catalyzes development and research around how our data-connected world is increasingly moving off the screen and into the everyday world of objects, buildings and activities.[18]

Using the same metaphor as Dunne, Turkel has argued that his fellow historians should begin to think of their work less in terms of the *digitization* and more in terms of *transduction*.[19] Turkel's focus is on the importance of original material artifacts, but he points out that text transcription and optical imaging of documents "are only two of a nearly infinite number of possibilities for digitization" (288). He then cites smell (because it has so often been the clichéd non-digitizable attribute of paper artifacts) as something that may actually someday be captured and replicated in digital surrogates. Meanwhile, digital humanities scholars have already "greatly expanded our sense of what the humanities can be" by working through problems in digitization and raising new questions as a result. But "what can be converted from analogue to digital can always be converted back into various analogue forms. These processes of *materialization* complement processes of digitization," and even distinguishing bits from atoms is complicated by the fact that "every bit is always encoded in physical form" (290–91; emphasis in original). Citing Kirschenbaum on the digital's illusion of immateriality, Turkel suggests that historians should "try to get beyond this illusion of immateriality, and to think instead in terms of *transduction*, the conversion of energy from one form to another" (291; emphasis in original).

This is, I think, an extremely useful suggestion. Once again, when archival artifacts, the important things behind humanities research, are digitized, they are not beamed up, atomized, blown to bits, and removed to another (digital) plane. Despite some bad examples out there in libraries and collections, in best practices, the originals are not inevitably destroyed in the process. Data are already attached to, already wrapping, the physical artifact (book, manuscript, fetish statuette, musical instrument, painting, game cartridge), which is to say the thing is marked by the record of its history, in total, as it has made its way through the world, and those data are merely captured, perhaps augmented, and transformed by digitization. These data include its appearance, its markings, any text it bears. The transformation is not really a one-way trip (to cite Gibson's "Agrippa" again), at least not from the point of view of the humans—researchers, students, interested lovers of art—who engage with the artifact and its surrogates. Digitization of physical things is about enriching and extending the data shadow cast by those things. It involves, or should involve, increased self-consciousness about the two-way acts of transduction that have been undergone and continue to be undergone as the objects reveal more explicitly their hybrid nature as both physical and data things, artifacts and their analog and digital representations and networked relationships. The seriousness with which the new DH plays with today's hybrid things—Arduino circuit boards, wearable computers, LED displays, remote-control drones, video games—is, I think, based on a sense of how important this complex process is today, and on a sense of a collective mandate to engage in the process and investigate its theoretical and practical consequences.

Play Things

One of the projects Limor Fried's Adafruit sponsored was Open Kinect (2010), an offer of a $3,000 bounty to the first person to create open-source PC drivers for Microsoft's wireless, motion-sensitive game controller. (The logo for the competition on the Adafruit Website featured Tux, the Linux penguin, with a Kinect sensor on his head.) Though it condemned the challenge at first, Microsoft soon claimed that the company had been misunderstood—that it had always assumed such experiments would be done using the open USB connection. After a winner was announced (he developed a Linux driver), and after Microsoft released an SDK (or software developer's kit) for Windows enabling further such experiments, a well-known Microsoft employee, Johnny Chung Lee, who had worked on Kinect development, beginning with a series of Nintendo Wii hacks, announced on his own blog that he had been involved in coming up with the idea and helping to finance the Adafruit competition.[20] Lee soon moved on to Google. It's possible Lee was acting with Microsoft's blessing, in a stealth marketing campaign, though he later claimed he did it to force the company's hand. (Adafruit acknowledged his involvement.) As *The New York Times* reported, the image of "a loosely knit band of outsider creative coders forcing a massive company to rethink a crucial new product is appealing. Especially when that company is Microsoft."[21] Either way, Microsoft was able to claim in a TV commercial the experiments with the controller were designed to happen all along, even including such hacks (the company prefers to call them experiments by tinkerers). A special version of Kinect for the PC was released early in 2012.

All the fuss was about the recognized potential of the Kinect sensors to fit into the existing ethos of Maker or hacker culture. Despite publicity that went big—Cirque du Soleil was hired to showcase the launch of the system at the E3 conference in 2010—the device was itself a kind of hack, a little robot-looking "head" that swiveled to keep the aim of its cameras on the player(s) standing out in front of the TV, composed of simple, off-the-shelf components, in competitive imitation of Nintendo's paradigm-shifting motion-control system of 2006, the Wii. Indeed, it seems likely that the Kinect was developed in part as a reverse engineering of the Wii, in more ways than one: Instead of your holding a device with CMOS sensors that detect LEDs arrayed up near your TV screen, with the Kinect, the cameras and sensors are placed at the TV and pointed out into the room, where they detect the light reflected off your body. It may be no accident that Johnny Lee's blog posts contained numerous Wii hacks during the time he was working on the Kinect development team, including tricks involving reversing the direction of the sensor, putting a Wiimote on top of the TV and wearing the LED array on his head (attached to a baseball cap). Although Kinect marketing slogans stressed the controller-free nature of the system, declaring, "No gadgets, no gizmos, just you!", the Kinect is the quintessential gadget, as the hacker or tinkerer community immediately recognized. Like the Wii when it was released, its components are tantalizingly close to what you might build yourself with parts from Radioshack (or Adafruit). The device that was touted on its release as a non-object—"Might the next step be an absence of an object?"—was precisely the kind of object (gadget, gizmo, thing) that Makers and hackers love to tinker with.[22] It might at first seem ironic, but it's more likely the result of an ad campaign attempting to assert a fantasy of object-free control by the gaming (or TV-watching) subject in the face of the contrary truth: that the Kinect is itself a product of the larger turn to gadgety things, a turn that was, in part, driven by the Wii in the first place, and that was part of the conceptual shift of the eversion. Motion-control systems such as the Wii and Kinect have been created with an attention to the controllers as things, devices with components such as CMOS sensors, RGB cameras, LEDs, accelerometers (in the case of the Wii), all working in a kind of local or personal network that turns outward to the physical room the player inhabits.

The Kinect is part of the trend I discussed in the previous chapter, started by the Wii and most widely experienced on mobile platforms, toward treating physical space as gamespace. It has more in common with the Nintendo platforms than with the fully immersive VR game systems some are still trying to develop (such as the Oculus Rift, for example).[23] The design thread that connects Nintendo's motion-control Wii, handheld 3DS, and tablet-based Wii U platforms is this turn outward to physical space, which involves the use of various gadgets, building on the tradition at Nintendo that includes products such as the Gameboy, Game & Watch, and Virtual Boy, but with a newly self-conscious attention to mixed reality or AR as the basis of console gameplay.

The handheld 3DS console uses accelerometers, like the Wii, and a glasses-free 3D display in a miniature system that puts the player's location in physical space at the center of attention—but also the gadget in one's hands, both too small and too big to simply "disappear" as an interface, so necessarily a platform for mixed-reality rather than fully immersive gaming experiences. The 3DS console has struggled commercially (though not as much as the Wii U), at least to match the high expectations with which it was released, but its conventional Gameboy-style play, and even the 3D versions of games, may be less significant in terms of the wider contexts of the future of creative technology than the small demo-like games that shipped with the system, the AR games. These work by superimposing animated digital objects on the visual field of the room you're in, with little characters appearing to walk around on, and emerge out of, your physical tabletop, as you aim at paper cards with QR-code-like triggers on them. You have to walk around the table, taking physical aim with the console as if it were a handheld weapon, in order to shoot at the virtual targets. Actually, the targets are part virtual and part physical. The paper card might look as if it's transformed by an image layer in the viewer into a pit below the tabletop, for example, out of which a dragon seems to lunge at you, with the 3D cameras working, as you move the device around in front of you like a magic window, to combine physical and digital worlds in one experiential field. Rather than delivering this mixed-reality media transparently, from the ether as it were (as Google Glass more or less aims to do), the 3DS openly makes playing with the gadgets—the encoded paper cards and the flip-top handheld device with its 3D slider, as well as the code on the tiny game cartridge—part of the game. Those things, the hardware and software components of the platform, augment and are augmented by the digital things you perceive as a result of the software and displays—mystery boxes, dragons, moving targets. The thingness of the 3DS is hybrid, openly mixed, digital and physical.

Nintendo's Wii U home console, released in November 2012, continues to build on this design idea (though it has been much less successful than its predecessor). Actually, it seems to have been designed to do a great many things, to cover a number of bases, in order to sell in an era that's increasingly dominated by mobile systems and the app ecology, rather than traditional living-room game consoles attached to a TV. In the event, the system seemed to confirm much of what George Thiruvathukal and I said in our book *Codename Revolution* about the direction the new system would represent, as a successor to the Wii on a similar design trajectory.[24] In that book, we began by citing Robert Putnam's *Bowling Alone* and suggested that the Wii was designed to address the problem of social isolation through a very Nintendo kind of retro-innovation, by using motion control and a collection of gadgets to turn the living room into a mixed-reality gamespace. Our playful icon for this design goal was the coffee table, which signifies old-school social gaming in shared physical space, the missing component of the system, we said, that has to be supplied by you and that only works, in a kind of Zen way, when you move it out of the way to make room for Wii gameplay (97, 117). In the Wii U announcement, the Nintendo president came right out and cited Sherry Turkle's book *Alone Together* on the isolating tendencies of today's technology, showing a slide with an image of a family sitting in a circle in the living room, all engrossed in their separate devices and screens, while he said that the goal of Wii U would be to counteract that tendency, to bring people together in local social interactions—to make the living room a better place, a physical space, for social interaction.[25] He even said that "together better" would be the system's slogan. Based on our work on the Wii, we think the goal is actually concretely tactical: to undermine the TV's tendency to monopolize its space, instead distributing gaming and viewing and control among a constellation of devices, including especially the new tablet-like touchscreen control pad. These can be used by someone as a personal handheld console while someone else uses the main console and TV (or just watches TV), it can serve as a touchscreen remote for the TV, and videos on the handheld can be "flicked" to the TV to share with everyone in the room. New game designs make use of the tablet controller for asymmetrical play—one player as the ghost chasing everyone else in the room (they're using Wiimotes), or a karaoke game that allows you to face the room when you sing, reading lyrics off the tablet, while others match dance moves on the big screen behind you and sing along at the right moments. There was a promised increased emphasis for Nintendo on online interactions in the "Miiverse," though in the event that hasn't been as prominent a feature as was suggested. But, aside from recapturing some core gamers (demos have been heavy on so-called triple-A titles, and there's even an Xbox-style gamepad with all the buttons), the real heart of the Wii U, from the point of view of innovative design, can be seen as an extension of the goal of the Wii: the deliberate use of the system as a constellation of devices, things such as the Wii U gamepad or the Wiimote and Nunchuk controllers, for reconfiguring the living room as a mixed-reality-possibility space, a space for digital-plus-physical social gaming.

This overall goal took a number of forms. In spring 2012, leaked video for the Wii U revealed that the game *Rayman Legends* would make use of small physical figurines, collectible toys as token objects that you actually place directly on the screen of the tablet controller to have them show up in the game, in much the way that Activision's *Skylanders* already does. Like *Pokémon*, this combines collecting (toys or cards) in the real world with affordances in the game world, shifting gameplay out into the world as the place where objects and data meet. If it does work like *Skylanders*, then each figurine will contain an RFID chip (or NFC chip) that the tablet can read, the Internet of Things directly applied as a hardware and software solution of game design.

Indeed, there may be no more vivid illustration at large of the nature of the eversion of the network we're all living through than that the children's game *Skylanders*, reportedly the best-selling video game of 2012.[26] The *Pokémon*-like collectible toys, plastic cartoony action figures, "come to life" inside the game when you place them on the Portal of Power, a small, round, glowing platform that the product Website calls "a gateway between our world and the amazing world of Skylands." The portal glows, the action figure glows, and the character appears in the game, moving and talking and fully playable, ready to go. You swap out the toy on the portal for another, and the new one appears. You can place two on the portal to activate co-op mode.

It's a neat trick, but when you look a little deeper into the development of the game and get over the stigma attached to toys, there's a lot more going on. As Roland Barthes said, 55 years ago (though he was talking specifically about French toys): "toys always mean something, and this something is always entirely socialized, constituted by the myths or the techniques of modern adult life."[27] Barthes would have hated *Skylanders*, I suspect, as he railed against the "bourgeois" significance of plastics, "graceless material, the product of chemistry, not of nature" (54). The game's figurines are the direct result of the spread of 3D printing and the resultant ability of a small shop to design objects in software that are then turned into physical objects. They can be painted and even have the round RFID tags inserted in their base to make them working, to-scale prototypes. (The later *Giants* game uses NFC chips.) Barthes ends his brief essay sounding like a grumpy old man, with a nostalgic panegyric to wooden toys. Modern plastic toys, he says, "die in fact very quickly, and once dead, they have no posthumous life for the child" (55). *Skylanders* might stand as a challenge to this claim. The game can be read semiotically as an exploration of the imaginative life of objects in transit between physical and digital worlds, software to plastic prototype (and back again). As the backstory motto goes, "frozen on the outside, alive on the inside!" The figurines are meant to be imagined as in suspended animation, their vitality stored as "memories," data on RFID chips, to be brought to life in the digital game world. Every time someone puts a little plastic statue on the glowing portal and it appears, animated, inside the game, the process recapitulates in reverse the way that very figure's prototype, at least, was produced: from drawings on paper and in a computer to a physical object hot off the printer.

FIGURE 5.2 *Skylanders* figurine

A 3D printer, when you think about it, is itself a kind of "portal of power" for everting digital objects out into the physical world. (The actual term used is "extruding.") It's commonly said that 3D printers, or "personal replicators,"[28] turn bits to atoms, which is a way of getting at how they turn software objects into physical (usually plastic, at present) objects. Although the basic technology existed earlier, the open-source, DIY, and desktop versions of these fabrication

FIGURE 5.3 *Skylanders* in-game characters

machines arrived with the eversion, with open-source CAD software and printer hardware and common design-file standards.[29] The first open-source desktop 3D printer was the RepRap, released in 2007. MakerBot Industries was founded in 2009 and made its DIY kits available that year. Large manufacturers now "speak the same language" as a small 3D printer such as MakerBot (G-Code), allowing prototypes to be tested, then sent to a mass-production line; so, after producing a design in CAD software, you can select options for printing "local" or "global" (Anderson, *Makers*, 360). The local option is a culture unto itself, now, tied to Maker spaces in many cities around the world, with affinities for the artisanal craft culture of Etsy, for example, and for tinkering with LEDs, Arduino boards, products by Sparkfun or Adafruit, remote-control drones, and other software and hardware combinations. In fabrication, "DIY culture has suddenly met Web culture," and "Physical products are increasingly just digital information put in physical form"—CAD software is like a word-processor for fabricating physical things (Anderson, *Makers*, loc. 957, 1041, 3331).

Neil Gershenfeld has explained that, for him, "personal fabrication" involves not just "the creation of 3D structures but also the integration of logic, sensing, actuation, and display—everything that's needed to make a complete functioning system" (*Fab*, loc. 73). This is the larger context in which the *Skylanders* developers' system was imagined. (And, to some degree, it is mirrored in the finished game system itself.) Besides the prototyping made possible by 3D printing, *Skylanders'* development depended on various wireless and hardwired communication channels, RFID and USB, for example (the portal platform conceals a circular copper wire that serves as a radio antenna). Significantly, apparently like the Kinect, the game was inspired by, and prototyped using, Nintendo's Wiimote, which had already begun to imagine the game system as a network of devices, and to configure physical space as a place for hybrid digital and physical gaming. Robert Leyland of Toys for Bob tells the story of how the team thought of doing what the Wii had done, how they "wanted something that would connect to the Wii to create a physical device."

> There was a period there where we said "But how are we going to connect it? Will we need to mount a Wii-mote in it?" And right around that time, on *MAKE* or *Instructables*, I can't remember where—we saw it on Gizmodo, somebody published a hack about how to use a Wii Nunchuck to control an R/C [remote control] helicopter and we thought: Whoa, that's really pretty cool. And we looked and sure enough they weren't just wiring to the potentiometers in the controller, they were using the output signals and there was a bunch of software published that showed that you could get the signal data from the Nunchuck controller. And I thought that was neat that they'd done that, but I also thought, if I can pretend to be a Wii Nunchuck controller I can talk to the Wii and we can go the other way.[30]

This interview itself appeared in *MAKE* magazine, and the developers at Toys for Bob are clearly intent to align themselves with the Maker subculture. (They also used easy-to-program, small Arduino boards to prototype the earliest models.)

> So, we got an RFID controller from Turkey, the Arduino from Italy, and the USB connection which was wired here in California with a software library from some guys in Germany—you can just pull all of these pieces together and gosh, you can quickly prototype something which is really neat.

Designer I-Wei Huang describes the hacker-like process of prototyping (though the mass-production manufacturing is a very different process, of course):

> Now we have a 3D printer in our studio, so we can do everything internally. We take our in-game model and we res it up in Z-Brush so it looks great and has all kinds of detail in it. Then as soon as we have the high-res version we put it in different poses because it's also an in-game model which already has a rig. We usually try about 3 poses and then we just export it, hit a button and the next day we have a 3D print.

Like the Wii, *Skylanders* is imagined as a distributed system in physical space—a constellation of small, portable processors and sensors—which mirrors the eversion of the network as a whole. But *Skylanders* is more far-flung than the Wii, truly cross-platform in significant ways, making the game feel to players like it's happening out in the world, rather than being trapped on DVD or on a console or on the screen. Each action figure carries its updated stats with it, so that it can be taken across town and brought to life in a friend's game, for example, or can travel from the Xbox or Wii or PC to the handheld 3DS, to an online game world (*Skylanders Universe*), or a mobile game, *Skylanders Cloud Patrol*. A new game was introduced in 2012, *Skylanders Giants*, with taller figures and using NFC technology (like the Wii U), so that the figures begin to glow when they are brought close to the Portal of Power (they have no power source of their own, just LEDs). Every starter pack of the original game comes with the game software, three action figures, and a Portal of Power, but also trading cards with the stats and special powers of your figures, stickers and a poster showing the complete group to collect (again reminiscent of *Pokémon*; you put the stickers on the poster as you build your collection), and cards with "secret codes" on them that are—what else?—QR codes that allow you to unlock characters for online and mobile play.

Early in 2013, Disney announced its own new game, *Infinity*, which is clearly based on the *Skylanders* model.[31] It has a portal of sorts, collectible smart figurines, and game worlds based initially on three major franchises: *Pirates of the Caribbean*, *The Incredibles*, and *Monsters, Inc.*, with more to come from the deep catalogue of Disney and Pixar animated characters and stories. But perhaps the most interesting feature of the Disney game is its sandbox mode, in which you can load characters using figurines from multiple franchises into a shared game world designed for building and interacting, as in *Spore* or *Minecraft*. The possible mashups are in some ways antithetical to the historical control Disney has exercised over its intellectual properties. They're an extension of the idea of combinatory possibilities afforded by the mixed-reality platform of data-enriched physical figurines moving into and back out of the digital game worlds.

If, as Barthes said, toys "prefigure the world of adult functions" (53), then the semiotics of *Skylanders* (and, presumably, Disney's *Infinity* when it comes out) suggests a world in which the normal relationship to the network and its data takes the form of repeated transduction back and forth across a porous boundary between the physical and the digital, in mixed-reality spaces, a world of well-connected data-transducing *things*, layers of things both physical and digital. Playing with them means digitizing them, interacting with them in both physical and digital environments, collecting and curating the data with which the things become tagged and annotated, sharing and collectively curating the experience of them with other users across a variety of platforms.

If that sounds like what I've been describing as the agenda of the digital humanities, it's no accident. There are obvious connections between this kind of game technology and the new DH—starting with a shared inspiration from Maker culture and its emphasis on open-source software *and* hardware. And video games are, after all, the most popular and widely experienced form of cultural expression of our time. As much as some people might be surprised to hear it, video games are an excellent example of the humanities in creative and expressive form, a form of popular or vernacular culture, out in the world. Why shouldn't scholars with expertise and an interest in digital technology turn their attention to video games (even those that are also very much toys)? In fact, some DH scholars have specialized in the study of games and video games, including, notably, Ian Bogost (who refuses the descriptor, DH, for his work), N. Katherine Hayles, Matthew Kirschenbaum, Kari Kraus, Jason Rhody, Mark Sample, Zach Whalen, and others. What's strange, when you think about it, is the residual academic pretentiousness (or status anxiety) that makes it seem unusual or unseemly for scholars to direct their research to such a worldly, popular form of new media. This seems especially strange when it's such a rich arena for creative experimentation with the very large cultural issues—and the emerging digital-and-physical platforms—that are at the heart of the humanities today.

★

Notes

1. William Gibson, "Google's Earth," *New York Times*, August 31, 2010, http://nytimes.com/2010/09/01/opinion/01gibson.html.
2. Bruce Sterling, *Shaping Things* (Cambridge, MA: MIT Press, 2005), 77.
3. Ian Bogost, "Elbow-Patched Playground," author's blog, August 23 and August 25, 2011, http://bogo.st/xy.
4. Kevin Ashton, "That 'Internet of Things' Thing," *RFID Journal* (July 22, 2009), http://rfidjournal.com/article/view/4986.
5. Neil Gershenfeld, Raffi Krikorian, and Danny Cohen, "The Internet of Things," *Scientific American* (December 4, 2009): 76–81 (76).
6. Bill Brown, "Thing Theory," *Critical Inquiry* 28.1 (Autumn 2001): 1–22. Summary from author's Web page, http://english.uchicago.edu/faculty/brown.
7. Henry Petroski, *The Pencil: A History of Design and Circumstance* (New York: Knopf, 1992); *The Toothpick: Technology and Culture* (New York: Knopf, 2007); and see, more generally, *The Evolution of Useful Things: How Everyday Artifacts—From Forks and Pins to Paper Clips and Zippers—Came to Be as They Are* (New York: Vintage, 1994).
8. Walter Benjamin, *The Arcades Project*, trans. Howard Eiland and Kevin McLaughlin (Cambridge, MA, and London: Belknap Press of Harvard University Press, 1999).
9. Martin Heidegger, *Being and Time* (New York: Harper Perennial, 2008).
10. Levi Bryant, "Alien Phenomenology, Idealism, and Materialism," Larval Subjects blog, August 22, 2012, http://larvalsubjects.wordpress.com/2012/08/22/alien-phenomenology-idealism-and-materialism. Ian Bogost, *Alien Phenomeology, Or What It's Like to Be a Thing* (Minneapolis and London: University of Minnesota Press, 2012), Kindle edition.
11. Ian Bogost, *A Slow Year* (Highlands Ranch, CO: Open Texture, 2010). For *Cow Clicker*, see Jason Tanz, "The Curse of Cow-Clicker: How a Cheeky Satire Became a Video-Game Hit," *Wired* 20.1 (December 20, 2011), http://wired.com/magazine/2011/

12/ff_cowclicker. For *Guru Meditation*, see Bogost's blog, http://bogost.com/games/guru_meditation.shtml.

12. Jennifer Howard, "Digital Materiality; or Learning to Love Our Machines," Wired Campus blog at *The Chronicle of Higher Education* (August 22, 2012), http://chronicle.com/blogs/wiredcampus/digital-materiality-or-learning-to-love-our-machines/38982.

13. http://adafruit.com/about.

14. Chris Anderson, "Q & A: Open Source Electronics Pioneer Limor Fried on the DIY Revolution," *Wired* (March 29, 2011), http://wired.com/magazine/2011/03/ff_adafruit.

15. Limor Fried, "Social Defense Mechanisms: Tools for Reclaiming our Personal Space," MS Thesis, MIT, 2005, http://ladyada.net/media/pub/thesis.pdf.

16. Douglas Rushkoff, *Program or Be Programmed: Ten Commands for a Digital Age* (New York: OR Books, 2010), Kindle edition.

17. Anthony Dunne, *Hertzian Tales: Electronic Products, Aesthetic Experience, and Critical Design* (Cambridge, MA: MIT Press, 2006), 101.

18. "About ThingTank Lab," http://criticalmaking.com/ddimit/?page_id=2.

19. William J. Turkel, "Intervention: Hacking History, From Analogue To Digital and Back Again," *Rethinking History* 15.2 (June 2011), 287–96.

20. Daniel Terdiman, "Kinect Developer Claims Credit for Hack Bounty Idea," Cnet, February 21, 2011, http://news.cnet.com/8301–13772_3–20034579–52.html.

21. Rob Walker, "Freaks, Geeks and Microsoft," *New York Times*, May 31, 2012, http://nytimes.com/2012/06/03/magazine/how-kinect-spawned-a-commercial-ecosystem.html?pagewanted=all&_r=0.

22. On the Kinect and its initial marketing, see Steven E. Jones and George K. Thiruvathukal, *Codename Revolution: The Nintendo Wii Platform* (Cambridge, MA: MIT Press, 2012), 149–70.

23. Adi Robertson, "Oculus Rift Virtual Reality Gaming Goggles Launched on Kickstarter (Update: Funded)," *The Verge*, August 1, 2012, http://theverge.com/2012/8/1/3212895/oculus-rift-virtual-reality-head-mounted-display-kickstarter.

24. Jones and Thiruvathukal, *Codename Revolution*, 162.

25. Sherry Turkle, *Alone Together: Why We Expect More from Technology and Less From Each Other* (New York: Basic Books, 2012).

26. Sales figures, of course, include the sales of the figurines. See Matt Liebl, "Skylanders Franchise Surpasses $500 Million in U.S. Sales," *Gamezone* (January 11, 2013), http://gamezone.com/products/skylanders-giants/news/skylanders-franchise-surpasses-500-million-in-u-s-sales.

27. Roland Barthes, *Mythologies* (New York: The Noonday Press, 1972), 53.

28. Neil Gershenfeld, *Fab: The Coming Revolution on Your Desktop—From Personal Computers to Personal Fabrication* (New York: Basic Books, 2008). Kindle edition.

29. Chris Anderson, *Makers: The New Industrial Revolution* (New York: Crown Business, 2012). Kindle edition, loc. 292–303.

30. Blake Maloof, "Alt.GDC: Developing Skylanders' Innovative 'Portal of Power,'" MAKE (March 13, 2012), http://blog.makezine.com/2012/03/13/alt-gdc-developing-skylanders-innovative-portal-of-power.

31. Chris Kohler, "Disney's Biggest Stars Join Forces for *Skylanders*-Style Gaming Mash-up," *Wired* (January 15, 2013), http://wired.com/gamelife/2013/01/disney-infinity.

6

PUBLICATIONS

One research topic for the new digital humanities has been the means of its own production, and of the production of academic discourse in general in the digital age. DH practitioners are in a good position to serve as subjects in their own experiments in publishing, and especially when it comes to exploring the relationship between print and digital forms. They're often directly involved in digitization projects in which they scan books and other printed materials, edit files, add metadata, and design or repurpose CMSs for online publication and tools for comparing, editing, and studying digitized texts. And they're involved in encoding texts in various formats and building applications for e-readers and mobile devices, as well as desktop computers. But even more importantly, many of them are rethinking the design and use of digital platforms for online scholarly communication and publication, ways to combine social networking and the sharing of research with peers and colleagues and some portion of a wider public. One minimal definition of DH has been the humanities done digitally, and DH has taken as one of its research questions: What might it mean for the humanities in general to publish on digital platforms?

Outside the disciplines of the humanities, networked electronic forms of academic publication, prepublication, post-publication discussion, sharing, and review have been in play for decades. By the mid 1990s, scientists in various disciplines increasingly made use of arXiv, an "electronic archive and distribution server for research articles."[1] A typical physicist, for example, reads at breakfast the latest research in her field in preprint form, with peer-to-peer discussion attached. University-hosted digital repositories, where researchers can self-archive their work in various stages for (usually) open-access downloading, have increasingly become important for the sciences, as well. The results of highly competitive and time-stamped scientific research often get communicated very quickly online and then sorted in various streams on their way to journal publication (or not). Multiple authorship by teams of researchers and the presentation of data through tables or graphs are other differences that have traditionally set apart scientific from humanities publishing. All of these features have begun to appear in some DH research, although, in the humanities in general, the dominant model to date has remained the article or book by a single author, written after relatively long-term research in the stacks and archives (or their online equivalent). Both articles and books undergo peer review to determine whether they're published—and publication often comes years after the research is completed—by a university press or in an established journal in a particular area of specialization.

That traditional model continues to characterize most publication in the humanities. In the past few years, however, many in the digital humanities have taken the lead in accelerated experimentation with new forms and venues, partly in response to the crisis in scholarly publication—which is not entirely new, but has been accentuated in the past decade by the rise of e-books, dedicated electronic reading devices and applications for reading and for buying texts, and by online publishing in general. The latest version of the crisis in scholarly publishing and the emergence of new forms of publication from within the new digital humanities are closely intertwined, and both are intertwined in turn with wider changes in commercial publishing and bookselling, and in the cultural response to these changes. Digital humanities scholars seem to be involved in an always-changing online ecosystem of blogging, microblogging, and more complicated forms of open-access and comment-friendly platforms for reviewing and publishing. To publish is to make public, to report openly and widely. As Jeremy Bentham said in 1827: "Who could be allowed to speak of secret publication?"[2] But the role of the public, or of any segment of the public, in determining the process of production (rather than just the reception) of humanities scholarship remains a sensitive issue for many in the humanities. Traditionally, public modes of production and consumption of texts have had very little to do with how the majority of academic scholarship is published (though there have been exceptions, such as the rise of new levels of marketing and book-jacket design for cultural studies titles in the 1980s). In recent years, this has changed, in not always comfortable ways, and in ways of which not everyone in the humanities has yet become aware, in response to the general eversion of the network. The eversion has included a new focus on networked, social, cross-platform distribution of texts, images, and data out in public, and this focus has been sympathetically manifest in DH, in the search for comparable new forms and new platforms for scholarly publication, as a process, not just a product whose forms are a foregone conclusion. One way DH has responded to the eversion (and the interrelated crisis in publishing) is by imagining the eversion of scholarly communication.

Crisis in Context

To begin, it's not only *scholarly* publishing that's in crisis, if crisis is even the right word for what has taken decades to develop and continues to develop. Academic anxiety over how scholarly research will be published and disseminated hasn't arisen in a vacuum. Commercial publishing has been experiencing a serious economic and institutional crisis for years, even decades, now, as everyone knows, with pronounced effects on retail booksellers, for example, producing succeeding waves of elegies for the book (yet again), as e-readers proliferate. As I write, superstore chains that once threatened independent shops are now themselves threatened by online sales from Amazon and Apple (and, perhaps, their own failures to mount online sales). Sites of closed Borders stores are haunting signs of the change: The former site of my closest local store was, appropriately enough, turned into a seasonal Halloween store. Barnes & Noble has its own online store, of course, but it has just announced that it will close one-third of its physical retail stores over the next 10 years.[3] The remaining Barnes & Noble stores are also changing, their main floors often becoming increasingly more spacious and open (looking more like Apple stores), as shelves are removed or pushed back and replaced by the company's Nook e-reader kiosk. The unofficial greeter of these stores is now the kiosk attendant, waiting expectantly to demonstrate the various models. Despite some encouraging upticks, local independent bookstores that predated the superstores have also declined over the past decade, leaving only hardy survivors—usually those with the most secure long-tail niches, with narrow genre focus, say, that people in a metropolitan area can support, or with the strongest ties to their local communities, or with a thriving online business that supports their brick and mortar operations. In my area, I think of Quimby's, with its focus on graphic novels and genre fiction, of the Seminary Co-Op on the University of Chicago campus, and of Women and Children First in Chicago's Andersonville neighborhood. Everyone can think of examples in their own cities of bookstores lost, and, if they're lucky to live in a large enough market, of independents hanging on. In my college town on the Chicago border, there are several losses that have affected me personally, including a small shop under the El track catering to local universities with books of literary and cultural theory, as well as selected serious literature, whose proprietors were themselves opinionated readers of such works (Great Expectations, closed 2001; the sign on the brick building is still visible from the El); and a labyrinthine, antiques-filled used bookstore located in a back alley, where I have sold books, some rare, as well as bought books, or just read them in comfort (Bookman's Alley, closed 2009; again, the sign remains hanging).

Crisis may be too loaded a term for these changes, too tied to Aristotelean ideas of plot (especially in the case of tragedy) and inevitable resolution. It's perhaps too easy to join the elegies for books and bookstores, too easy to fall into what have become clichéd narratives of decline and displacement when it comes to

FIGURE 6.1 Bookman's Alley sign, Evanston, IL

book publishing that seem to cede agency and an essential, linear historical destiny to the medium of "print" itself. We should remain skeptical when it comes to such narratives about books, just as Lisa Gitelman and others have argued we should be when it comes to narratives about the history of other media.[4] Gitelman argues persuasively that media are "the results of social and economic forces, so that any technological logic they possess is only apparently intrinsic." On the other hand, as she says, media can have a powerful influence on society, "and their material properties do (literally and figuratively) matter, determining some of the local conditions of communication amid the broader circulations that at once express and constitute social relations" (10). The nature of medial change is social and has social effects, but it's not a simple story of the inevitable succession and supercession of media regimes, as the very term "print culture" might lead one to believe.[5]

In the case of books at our own present moment, large mergers, for example, and the very fact of Barnes & Noble's successful Nook device, or the adoption of the Kobo e-reader by many independent booksellers, and the shifting relative popularity of dedicated e-reading devices versus software applications for phones and tablets should remind us that the contemporary history of books, including publishing and bookselling, continues to unfold in complicated and volatile ways. *The New York Times* reported that independent bookstores seemed to enjoy a kind of upsurge at the end of 2012, perhaps connected to an apparent fashion for championing books on paper, even sometimes an analog backlash, which in turn may have arisen precisely because e-books are becoming so established in the commercial mainstream.[6] There are many reasons for book retailers to have failed besides the rise of electronic publishing, including Borders' attempt to sell music CDs at just the wrong time, for example. But it's undeniable that the book market has been undergoing a major shift in its means of production and publishing, thanks to the normalizing for a mass audience of online retail sales and the development of more effective dedicated readers and applications for e-books. Publishers' experiments with new electronic models often have a slightly— sometimes more than slightly—desperate air. But they are trying new models, now, because the (electronic) writing is on the wall, and e-book readers are selling so well. Devices for reading e-books, whether dedicated e-readers or tablets and phones using reading applications, are finally becoming familiar enough to consumers to create serious market effects.[7] Amazon's Kindle remains, for the moment, the closest thing to an iconic product (though that may well have changed by the time you are reading this book), so much so that the reaction against e-books in general often takes the form of attacks on "the Kindle" or, in what's surely the sincerest form of marketplace flattery, by championing some particular example of the "anti-Kindle."

All of this is part of the larger cultural context—much more than a mere "backdrop," as academics often figure it—for the latest *sense* of crisis in academic publishing, a crisis experienced perhaps more intensely and widely than in earlier phases of this long-lived problem of what scholars publish, and how, for whom, and to what ends. The academy's discussion can seem parochial and insular, but its concerns about publication are ultimately connected to extramural trends and cross-currents. The loss of subsidies for university presses, cuts in library budgets at the same time that large commercial vendors have raised subscription rates for bundled e-journals (especially in the sciences), while at the same time universities have maintained and even inflated the publication requirements for hiring, tenure, and promotion—all have contributed to a problem that has been developing for decades. This has affected all humanities disciplines, but perhaps my own, literary studies, has the greater stake in the subject of publishing itself. A report of the MLA's Ad Hoc Committee on the Future of Scholarly Publishing (2002) summarized the crisis as such, but remained ambivalent about whether electronic publication was "the solution," though it agreed that it was "an important new component of the problems that it has set out to examine."[8] Since that report appeared, the acceleration of electronic publication in the world at large, as well as in the academy, has generated a new urgency.

More pressing than mere commercial success or failure, the problem of scholarly publishing is at the heart of what academics do: engage in discourse, make public our research, engage in a larger conversation with scholars, and sometimes the non-academic public, about that research, about ideas, theories, readings, interpretations, evidence from archives, data and its analysis. What humanities scholars make public (in theory) when they publish is knowledge, including the record of the ongoing research and conversations that produce new knowledge. To publish is to propagate, to share, first with one's peers, but potentially with other readers who might play the role of peers on one level or another. In this era of social media, there is no shortage of platforms for doing *that*, for sharing and propagating. But, of course, the question is how new digital platforms might articulate with the centuries-old, paper-based cultural heritage, and how the new platforms might serve the often guild-like professional requirements of humanities disciplines, which are so much based on the protocols of print publication. As Kathleen Fitzpatrick, digital humanities scholar and the first Director of Scholarly Communication for the MLA, playfully figures it, the scholarly monograph, in particular—the single-author book on a single subject that has been the basis of academic careers in the humanities for the past century or more—"isn't dead; it is *undead*."[9] As a form of publication, she mordantly observes, it's just "not viable," not truly alive, and yet it's "still required" for promotion and tenure, advancement in the academy (4). In this sense, "contemporary academic publishing is governed by a kind of zombie logic"—it haunts us "from beyond the grave" (and is after our brains, as she wittily observes) (4–5). Fitzpatrick's own, newly created position at the MLA is itself a sign of a new seriousness in the debates, and I'll have more to say later about her important interventions and about efforts by her and others to engineer new platforms for academic publishing. But first, I want to add a dimension to the context: the reaction against the rise of electronic publishing, a public reaction to (yet again) the specter of dead bookstores and lost codices. In the end, I'll agree with Fitzpatrick—we do inhabit a landscape haunted by apparently undead modes of publication, and many are in denial about their true state. But, as I'll argue, I think these undead, bookish modes of publication are maybe best understood, less as zombies, and more as monsters of our own making—more like the famous creature animated with unanticipated consequences by Victor Frankenstein.

Analog Backlash?

I'll come back to *Frankenstein*, but first I want to consider what looks like a recent countermovement, a symbolic "return" to paper-based reading, codex pages, emphatically *analog* books, as a form of protest or as an artistic and cultural statement. At this vexed moment in the history of publishing (in the broad sense of the production and transmitting, the making public, of texts of all kinds), it would be surprising if there were no such reaction, no backlash against e-books and digital text and the digitization of print texts. In fact, there have been successive waves of reaction, going back decades. One familiar version in the 1990s was often self-identified as neo-Luddite, as exemplified by Sven Birkerts' *The Gutenberg Elegies* (1994). It was accompanied by cautionary warnings, even dire jeremiads, against the Internet in general and the burgeoning interest in hypertext in particular, often as part of a principled call to resist Technology (with a capital T) that was echoed in popular culture and political activism, such as the anti-World Trade Organization protests at the end of the century. Kirkpatrick Sale was famous at the time for lectures at which he smashed beige PCs with a sledgehammer like that used by the Luddite machine breakers of early industrial England.[10]

Some recent resistance to e-books, digital texts, and the effects of the Internet on reading in general continues this tradition of cautionary neo-Luddism, especially in the hands of technologically sophisticated critics such as Jaron Lanier, Sherry Turkle, and Nicholas Carr.[11] Often the resistance takes the form of an appeal to the tactile qualities of books—and, with the kind of repetition that suggests a symptom, the olfactory qualities; the smell of books remains an emotional touchstone for many—as meaningful affordances missing in electronic forms of text. Appeals to paper and boards and glue and thread, and the weight and feel and smell of those things, have recently been made in the context of an artisanal turn in general, and not always, or not only, in simple opposition to electronic texts.

Andrew Piper explores the boundaries of our cultural attachment to physical books and our collective move toward digitization in *Book Was There*.

> It is time to put an end to the digital utopias and print eulogies, bookish venerations and network gothic, and tired binaries like deep versus shallow, distributed versus linear, or slow versus fast. Now is the time to understand the rich history of what we have thought books have done for us and what we think digital texts might do differently.[12]

Piper argues for more inventive electronic interfaces, against "faking it" with skeuomorphic imitations of the codex, page-turn animations, and indeed the page itself. He wants to avoid what he aptly calls the "virtual fallacy"—the notion that e-books are immaterial (loc. 345)—but he also notes the powerful pull in the other direction in our transitional moment: "The more screenish our world becomes, the more we try to insert tactility back into it" (loc. 355). There seems to be a growing interest in "language as a visual and material medium," a cultural compensation: "the more we lost in this area electronically, the more we are learning to value it."[13] Even Piper, however, goes on to make sometimes tendentious claims for the experience of reading books versus reading on "acrobatic screens," including scenes of reading to his children in a mutually relaxed posture, "the book our shared column of support," a scene that he laments "could never happen" using an e-reader (loc. 451). It's not clear why the family couldn't gather around and lean into a shared Kindle or Nook or Galaxy tablet. Mostly, however, his extended essay usefully complicates the relationship of book to e-text by exploring some of the anxieties surrounding competing ways of reading. Piper is surely right to see ours as a transitional or "translational" moment, requiring increased humanistic *and* technical understanding of what is at stake in the different materialities of our different platforms for reading.

In fact, the most interesting instances of the analog backlash, the bookish resistance to digitization, often contain within themselves the evidence of the very complications that may seem at first to be trying to escape. Dave Eggers' McSweeney's Publishing has produced a number of books with flagrantly physical bindings, for example, not the least of which is Eggers' own 2012 novel, *A Hologram for the King*, with a textured, gold foil-stamped cover, designed by Jessica Hische and printed by Thomson-Shore printers outside Detroit. It's a book that says "Book" in no uncertain terms, no accident in a novel that tells the story of a crazy boondoggle to set up a hologram-based communication link in the Saudi desert. McSweeney's interest in this general area is well established. In December 2012, it published independent musician Beck Hansen's latest "album," *Song Reader*. Its advertising says the album "comes in an almost-forgotten form—20 songs existing only as individual pieces of sheet music, never before released or recorded."

> Complete with full-color, heyday-of-home-play-inspired art for each song and a lavishly produced hardcover carrying case, *Song Reader* is an experiment in what an album can be at the end of 2012—an alternative that enlists the listener in the tone of every track, and that's as visually absorbing as a dozen gatefold LPs put together.[14]

If you want to hear the songs, the announcement concludes, "bringing them to life depends on you." In a digital era when analog synthesizers, vinyl records, and analog tape recordings are retro-hip, Beck has out-analoged the analog fetishists (he is, we recall, the grandson of a Fluxus artist). The final twist to the project is that (of course) performances of the songs are being recorded, by known artists and unknown amateurs, using digital technology (of course), and selections of these performances are posted as videos for download on the album's official

Website. So the event or happening that the album is meant to cue is very much a hybrid analog–digital affair, totally dependent on the Internet for its own "publication."

Take another example, Jonathan Safran Foer's 2010 experimental book, *Tree of Codes*. It was treated by marketing and many reviewers as an act of resistance, openly called "the anti-Kindle," as well as a "true work of art," and "delightfully tactile."[15] One artist–reviewer (cited in a jacket blurb for the 2012 edition) commented: "In our world of screens, he [Foer] welds narrative, materiality, and our reading experience into a book that remembers it actually has a body." It's a by-now familiar opposition: the body, materiality, and tactile artistry on the one hand; "screens" and "the Kindle" on the other. Foer himself, however, has characterized the function of *Tree of Codes* in somewhat more complicated terms, as "a way of remembering something about books," and suggests, as others have, that the desire to so remember has recently increased in response to the mass-digitization projects of Google and HathiTrust, and the marketing of e-books represented by Amazon: "I think that's going to be something that happens now, where books move in two directions, one toward digitized formats and one toward remembering what's nice about the physicality of them."[16] Though he may be guilty of too easily dividing the physical from the digital, Jonathan Safran Foer clearly expects the two to continue together in the culture for some time, intertwined in a kind of double-helix structure of experiment and remembering.

If you look closely, you quickly see that *Tree of Codes* was created through a complicated process that belies any easy characterization of it as an arch-analog object. The credits name a Belgian printer, a die-cut design shop in the Netherlands, and separate hand-finisher and binder. The publisher's note says simply that, "the author took an English language translation of Bruno Schulz's *The Street of Crocodiles* and cut into its pages, carving out a new story." The result is a book whose pages have holes cut into them, as if someone had redacted the text with a razor blade. Sometimes text from pages below shows through on the page you're reading, but the main Foer text you are meant to read is made up of the remains of the process, the sparse text that was not cut away from any page. So an entire page in Schulz's story is reduced at one point (63) to "the whole of that year a / day, / a transcendental hour / a moment / forever. / But the future lay open." (My slashes are not in the original, but indicate line breaks and the sparse arrangement on the page of the remaining lines and fragments of lines.) If you do not block from view the pages beneath (using a blank sheet of paper, for example), you see excavated a busier and sometimes more garbled text, including the phrase, "a small quick heartbeat" showing through in the third line of the cut page (which actually appears on page 64). These aleatory or chance-exploiting combinations can be manipulated by shifting the location of the loose sheet of paper, so that multiple texts, of varying coherence, are discoverable. An affecting verbal text results, in part because the initial act of cutting was presumably carefully considered and intended by Foer as the author of this new work, though in collaboration, of course, with Schulz's original text. This deliberate and intentional authorial design sets *Tree of Codes* apart from Brion Gysin's and William Burroughs' earlier cut-ups, for example, or famous Dadaist experiments with random constructions, such as *The Exquisite Corpse*. And, to some degree, this technique makes it different from the work of the Oulipo group, such as *Cent Mille Milliards de Poèmes* (a hundred thousand billion poems), a similar device for controlling and constraining the recombinatory effects of layered pages of text.[17] In contrast, Foer deliberately plays the role of author as sculptor or master artisan, carving away everything that is not his new, intended text, though leaving contour lines as it were—the layered holes in the stacked bound pages—that reveal some surprises, as well.

But, of course, the actual books required a team of specialists to produce, as I've already indicated. They were produced for a trade if not a mass market, and the producers used sophisticated machinery of various kinds, including computers and design software for creating the very dies that were used to stamp-cut the pages. A video made available by the printer shows stages of the process in loving detail.[18] At about one minute in, we see the large computer screen of the designer at work, and then what looks like a laser cutter producing the dies.

It's possible, I suppose, to see all of these examples, and others I haven't described, as part of an analog backlash, a collective gut reaction against the digitization of everything. But I just can't see these experiments as reinforcing any easy opposition of print versus electronic, analog versus digital publication. They seem both more and less than that kind of opposition. These flagrantly physical publications are interestingly symptomatic, signs of a more complex condition, the transitional state I associate with the eversion. Much of what looks like an analog backlash, whether consciously or not, actually reflects a deep and justifiable concern in the shared public imagination with the ideology of disembodied textuality, but a concern expressed from the belly of the beast, from the very midst of the world of digital publication. Foer and others have a good deal of experience, of course, with digitized text, beginning with their own submitted manuscripts. In that context, they're working to remember the physical "body" of books, the material existence of all texts, including, ultimately, all digital texts. Behind the apparent nostalgia, there's a real concern with what might be lost with physical books, and this is a concern to which humanities scholars should pay attention, especially as the humanities (which now includes the digital humanities) has a centuries-old relationship—starting with early recoverers of manuscripts in the fifteenth century, such as Poggio Bracciolini, scholars such as Erasmus, and publishers such as Aldus Manutius—to textual and artifactual forms of materiality and how to publish them, make knowledge of them public.[19] More generally, we need to take seriously cultural representations, metaphors, affective responses to technological change. If we're really interested in gaining a humanistic understanding of the culture's relationship to technology at the moment, then how people (individually and collectively) *figure* the shift to digital publication, how they think about it using metaphors and images, is as important as what they explicitly say about it, or measurable data about behavior in response to it. Once we look closely in this way, we see that the so-called crisis in publishing, or the death of the (print) book, appears as an ambiguous event, one characterized by the promises of the digital and the pull of the analog, and characterized in the end by the mixed materialities, the composite body, of any text, whatever its form, in any medium.

Not Dead Yet

During 2012, a shakeup at Apple raised questions about the overall design of the company's software, which is being reassessed, perhaps in the wake of Steve Jobs' death and perhaps driven in part by the competition from Windows 8. Some speculate that a new era is now opening that may take iOS software in the direction of Jonathan Ives' signature minimalism, rather than the highly skeuomorphic textures and a/illusions that have characterized the interface on iPhones and iPads, especially, but also on Macs.[20] When I want to explain the meaning of the word skeuomorph to my students (the continuation of a previous behavior of a technology platform, often as a visual metaphor, when its function no longer exists), I just remind them of the page-turn animations in iBooks, or the torn paper left on their iCal calendar when the month is changed, or, for that matter, the weirdly photorealistic image-skins of leather and paper and linen that characterize Apple's native iOS apps. There may be good ergonomic and HCI reasons that some sort of visual transition is useful when reading "pages" on screen, but why would anyone want to wait a second for the page of an e-book to curl and "turn" when it's swiped? (And this is not to mention the more extreme version in some independent apps that provide audio "rustling" when a "page" is "turned.") Is this mere nostalgia, like the famous first public demo by Jobs of iBooks on an iPad, sitting in a leather armchair and performing the role of traditional "reader"? (The scene had everything but a pipe and slippers.)[21] Is it a mark of cultural remediation (to use a term developed by J. D. Bolter and Richard Grusin[22]), as books overlap with the emergence of e-books? To some degree, it's likely a mixture of nostalgia and remediation. Among DH scholars, one in-joke circulating on Twitter associates a relatively unthinking or reactionary nostalgia for books with their smell or with the ability to read in the bathtub. These images go back to the first era of anti-technology reaction against electronic texts in the 1990s. The page-turn animation is no more sophisticated, really, than the bathtub argument, a kind of nostalgic simulation of forms of materiality no longer active and no longer needed in iBooks, merely represented there as a concession to the emotional needs of certain users. Johanna Drucker has called this "simulacral page drape" a "kitsch" element of remembered book reading, and argued that it has distracted attention away from the more substantive affordances in electronic reading environments, such as "rapid refresh and time-stamped updates or collaborative and aggregated work."[23] Instead of worrying about how a book looks, she suggests, designers should pay more attention to how books work, to their functions as "performative space[s] for the production of reading." She emphasizes what she calls the "phenomenal book," as a "complex production of meaning and effect," the result of the reader's "dynamic interaction with the . . . work," but then refers to this as taking place in "e-space" or a "virtual" space of reading. I would just suggest that the term "phenomenal book," as applied to reading e-books or print codices, is already a more complex—more mixed-reality—concept than "virtual" alone can cover. The "virtual reality" of reading is always already a product of dynamic interactions between our human imaginations and the material conditions of the texts with which we engage, always already a mixed-reality experience in the most fundamental sense.

Since Drucker made this argument, the use of e-readers has escalated, reaching the tipping point in 2011, when Amazon sold more e-books than paper books.[24] But, of course, Amazon has its own reasons for reporting these numbers (in the spirit of ongoing "creative destruction"), and we should remember that they already reflect e-book sales versus *online* sales of paper books. More fundamentally, as I suggested earlier, the (digital) devil is often in the details of the apparent analog backlash to this development. Indeed, a number of people promoting the virtues of print today are often also questioning the opposition of analog and digital, book and e-book.

Take journalist Tim Carmody, for example, who published "A BookFuturist Manifesto" in *The Atlantic* in 2010.[25] He took the term, appropriately enough, from a Twitter list and with reference to the Institute for the Future of the Book (the co-founder of which writes a blog called Bookfutures). Bookfuturists, Carmody says, are not reactionary bibliophiles, or "bookservatives." Nor, he insists, are they utopian technofuturists. Instead, they're part of what he sees as a "movement" that refuses such oppositions.

> Bookfuturists refuse to endorse either fantasy of "the end of the book"—
> "the end as destruction" or "the end as telos or achievement" as Jacques
> Derrida would have it. We are trying to map an alternative position that
> is both more self-critical and more engaged with how technological change
> is actively affecting our culture. . . . [Bookfuturists] try to look for the
> technological sophistication of traditional humanism and the humanist
> possibilities of new tech.

The clever chiasmus of that closing sentence—"the technological sophistication of traditional humanism and the humanist possibilities of new tech"—echoes "the digital humanities." Carmody identifies his movement with the term coined by blogger and designer Jason Kottke, "Liberal Arts 2.0," and he edited a collection of essays in 2009 called *New Liberal Arts*.[26] Carmody's project and the social network affiliated with it are, in fact, a kind of extramural digital humanities.

Anyway, the wall between academic and non-academic developments when it comes to new forms of communication and publication—and especially where the new DH is involved—is often hard to locate. It's permeable and, to extend the metaphor, is covered in graffiti on both sides. Partly this is because actual people cross over all the time, from academic training out into technology research and development, game design, writing, and journalism—and sometimes back in the other direction, into the academy, especially in the arena of DH. As I have suggested already and will pursue further in the next chapter, many of the newer forms of DH were produced in the first place by younger scholars keenly aware of the developments in the wider world, developments I've been calling, after Gibson, the eversion. One of the premises of this book is that the so-called Web 2.0, movements such as Liberal Arts 2.0 and Bookfuturism, *and* academic DH are all parts of a continuum of emergent practices and theories, evident on blogs and in journalism, and among designers and novelists, as much as in academic departments or interdisciplinary centers. Tim Carmody himself, who exemplifies the trend, has said that he considers himself a "digital humanist" in precisely these terms. As he expressed it in a 2010 essay written for the crowdsourced open-access book project, *Hacking the Academy*:

> For my own part, I tend to see digital humanism less as a matter of individual or group identity, or the application of digital tools to materials and scholarship in the humanities, but instead as something that is happening, continuing to emerge, develop, and differentiate itself, both inside and outside of the academy, as part of the spread of information and the continual redefinition of our assumptions about how we encounter media, techno-logical, and other objects in the world.[27]

Carmody's own 2009 *New Liberal Arts* collection is a kind of digital chapbook containing short pieces taken straight from the blog format. As an act of publication, it's an interesting and typical example. It began as a group blog, was printed as a limited edition chapbook (which sold out), and was also made available online in PDF and HTML forms under a Creative Commons noncommercial license. The physical-book version, the editors said, was meant to be "a beautiful object," their way of "keeping faith with the past. For all this fuss about new-ness, we know the score: Books are pretty great *techne*." The term itself implies making, a technology that's also craft, and the statement deliberately bridges a kind of vernacular book history with experiments in new forms of electronic publishing. This bridging of print and digital platforms is in fact widespread, more common than pure forms of either option, once you look beyond the clichéd oppositions. Carmody's co-editor in the *New Liberal Arts* project was Robin Sloan, who called himself at the time a "Generalist Media Nerd" and had worked for the media network Current, and would soon work as a social-media specialist for Twitter. He contributed his own short piece to the collection, "Iteration," an essay on the creative process of "making things" in general. He later developed his own free iOS app, Fish—a short "tap essay" in a series of brief lexias or text-slides, looking like a well-designed PowerPoint presentation, with different background colors, typefaces, and occasional dynamic layout animation effects (words are struck through and replaced by other words, for example)—that you read by tapping through it. Its topic is the difference between "*liking* something on the internet and *loving* something on the internet." The essay is about online media and the problem of attention. Sloan also mounted a crowdfunded Kickstarter campaign to help finance his first novella, a geeky "detective story set halfway between San Francisco and the Internet," in which the Watson-like sidekick to the female detective is a sentient AI program, running on a server across town but whispering to her through a speaker in an earring. Sloan's first full-length novel, *Mr. Penumbra's 24-Hour Bookstore*, was published in 2012, based on a short story Sloan had first published for the Kindle and online. Again, in a familiar pattern, it emerged from a series of self-conscious media experiments across different publishing platforms, including physical books and e-books in various formats, in the context of the idea of the New Liberal Arts. It's a novel produced out of the social context of a non-academic version of the new DH. On Twitter, Matthew Kirschenbaum called *Mr. Penumbra* "quite likely the first novel of the digital humanities"; shortly after the tweet appeared, Sloan himself responded: "Dunno if it's the first, but I definitely had the digital humanities community in mind while writing it" (November 26, 2012).

Mr. Penumbra's 24-Hour Bookstore is about a book-obsessed secret society coming into conflict with the dominance of digital technology, the latter represented by e-books, the Kindle, Google Books, data mining and visualization, and video games. The cult of the book survives and in a sense triumphs as characters learn, as Carmody and Sloan put it, to respect the "pretty great *techne*" of print books. Sloan often says explicitly in interviews that he wrote the book to overcome the false binary opposition implied in the choice of books versus cool technology.[28] He worked for Twitter; his fictional protagonist, Clay Jannon, tells a Google employee he works in "the opposite of Google"—and the Googler responds knowingly, "Ah, books" (loc. 1165). At another point in the story Clay remarks,

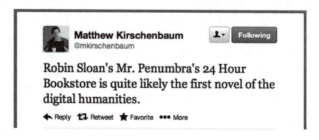

FIGURE 6.2 Twitter conversation, Kirschenbaum

Matthew Kirschenbaum
@mkirschenbaum

MT @robinsloan @mkirschenbaum Dunno if it's the first, but I definitely had the digital humanities community in mind while writing it.

← Reply ↕ Retweeted ★ Favorite ••• More

1
RETWEET

11:35 AM - Nov 26, 2012

FIGURE 6.3 Twitter conversation, Sloan

"books used to be pretty high-tech, back in the day. Not anymore" (loc. 1257), but the rest of the novel works to complicate that judgment.

In one interview, Sloan was asked whether books are now part of a hip analog backlash, amounting to "the new vinyl" in the context of the "print vs. digital" conflict. He thought not, adding:

> People think the e-book debate is about books versus computers, but as it goes on, you realize that they actually have a lot in common. One of the things I'm trying get across is that books are just as much technology as your iPhone. When books were new, the scene felt just as chaotic and confusing as what's happening in San Francisco right now.[29]

The MacGuffin of the novel's plot turns out to be not just printed books but the metal type punches created at the Aldine Press in the fifteenth century that allowed the early books to be made. An original set of these punches turns out to contain the key to a code that all of Google's computing resources—including advanced crowdsourcing and parallel-processing applications, along with large-corpora text mining and data visualization—fail to crack. The trouble, Clay implies, is that the digitization process has erased the material evidence embedded in the physique of the books, turning their texts into something altogether different, a mere disembodied "data dump" (loc. 3121). Although this may be good for running large-scale analyses and utilizing massive resources such as Apache Hadoop, it misses the literally microscopic details of the book's historical analog technology, details only accessible to a mixed-reality, hybrid, digital-and-physical forensic approach. As Clay admits late in the story, "we were looking at digitized text in a different typeface entirely. We were looking at the sequence, not the shape. . . . To crack this code, you need to think typographically" (loc. 3788).

They may need to think typographically, to think like type designers (or even to think like type), but they also need to think like gamers. The characters in the book live in San Francisco, and many of them work in technology jobs, and, of course, they play video games in their spare time, as the novel reminds us more than once. One of them has made "a dot-com fortune" creating software for simulating the motion of players' breasts in a "terrible" 3D beach-volleyball simulation game (a reference to a well-known real-world example). At one point, Clay helps his friends digitally capture the bookstore itself in order to model it in software, taking many photos until his hands are cramped and he feels, he says, as if he's been playing video games for too long—and "this is a terrible videogame" (loc. 2478). Games provide the contrast between the superficiality of the 3D simulation of the bookstore versus the depth provided by the combined contents of all the books. The former may make for a playable video game someday, but its limitations will remain obvious.

> We didn't capture the pages inside, of course—that would be a project of a different scale. If you're ever playing Super Bookstore Brothers, navigating a 3-D simulacrum of Penumbra's bookstore with pink-yellow light coming in the front windows and a foggy particle effect rising in the back, and you decide you want to actually read one of the beautifully textured books: too bad. Neel's model might match the store's volume but never its density.
> (loc. 3053)

Just as Clay works in the "opposite of Google," in a bookstore, you might think from this passage that the novel makes books the opposite of games. But it's more about recognizing the unique affordances of both technologies, starting here, with the inability of digital simulations to capture in simulated form the layered "density" of inherited print culture. But it can become part of that density, adding its own set of layers. The scene takes place, after all, during an intensive collaborative digitization session.

The whole point of the novel is to promote a mixed-reality culture—out in the world or in the stacks, among physical books and metal type and social groups, but also online, using digital tools and algorithms (as far as they go), DIY book scanners, e-readers, and networks. Games are central to this culture. At a different scale, the overall plot obviously unfolds like a big game, an ARG, actually, involving digital and physical clues, locative and mixed media, crowdsourcing, collective intelligence, and collaborative play by a team representing diverse expertise, with a gamemaster behind the scenes (and beyond the grave)—in this case a fictional type designer, Griffo Gerritzsoon, who is said to have worked with the historical printer at the wellspring of print culture, the humanist Aldus Manutius. Penumbra says it near the novel's conclusion: "all this time, we were playing Gerritszoon's game" (loc. 3829–39). His typeface, which is still used everywhere in the modern world, is a set of signs, meaningful pointers to the physical marks that he left as meaningful keys to the code embodied in countless books.

But this emphatically analog key to the mystery—marked pieces of metal—is discovered in part through digital means. These include a robotic shelving system in the archive (like those used in Amazon's warehouses, for example) and high-resolution digital magnification, and they do not lead in the end to a neo-Luddite solution, in which e-books are smashed and the magical bookstore is restored as it was, but to a kind of movie ending that has all the characters involved in ideal projects that combine an artisan's attention to physical artifacts, including books, with a coder's facility with cool technology. This is *Mr. Penumbra*'s openly tendentious summation. The bookstore of the title is converted into a climbing gym, which seems absurd but, ironically, may be the most realistic San Franciscan detail of the story. Clay and his gang decide to form, not a new bookstore or publishing company, but that most tech-industry type of business entity—"a consultancy: a special-ops squad for companies operating at the intersection of books and technology, trying to solve the mysteries that gather in the shadows of digital shelves" (loc. 3923). That the digital shelves cast or retain "shadows," areas of blindness, is the point of the book's interest in reviving or keeping alive interest in print technologies. The consultancy's first contract is to design a "marginalia system" for a new, Google-sponsored e-reader, the improved affordances of which include a cloth skin, "like a hardcover book" (loc. 3917). The new company's offices are lined with books salvaged from the old shop, and the consultancy also, improbably, indulges in a new model of bookselling: "Every few weeks, we'll cart the books out into the sunlight and hold a pop-up sidewalk sale, announced on Twitter at the last minute" (loc. 3927). Of course, Clay's own book (the one we're reading) is published and made available in "all the places you find books these days: big Barnes & Nobles, bright Pygmalion, the quiet little store built into your Kindle" (loc. 3950).

It's a deliberately aery fantasy of an ending, reminiscent most of all of Hollywood movies in which the characters' futures are told in a series of tableaux, a "where-are-they-now" epilogue played out while the extended credits roll.[30] Caricature and comic exaggeration are licensed by the convention. But I also detect in the novel's epilogue a more poignant desire, which runs throughout the novel, for a mixed physical and digital creative culture, as when two of the designers in the story end up starting "a production company that uses pixels, polygons, knives, *and* glue" (loc. 3889). This is a desire expressed in almost every interview Sloan has given about the book, a desire he seems to have faithfully recorded from the midst of the real physical/digital Maker culture of which he's a part. This aspect of the technology culture over the past decade amounts to an ethos, one that's only recently starting to be widely reported. In its sometimes naive desire to resist the easy oppositions that have riven publishing as a broader cultural problem in the past couple of decades, this ethos has much in common with emerging DH scholarship, which is in the midst of reinventing its own forms of publication and scholarly communication, while also turning outward, to address developments in the world at large.

It's (Still) Alive!

I agree that Sloan's novel is the first DH novel of our new era, mostly, as I've indicated, because it expresses a desire shared by DH for a mixed-reality, physical and digital perspective on creative and scholarly culture. It's not that I believe the eversion has brought about such a millennial world; but I think the impulse driving the eversion (and driving DH) has a trajectory of desire in that direction.

And, as I described above, as part of this desire, *Mr. Penumbra's 24-Hour Bookstore* gestures to traditional humanities. The fictional type designer's name, Griffo, is taken from the historical Manutius' actual type-cutter for the Aldine Press in fifteenth-century Venice, Francesco Griffo (who is credited with creating the italic typeface). The Aldine Press was famous for its elegance of design and for printing books in the smaller, relatively inexpensive, octavo format. Aldine books were innovations at the time, presumably meant to further the general humanist aim of disseminating learning, editions of Greek and Roman texts, to more readers. The Aldine Press of Manutius, in other words, at least as it has traditionally been characterized, emphasized the public in its publications, and has been made into a symbol of the public-facing spirit of the humanities and liberal arts (as they have been constructed later, as academic metadisciplines). At the same time, Aldus can be construed as a technologist, as an inventor. The Bay-area Bookfuturists even like to say (stretching the historical analogy a bit to connect with contemporary start-up culture), that he was an entrepreneur. That somewhat anachronistic market celebration aside (such characterizations rarely deal with the problem of patronage, for example), it's true that Aldus was a printer with a refined design sense, a true artisan, as well as a successful publisher. So the Aldine Press was chosen by Sloan as an antecedent for the productive doubleness—the mixed combination of physical and informational—that, as Sloan has repeatedly said, lies behind his novel.

Mr. Penumbra's 24-Hour Bookstore might easily enough be deconstructed as nostalgic, itself skeuomorphic—a representation of book fetishism wrapped in digital denial. Part of what bothers many people (myself included) about some bookish skeuomorphs is how they trivialize, turn into mere cartoons, the real and robust affordances provided by books. If you love the weight of a page in a properly formatted book as you turn it with your hand, you may be annoyed at the page-turn animation on your gleaming tablet. Parts of Sloan's novel are open to the same charge, of reductionism, or caricature, as being a kind of Harry-Potter book history.[31] Despite the novel's evident bibliophilia, it also seems wryly to embrace the creative destruction by which the historically aware independent bookstore is turned into a hipsters' gym, with mere images of the old store left on the walls as superficial decor. But, as I've indicated, it's also possible to read the general phenomenon of skeuomorphism more generously, as an attempt at expressing real needs on the part of the reader, and as a not-always conscious symptom of a deep and meaningful ambivalence in the culture. Likewise, instead of bibliophilic nostalgia, Sloan's novel can be read as expressing an ambivalent desire—to preserve aspects of print culture even as we build new digital technologies, and, even more significantly, to recognize the material conditions that shape all publishing, including digital publishing. There's no magic in the ending of the novel, just competing technologies—print and digital—and the cultures that emerge with them. The sometimes light, playful plot is based on a vision—we might recognize it as the shared vision behind much of DH—of the humanities thriving as a vital force in the digital age. One construction of the humanities chooses as it founders humanists such as Aldus Manutius, who printed elegant editions of recovered texts, which had earlier been "copied, edited, commented upon, and eagerly exchanged, conferring distinction on those who had found them and forming the basis for what became known as the 'study of the humanities'."[32] This is the kind of culture of the book many have in mind when they worry today that digital publishing is irrevocably changing the nature of humanities publishing. On the other side, the question is how far archival, book-based forms of discourse can be integrated with newer modes, how they can remain socially vital, intellectually alive, rather than, as Kathleen Fitzpatrick has suggested when it comes to the academic monograph, (metaphorically speaking) merely undead.

Again, the problem with skeuomorphs is that they are—almost literally—mere shadows of what makes books work so well, that combination of tactile and visual cues, and in this way the animations often feel uncanny, like diminished and monstrous husks of print realities, zombie features in the media landscape. Here, I'm extending Fitzpatrick's metaphor for existing academic publishing, especially in the humanities and based on the dominance of the monograph, as "governed by a kind of zombie logic . . . undead, haunting the living from beyond the grave" (4–5). As she points out, zombies have already been read as a metaphor for the self-contradictory forms of late capitalism, or for the modern subject living those contradictions. By a kind of analogy of scale, she applies the metaphor to the prospect of "death-in-life" for academics, as "certain aspects of the academic publishing process are neither quite as alive as we'd like them to be, nor quite as dead as might be most convenient" (5).

> If the monograph were genuinely dead, we'd be forced to find other forms in which to publish. And if the book were simply outmoded by newer, shinier publishing technologies, we could probably get along fine with the undead of academic publishing, as studies of forms like radio and the vinyl LP indicate that obsolete media have always had curious afterlives.
>
> (5)

The analogy isn't perfect, she admits. We don't have real replacement forms for scholarly books, and they're not going to become merely a niche technology in academic publishing any time soon. But Fitzpatrick's metaphor has the added virtue of opening up connections between the academic problem and the larger media landscape. It applies a wider lens to the academic crisis, starting with a broad definition of publishing. As she says, "all publication is part of an ongoing series of public conversations, conducted in multiple time registers, across multiple texts" (199). What zombie scholarship lacks is precisely what should be at the heart of publishing as a conversation: actual social relations.

In that same seriously playful vein, I want to extend Fitzpatrick's zombie metaphor to suggest that the zombie failures of the academic monograph system, which is part of a larger crisis in models of publishing in a digital age, can also be understood with reference to a different metaphor and a different myth: Frankenstein's monster. Victor Frankenstein's scary creature, as told by Mary Shelley in 1818, was made in a "workshop of filthy creation," apparently from salvaged parts of corpses, through chemistry with the addition of electricity. Intended as beautiful, the creature appears hideous to its creator. Frankenstein infamously spends the rest of the story in a kind of strange denial about his responsibility. The creature only turns murderous when he is abandoned and it turns out he has no place in society.[33] Victor famously denies his own responsibility for what he has made, and has an initial, viscerally horrified reaction to the creature's cobbled-together appearance, which reveals his salvaged origins among the dead, but also the fact that he has been stitched together by Victor himself. Instead of exulting, as he is made to do in the 1931 Hollywood version, that "it's alive!," in the novel Victor panics at the uncanny prospect that what he has made is neither fully alive nor fully dead. His creation reveals too clearly that it has been made, not born, constructed in the "workshop" and set loose out in a world that may not be ready to offer it an appropriate reception.

The novel has been read in countless ways, among them, as an allegory of Technology (with a capital T) run amok. But I'd like to see it for a moment as an allegory for the anxieties of publishing—something about which the young Mary Godwin knew a great deal—as a kind of technology (with a lower-case t), one that requires, but cannot guarantee, a social network for it to succeed. After all, Victor was an academic, one who never completed his course of study at the university at Ingolstadt, instead withdrawing into "a solitary chamber, or rather cell, at the top of the house" (81), and cutting himself off from other people, his family and friends, but also his professors and fellow students at the university, in order to create something on his own, with no peer or public vetting. Victor later admits of his lone research that it "had secluded me from intercourse with my fellow-creatures and rendered me unsocial" (94). The creature is an extension of Victor's solitude. One way to explain why the creature goes wrong, what makes him a monster, is that Victor fails to socialize him, fails to imagine him as a social being with a life in the world.

Our experiments with new forms of publication in the digital age are in this way like Frankenstein's creature: We're often in denial about the fact that what we make as scholars is always inherently social. Down deep, we fear we are turning out work in now-monstrous forms, lingering, neither alive nor dead. Perhaps the answer is to take pragmatic responsibility for the necessarily hybrid nature of our creations, and to make them from the start fit for a reception out in the world as it is. When it comes to new forms of publication at our own transitional moment, a certain mixture of dead and living forms (a state we can glimpse in the uncanny persistence of skeuomorphs) may be inevitable, as we stitch together new platforms for publication based on existing and emerging social structures as much as on technologies, based in fact on recognizing the social basis of new technologies. As Fitzpatrick observes, "the issue of engagement . . . is not simply about locating the text within the technological network, but also, and primarily, about locating it within the social network" (119). She cites in this regard Matthew Kirschenbaum, who exhorts scholars to attend to "the fundamentally social, rather than the solely technical mechanisms of electronic textual transmission, and the role of social networks and network culture as active agents of preservation" (2008, 21; cited in Fitzpatrick, 129). Kirschenbaum is here addressing the problem of preservation, but, as his work on Gibson's Agrippa, for example, demonstrates, publication also turns on the social nature of textuality. The social nature of publication is the point of recent experiments in using social-software models for DH scholarship. Digital publishing platforms are alive in the sense that they are made (often from existing parts); in the sense that they are made up of layers of mixed-reality materialities; and in the sense that they are open to remaking within public, social networks, which is where they find their realized existence (if at all).

Platform Thinking

What Fitzpatrick's *Planned Obsolescence*, which is about (mostly academic) publishing, expresses so well is that publishing in the digital age has to begin by thinking in terms of practical constraints and affordances, not just of e-books or "screens" versus print or "paper," but of new publishing platforms. Those platforms, when they function as they should, are fundamentally social, mixed-reality systems, layered "stacks" that connect various materialities of research, writing, reviewing, and reading that, for now, will continue to include and participate in book culture, even as they bridge to other forms of communication, other emergent forms of making public humanities scholarship.

   Planned Obsolescence was itself a kind of participant–observer test case, published by NYU Press in 2011, but only after an interesting pre-existence. The manuscript was posted online in 2009 at the MediaCommons Press, using the open-source CommentPress theme for the WordPress blogging and publishing platform, where it underwent open peer review. Comments were tied to individual paragraphs of the book in progress and were not only taken into account by the author during revisions, but were sometimes addressed by her via the same platform. In 2004, Fitzpatrick had begun to speculate about creating an all-digital, community-based scholarly press, and first the MediaCommons Press and then the MLA Commons platform were the results (7). She has said that the idea was based, in part, on previous experiments in open peer review, such as the widely reported one in 2010 for *Shakespeare Quarterly* (9). She openly sought to build, not just an online journal or online press, but a platform, what she imagined as a "peer network backbone" for a kind of "Facebook for scholars" (9). The MLA launched MLA Commons during the January 2013 convention in Boston, announcing it as "a platform for the publication of scholarship in new formats." It was built with a software suite known as Commons in a Box, which includes the BuddyPress extension for WordPress (which, in turn, is built on a Linux–Apache–MySQL–PHP LAMP open-source stack, as Matthew Kirschenbaum pointed out in a talk at the same MLA meeting[34]). The experiment was, from the start, like much digital humanities work, a way of reconceiving the platforms available for scholarly publishing, but even more important, perhaps, were the basic premises behind the experiment: that publishing always takes place on one platform or another, and that successful platforms are inherently social infrastructures.

In the foreword to the Platform Studies series they created and co-edit, Ian Bogost and Nick Montfort assert that, "it is time for those of us in the humanities to seriously consider the lowest level of computing systems"—the platform—in order to better "understand how these systems relate to culture and creativity."[35] Although computing platforms are often thought of as hardware-based, in fact, there can be hardware-only platforms, hardware + software platforms, or software-only platforms (the editors cite Java as an example). Ultimately, platform is an "abstraction," a way of conceiving of a system as a designed and programmable foundation or infrastructure on which digital artifacts can be developed—including creative and expressive works based in software. The editors' operational definition of platform is: whatever it is that developers require in order to make what they make. An operating system such as OSX can be a platform, but so can a video-game console such as the Xbox, or the Web itself, for example.

However, the emphasis of platform studies is on infrastructure and what it enables and constrains in the way of other kinds of development. By the "lowest level of computing systems," they mean the circuits and processors and code, as opposed to the higher-level software that runs on a computing system—games, electronic literature, video—which is the usual limit of humanities scholarship. The idea is to redress an area of relative neglect in media studies by turning to the usual approach of computer scientists and programmers to a computing system: as vertically organized in a way that's analogous to the data-type and computing architecture of the "stack." Higher-level components and the operations involving them take place closer to the end-user, at the interface, for example, whereas lower-level components are closer to the machine. Each higher level is built on the levels below it in a series of codependencies: hardware architecture, machine code, operating system and other software frameworks, application programs, screens and controllers (with their own hardware and software configurations), software interface, and expressive or creative applications, such as games or spreadsheets or digital literary works.

The whole basis of the idea of a computing platform is that diverse material-ities of machinery and code and creativity are interrelated. As a platform can be a kind of constructed thing made of code, it's clear that there's no essential division between circuits and scripts, machine and creativity. Culture shapes every layer, and the layers themselves are culturally conceived as interrelated. Nonetheless, like the OHCO thesis regarding text markup (which sees texts as Ordered Hierarchies of Content Objects), this metaphor of a vertically organized platform may seem to brush against the grain of certain humanities assumptions about texts and other objects of attention, or about cultural expression in general.

Partly in anticipation of such resistance, in our book for the Platform Studies series on the Nintendo Wii, George Thiruvathukal and I deliberately paid attention to the higher-level aspects of the system, such as the configuration of its motion-sensitive game controllers, expectations for the user experience, and the projected social situations in which the games would be played. We also took into account—as an imagined feature of the overall platform—the notional space of the "living room" as the center of gameplay, which, we argued, Nintendo designers deliberately emphasized in opposition to the virtual world of the game "behind the screen." In this way, we explained what was unique about the Wii as a gaming platform—its design as a system for encouraging social gameplay, not by creating immersive game worlds but by saturating the living room (using wireless and wired connections) with the distributed system, extending the console's reach out into the physical space between the couch and the TV. That was the point of our joke about the coffee table as the missing component of the system when it came to Wii gameplay. This design on social space was implemented through marketing as much as hardware and software architecture, we suggested. But we were only drawing attention in an exaggerated way to the fact that all platforms are socially constructed phenomena.

On the other hand (or at the other end of the platform), Nintendo's strategic shift of focus to the living room as the site of social gameplay was afforded by particular technical features of the system, from the power-sipping processor and elegant design of the console (which made it attractive to the projected "moms" who would supposedly purchase it for their family's living room), to the MEMS (micro-electronic–mechanical system) accelerometers in the slender Wii remote controller that measure player movements and translate them into in-game actions. As we argued, every layer of a platform such as the Wii is saturated with cultural presuppositions and connected to cultural effects. So the marketing of Nintendo games as family fun shaped the emphasis on the living room as gamespace, which in turn led to experiments with accessible, simplified controllers; or the cartoony, manga-inspired designs of famous Nintendo icons (such as Mario), which arose out of a combination of practical necessity and creative flair, led to the Miis, cartoon avatars for the Wii that were also, not coincidentally, easier for the low-powered graphics of the system to render than more photo-realistic characters would have been. Platform may be organized in a vertical stack of hardware and software components, but all the components and features are culturally conditioned. Platform is, at every level, cultural and social.

I cite this example of a well-known gaming platform and once-popular consumer device in order to illustrate how the interpretive approach of the humanities can work alongside more technical analysis, how combined approaches can illuminate the connections between technical aspects of a system and social and cultural contexts, the ways in which hardware and software and cultural expression are interconnected. In this sense, the idea of platform goes to the heart of the new digital humanities and its own platforms for scholarly communication and publishing. It has always been possible to describe publishing as a system at least loosely analogous to platform, with hardware-like components—from the tools of the scriptoria to moveable type and presses, to later automated typesetting machines, and, still later, computers—and software-like printers' instructions, style guides, and works of literature themselves, with their paratexts, including blurbs, advertisements, and reviews, not to mention hybrid hardware–software-like ISBNs and other inventory encoding systems.[36] Thinking of publishing as taking place via "platforms" in this largely metaphorical way is useful for understanding the bigger picture of the production, transmission, and reception of texts, as a system of components with specific affordances and constraints, as opposed to just referring to some vague entity called "print."

In recent years, however, a more precisely defined notion of platform, as a layered *computing* system, has found its way to the heart of the digital humanities. This new centrality of (computing) platform thinking is what lies behind Kathleen Fitzpatrick's work on the future of scholarly publishing, including her own book project and the larger project it led to, the MLA Commons. (In fact, she once began work on a grant proposal explicitly for the development of digital platforms for new forms of scholarly publication.[37]) She's just one of those who are leading a professional community to reimagine scholarly communication specifically in terms of particular computing platforms, and to imagine decisions about the design and use of platforms as central to humanities publication and communication.

The CMS-like blogging platform WordPress has been adopted for a good deal of online publication in the humanities in recent years; for example, especially as modified with specialized open-source plugins developed by DH scholars, such as Anthologize, produced by a group of collaborators during an NEH-funded challenge for the easy production of e-books, formatted in e-Pub or PDF, from a WordPress blog. On the WordPress plugins site, Anthologize is described as "a free, open-source, WordPress-based platform for publishing."[38] Another, more comprehensive publishing platform was initiated in part by Bob Stein of the Institute for the Future of the Book, Scalar. The official Website of the Alliance for Networking Visual Culture describes it as "a free, open source authoring and publishing platform that's designed to make it easy for authors to write long-form, born-digital scholarship online."[39] Scalar means to enable the use of images, videos, media files of various types, as well as text, and to provide built-in visualization tools and multiple pathways through a work. The digital media journal *Vectors* is a partner in developing the platform. As I write, it has scheduled a public beta release for the first quarter of 2013.

Finally, a number of books slated for publication by university presses, such as *Planned Obsolescence*, have been published via the CommentPress platform. One impetus for the use of such platforms has been the DH community's interest in new models of peer review, everything from fully open review to limited-group peer-to-peer review, and post-publication comment and review. The tendency of such models is to treat new scholarly texts as more or less collaborative objects, and more or less fluid works-in-progress, with publication conceived of as more a process than a product. These models are sometimes being driven by the increased importance of data—with the attendant use of graphs, tables, arrays, and visualizations in general—in digital humanities research, or even the sharing of programming code itself, as opposed to all humanities research being presented discursively in finished, polished essays and monographs.

The quiet infiltration of platform thinking into the design of humanities infrastructure is even better illustrated by the popularity of GitHub, a codebase-hosting Website using the Git distributed version control system, which was developed initially by the open-source software community as a way to enable collaborative programming by allowing for "forking" of a codebase, copying a given repository in order to modify it and create a new "branch," the revisions in which could then be noted in a "pull request" to be incorporated into the shared repository (or not).[40] Every new pull request in the Git system to any given shared repository is thus a potential first step to collaborative editing of the codebase and a new release with incorporated changes. It's easy enough to see how the Git architecture, meant to facilitate collaborative coding, could have been adopted for actual DH software projects, but it's also increasingly used for collaborative writing and revision of texts. The platform is popular among DH scholars (and others) beyond its practical utility—or at least beyond the explicit practical purpose of sharing code—and I think that popularity can be explained in symbolic as well as practical terms.

More than a blogging platform such as WordPress, Git offers a structural model of collaboration based on the FOSS (free and open-source software) movement. Some of those publishing simple text documents on GitHub might be doing it because it's the cool thing to do (for the moment). Some may be just making a gesture of support for open source (a gesture that, in itself, may be socially valuable, of course). There are cases of manifesto-like public documents being published to GitHub with a more or less explicit invitation to rewrite the text instead of merely commenting on it. In that case, one critic filed an "issue report"—as if he were reporting on a problem with code, when he was really critiquing the document's rhetoric and arguments.[41] GitHub does offer a faster and more accurate version control system for collaborative text documents than a wiki or blog, and this has led to its adoption by a range of different groups, including, for example, the city of Chicago.[42] And there have been claims by some tech-journalists for the platform's signaling a "revolution" and "the birth of a new culture," based on widespread adoption of FOSS premises and (as important) the platform architecture and interface that make implementing them convenient and easy. GitHub's "low barriers to contribution," allow "less-technical users" to directly intervene and improve new software.[43]

Undoubtedly, a good number of DH users (and others) are, for the moment, using the platform as a kind of public performance of support for open-source culture and its practices. It's something like putting a sticker on their laptops. But it's not *all* symbolism and (sub)cultural identification. Some DH practitioners are themselves also programmers who have, for a long time, already been depositing their code at GitHub. So for them it's just a practical convenience to also publish text documents, including their own blogs, for example, on the same platform. Late in 2012, a prominent DH scholar at the University of Nebraska, Stephen Ramsay, gave a lecture at Loyola's Center for Textual Studies and Digital Humanities in Chicago. After the talk, as a matter of course, he dropped into our lab to log on, open a command line, and access GitHub, where he uploaded and published the full text of his lecture. Then he tweeted the link to it. We all headed off to dinner, and, in the car on the way to the restaurant, Ramsay's phone began to ping repeatedly as people downloaded the lecture and retweeted the link. Ramsay—who is a programmer and advocates teaching programming to humanities students—treated his lecture in the most straightforward way as yet another release event. He publishes a good portion of his own research and writing, including his blog, via the GitHub platform, using his own domain and by way of the streamlined text-encoding markup language, Markdown, and so publishing this talk in this way was nothing out of the ordinary for him. A platform designed to share source code was used in this case to share discursive text, but the text was treated as if it were source code, published under the kind of Creative Commons license that meant that one of those who downloaded it might well have re-encoded it in e-Pub format and made it available as an e-book, for example. As he is in the habit of doing, Ramsay thought of the text of his talk as something theoretically open to input and reuse by members of a distributed, engaged audience, a peer community. To some degree, his choice of publishing platform made this openness known and more likely to happen.

I could use this example to expose tensions within the digital humanities community: between those who program and those who only collaborate with programmers,[44] between those who publish in new ways—often influenced by the example of open-source software developers and their need for shared code repositories—and those who continue mostly to publish articles and books (like this one) through more traditional channels of peer-reviewed journals and university presses or presses with a focus on academic subjects. Those tensions are real, and they show up as debates at conferences or online, as what DH is, what doing DH entails, continues to remain contested. But DH scholars are experimenting with using platforms such as GitHub for sharing both code and documents, and this is a way to register at least a conceptual parity between the two forms of production, the two forms of publication. The choice of platform goes beyond matters of interface to the underlying architecture and design attitude, including the social architecture of the kinds of group who use the different platforms. Just the fact that it's now plausible, and becoming more common, to think about humanities publication as something that can take place via a code repository and version-control system is a significant contribution made by DH in recent years.

A new, interdisciplinary kind of platform thinking is infiltrating humanities disciplines and affecting their practices, across the boundaries of such disputes, even outside of DH. The value of this turn to platform thinking for humanists who are not used to thinking in this way is different from the value for computer scientists, for example. For some in DH, the value is practical, tied to the specific material conditions of workflow, for example, or of access to the results of scholarly research. But platform is also a metaphor and framework for thinking. It shifts the way humanists conceive of what they're doing when they publish, when they make scholarship public. Platforms are systems to be built on, not receptacles to be filled with text. Platforms are based on meaningful connections between the material means of production—host machines and wider networks, content management and version control, storage and services, text and image encoding, and metadata—and the forms taken by the higher-level expressions, creative, interpretive, and analytical, built on top of these material means of production. Not everyone will be able to hack or modify every level of the platform, but, collectively, DH practitioners approach platforms as makers rather than users, and this involves thinking of digital materialities, at different levels, as intertwined, worldly, and social realities.

Platform thinking is another part of the eversion, an example of the network's turning itself inside out by revealing its innards in various matter-of-fact ways, revealing and making a part of the process of publishing the infrastructure or scaffolding that makes online publishing possible. It's not simply replacing printed, paper books and articles with digital venues for publishing e-books and articles. It's a conceptual shift and an increased attention to infrastructure. Publishing is always a mixed-reality process, including paper-based as well as digital forms, varieties of both (and it will remain so for some time to come). The key debates are about competing attitudes toward reading, scholarship, publishing, and communication in the digital age. These attitudes can be represented with competing metaphors: On the one hand, we might imagine zombie pages, turning in skeuomorphic animations, tinged with nostalgia and regret; on the other hand, socially oriented monsters, made in workshops, not "filthy" in Frankenstein's neurotic sense, but perhaps messy in the sense that they're hands-on and experimental, workshops of creation that are collaborative rather than isolated. The results of such lab work are layered systems, built and rebuilt by maker–scholars as starting places, platforms on which to build future things, scaffolding for new forms of research and communication, connecting born-digital media with digitized objects, networks with physical archives. This kind of platform thinking requires the turning inside out of scholarly communication, working with and along the stitching, seams, and imperfections. As Kathleen Fitzpatrick suggests, an emphasis on open-source and open-access platforms over closed and proprietary ones affords the possibility of "drawing the academy back into broader communication with the surrounding social sphere" (56). In the end, an emphasis on social infrastructure is more important than any particular form of new technology, but platforms such as GitHub or WordPress (with its evolving plugins and variations), are designed in favor of exposing social infrastructure. Platform thinking is about acknowledging that scholars themselves are the ones to make and remake—not just inherit—the means of production when it comes to their own research: fewer zombies, more Frankenstein's monsters that we stitch together ourselves and for which we take responsibility. In this way, the digital humanities may well play a leading role in reconceiving scholarly publishing.

Colophon

Acts of publication on these new platforms can take many forms. MLA Commons, still new as I write, has been the site for publication of conference papers, essays, multi-author anthologies, as well as social-media communications of various kinds. What about the book you're reading? It is a more conventional form of scholarship, to be sure, a monograph (in the sense that it's a book on a single, unified topic), published by a commercial press known for its cultural studies and media studies lists. It's not open access (as you, the reader, well know). It's an extended essay, as I've said, and for that and other reasons, it seemed to me material best suited for the book format and the publishing apparatus that goes with it. But even in this conventional form, it was, of course—like almost every academic book these days—produced as electronic files, and its notes and references contain a preponderance of electronic sources. Until the final stages (when MS Word was required), I wrote it almost entirely on an iPad with an external keyboard, as I always had that device with me. It was backed up automatically to Apple's cloud service, iCloud, so I could also get to it from my phone or from other computers. There's nothing special about any of these features these days (just one more sign that the binary of "print" versus "electronic" is a misleading fiction). Nor is it unusual that I drafted portions of the book on two different blogs (on WordPress and Tumblr), often expanding a blog entry to produce a chapter. Comments on both blogs, as well as on Twitter, where I called attention to new posts and sometimes carried on conversations about them, helped shape the book.

But I also contributed an essay based on the book's introduction to the open-access edition of *Debates in the Digital Humanities*, edited by Matthew Gold and produced via CommentPress for the University of Minnesota Press, but then moved for release to a new publishing platform at the GC Digital Scholarship Lab at the Graduate Center, CUNY.[45] The piece was vetted via an extensive process of "peer-to-peer" review, receiving detailed responses by specific paragraph from a diverse range of DH scholar-practitioners (drawn from those who were also contributing or had contributed to the volume). Then it was reviewed again by the press, on the way to approval for inclusion in the online and open-ended OA volume. The comments from this review process, as well as from conferences and talks where I presented the material (often in the form of slide shows), really helped me think through and revise the book in the early stages. The process by which this book was made was normal, in other words. It's clear that "print" would be an inaccurate term to describe the messy, collaborative *techne* of its production and transmission, which included digital as well as print files and frameworks, across multiple platforms, conceived of as social structures as much as technological ones, many still emergent in the current mixed-reality environment.

★

Notes

1. Cornell University Library, arXiv, http://arxiv.org/help/general.
2. "Publication," OED Online, Oxford University Press, http://oed.com/view/Entry/154060?redirectedFrom=publication,1827: J. Bentham Rationale Judicial Evid. II.iv.v. 577.
3. "B&N Aims to Whittle Its Stores for Years," *Wall Street Journal* (January 28, 2013), http://online.wsj.com/article/SB10001424127887323854904578264400822084708.html.
4. Lisa Gitelman, *Always Already New: Media, History and the Data of Culture* (Cambridge: MIT Press, 2006), 8–10. And compare Jay David Bolter and Richard Grusin, *Remediation: Understanding New Media* (Cambridge, MA: MIT Press, 2000).
5. On debates about print culture within the field of book history, see Elizabeth Eisenstein, *The Printing Press as Agent of Change* (Cambridge: Cambridge University Press, 1980), and Adrian Johns, *The Nature of the Book: Print and Knowledge in the Making* (Chicago: University of Chicago Press, 1998).
6. Leslie Kaufman, "No Big Hits, But Bookshops Say They're Thriving," *New York Times* (December 17, 2012), http://nytimes.com/2012/12/18/books/small-bookstores-say-theyre-thriving-even-without-big-hits.html?_r=0.
7. Lee Rainie and Maeve Duggan, "E-Book Reading Jumps; Print Book Reading Declines," Pew Internet and American Life Project, December 27, 2012, http://libraries.pewinternet.org/2012/12/27/e-book-reading-jumps-print-book-reading-declines.
8. Report of the MLA Ad Hoc Committee on The Future of Scholarly Publishing, *Profession* 2002 (New York: MLA, 2002), 172–86.
9. Kathleen Fitzpatrick, *Planned Obsolescence: Publishing, Technology, and the Future of the Academy* (New York: New York University Press, 2011), 4.

10. Steven E. Jones, *Against Technology: From the Luddites to Neo-Luddism* (New York: Routledge, 2006), 19–24.

11. Jaron Lanier, *You Are Not a Gadget: A Manifesto* (New York: Vintage, 2010); Sherry Turkle, *Alone Together: Why We Expect More from Technology and Less from Each Other* (New York: Basic Books, 2012); Nicholas Carr, *The Shallows: What the Internet Is Doing to Our Brains* (New York: Norton, 2010).

12. Andrew Piper, *Book Was There: Reading in Electronic Times* (Chicago: University of Chicago Press, 2012). Kindle edition (loc. 113).

13. Andrew Piper blog: http://bookwasthere.org.

14. McSweeney's Publishing, "Song Reader: Beck page," http://mcsweeneys.net/pages/song-reader.

15. From *New York Magazine*, *The Times*, and *Vanity Fair*, respectively, the last two cited as blurbs for the 2012 edition.

16. Boris Kachka, "Reinventing the Book: Jonathan Safran Foer's Object of Anti-Technology," *New York Magazine* (November 21, 2010), http://nymag.com/arts/books/features/69635.

17. For a convenient anthology of some of these aleatory experiments, see Noah Wardrip-Fruin and Nick Montfort, eds., *The New Media Reader* (Cambridge, MA: MIT Press, 2003).

18. The making of *Tree of Codes*, by Jonathan Safran Foer, http://youtube.com/watch?v=r0GcB0PYKjY.

19. The examples are taken from the account of the early humanities by Stephen Greenblatt, *The Swerve: How the World Became Modern* (New York and London: Norton, 2011).

20. See "Apple Shakeup Could Lead to a New Design Shift," Nick Wingfield and Nick Bilton, *New York Times* (October 31, 2012), http://nytimes.com/2012/11/01/technology/apple-shake-up-could-mean-end-to-real-world-images-in-software.html?pagewanted=all.

21. For an astute "reading" of the Apple iBooks event in relation to the bibliography of e-books, see Alan Galey, "The Enkindling Reciter: E-Books in the Bibliographical Imagination," *Book History* 15 (2012): 210–47; doi: 10.1353/bh.2012.0008.

22. Bolter and Grusin, *Remediation*.

23. Johanna Drucker, "The Virtual Codex from Page Space to E-space," in *Companion*, eds. Schreibman et al., http://digitalhumanities.org/companionDLS.

24. Amazon press release, May 19, 2011: "Since April 1 [2011], for every 100 print books amazon.com has sold, it has sold 105 Kindle books. . . . Less than one year after introducing the UK Kindle Store, amazon.co.uk is now selling more Kindle books than hardcover books, even as hardcover sales continue to grow," http://phx.corporate-ir.net/phoenix.zhtml?c=176060&p=irol-newsArticle&ID=1565581&highlight=. How readers will read the electronic texts, whether on dedicated devices or software apps for tablets or mobile phones, remains an open question.

25. Tim Carmody, "A Bookfuturist Manifesto," *The Atlantic* (August 11, 2010), http://theatlantic.com/technology/archive/2010/08/a-bookfuturist-manifesto/61231/.

26. *New Liberal Arts*, eds. Tim Carmody and Robin Sloan (Snarkmarket/Revelator Press), http://snarkmarket.com/nla/new-liberal-arts.html.

27. Tim Carmody, "The Trouble With Digital Culture," first posted on the Snarkmarket blog, May 28, 2010, http://snarkmarket.com/2010/5624. On *Hacking the Academy*, eds. Tom Scheinfeldt and Dan Cohen, see http://hackingtheacademy.org/what-this-is-and-how-to-contribute.

28. For example, see Nick Bilton, "One on One: Robin Sloan, Author and 'Media Inventor'," *The New York Times* (October 12, 2012), http://bits.blogs.nytimes.com/2012/10/12/one-on-one-robin-sloan-author-and-media-inventor.

29. Bilton, "One on One," *The New York Times*.

30. I take the term for this convention from TVTropes, http://tvtropes.org/pmwiki/pmwiki.php/Main/WhereAreTheyNowEpilogue.

31. This is essentially the charge made in a *New York Times* review, which accuses the novel of suffering from "an excess of convenience." Roxane Gay, "Bookworms and Apples," *The New York Times* (December 14, 2012), http://nytimes.com/2012/12/16/books/review/mr-penumbras-24-hour-bookstore-by-robin-sloan.html?ref=books&_r=1&. I obviously disagree with the review's claim that the epilogue is "unnecessary." Gay also briefly mentions Fitzpatrick's work in connection with the issues raised by the novel, reinforcing for me the connection I had already drafted when the review appeared.

32. Greenblatt, *The Swerve*, p. 23. And see Anthony Grafton and Lisa Jardine, *From Humanism to the Humanities: Education and the Liberal Arts in Fifteenth- and Sixteenth-Century Europe* (Cambridge, MA: Harvard University Press, 1986).

33. Mary Wollstonecraft Shelley, *Frankenstein; or, The Modern Prometheus* (Peterborough, Ontario, CA: Broadview, 2012 [first published 1818]).

34. Matthew G. Kirschenbaum, "Distant Mirrors and the LAMP," talk delivered January 4, 2013, http://commons.mla.org/docs/distant-mirrors-and-the-lamp.

35. The Foreword first appeared in the editors' own initial contribution to the series, Ian Bogost and Nick Montfort, *Racing the Beam: The Atari Video Computer System* (Cambridge, MA: MIT Press, 2009). And see the FAQ they prepared: http://bogost.com/downloads/bogost_montfort_dac_2009.pdf.

36. On bar codes, UPCs, etc., in book publishing and bookselling, see Ted Striphas, *The Late Age of Print: Everyday Book Culture From Consumerism to Control* (New York: Columbia University Press, 2009), 91–99.

37. Conversation with Kathleen Fitzpatrick, February 13, 2012.

38. http://wordpress.org/extend/plugins/anthologize.

39. http://scalar.usc.edu/scalar.

40. For an introduction, see the book by Scott Chacon, *Pro Git* (New York: Apress, 2009), available on GitHub as an e-book under a Creative Commons License (CC BY-NC-SA 3.0) at: http://git-scm.com/book. For one blog post arguing for the potential value of GitHub for DH, see Timothy Nunan, "Sticking a 'Fork' in the Humanities? Some Thoughts on Digital Humanities," author's blog, July 16, 2011, http://timothynunan.com/2011/07/16/sticking-a-fork-in-the-humanities-some-thoughts-on-digital-humanities.

41. Steve Kolowich, "Authors of 'Bill of Rights' for Online Learners Face Criticism," *Chronicle of Higher Education*, Wired Campus, January 25, 2013, http://chronicle.com/blogs/wiredcampus/authors-of-bill-of-rights-for-online-learners-face-criticism/41971.

42. http://digital.cityofchicago.org/index.php/chicago-on-github.

43. Mikeal Rogers, "The GitHub Generation: Why We're All in Open Source Now," *Wired* (March 7, 2013), http://wired.com/opinion/2013/03/github.

44. Stephen Ramsay notoriously argued at one conference that, to be a digital humanities scholar, "you have to program." In a thoughtful blog post, he later generalized the claim to "you have to build something." Stephen Ramsay, "On Building," author's blog, January 11, 2011, http://stephenramsay.us/text/2011/01/11/on-building.html.

45. *Debates in the Digital Humanities*, Open-access volume, http://dhdebates.gc.cuny.edu. GC Digital Scholarship Lab, http://gcdsl.commons.gc.cuny.edu.

7

PRACTICES

It was at the MLA's annual convention in 2009 that the digital humanities first came to the attention of a wider academic and general public and was hailed as the next big thing. Four years later, the annual meeting in Boston in January 2013 offered something like 66 sessions on the digital humanities, panels and workshops "that in some way address the influence and impact of digital materials and tools upon language, literary, textual, and media studies, as well as upon online pedagogy and scholarly communication," as Mark Sample put it in his annually compiled list, roughly 8 percent of the total sessions at the massive event.[1] One of the best attended and widely reported was a session on "The Dark Side of Digital Humanities," which explored issues of labor, institutional power, corporatism and instrumentalism around the rise of the digital humanities, and considered DH from the point of view of university administrators and trustees as much as practitioners themselves. The session's description called on participants to offer "models of digital humanities that are not rooted in technocratic rationality or neoliberal economic calculus." The implication may have been that DH could be particularly complicit in that regard, more so than, say, English or comparative literature, given its central reliance on digital technology, but also, perhaps, its self-definition as a set of practices, which are theoretically applicable to many ends. In the event, however, a portion of the talks and most of the discussion afterward turned out to be about the then-timely topic of the impact of MOOCs on the humanities, courses that many in the digital humanities community had been critiquing online for months before the convention as not really innovative, not really "DH" *enough*. Not everything academic with "digital" in it is automatically the result of DH, in other words, and the distinctions are, perhaps, more important the closer one is to the making and doing under consideration. Digital humanities sessions at the MLA in Boston were, in general, well attended, and for another year of several in a row, now, produced the most lively back-channel discussions on Twitter. Among the 66 were a diverse range of approaches and topics, including some that addressed issues such as those highlighted in the Dark Side panel, but one underlying issue went mostly unspoken: the assumption that what's politically and institutionally questionable about digital humanities is its practical orientation—an assumption potentially reinforced every time DH is defined as "a set of practices." It's true that, in the DH list of MLA sessions, the word "practice" appears 12 times, with 5 of the occurrences coming in session titles. (Searching the MLA program as a whole turns up only a few additional instances of the word beyond the DH sessions).

The new DH has, in fact, often been defined as a set of practices—ways of doing and making, tinkering and coding. One implication that might be drawn from the Dark Side session's description, at least, is that this practical orientation, the insistence on doing and making and generally understanding technology, might make DH complicit in a utilitarian and instrumentalist agenda, a program that would trade off traditional humanities research and teaching against brave, new, low-overhead digital versions of the humanities (which might incidentally bring in more external funding), in the ruthless spirit of "disruption" and "creative destruction." Or worse, it might contribute to a general techno-utopian booster-ism in a technocratic society, might substitute celebratory studies of media and the use of computers for critique, making the academic humanities an uncritical extension of the military-entertainment complex.

These are serious concerns, worth taking seriously. Critique of power, but also the preservation of cultural heritage, no matter what the content or its perceived usefulness in the present, and support for exploring certain "monastic" forms of knowledge, the particulars of early-modern book history, for example, as well as potentially threatening forms of historical exploration or contemporary cultural theory—or (I can't help adding) a detailed understanding of historical, now obsolete computing platforms—are vital to the calling of the humanities as a counterforce to much in contemporary society.

But it should not be assumed that, because DH emphasizes practice and makes use of computers, it's therefore naively instrumental or positivist in its assumptions, or that its hands-on doing necessarily precludes theory. Only an impoverished view of theory as pure verbal and written discourse, separate from practice, would produce such assumption on the face of it. The *Digital Humanities Manifesto 2.0*, produced on CommentPress by multiple hands (but initiated out of UCLA in 2009), spells this out pretty clearly:

> The dichotomy between the manual realm of making and the mental realm of thinking was always misleading. Today, the old theory/praxis debates no longer resonate. **Knowledge assumes multiple forms**; it inhabits the interstices and crisscrossings between words, sounds, smells, maps, diagrams, installations, environments, data repositories, tables, and objects. Physical

fabrication, digital design, the styling of elegant, effective prose; the juxtaposing of images; the montage of movements; the orchestration of sound: they are all *making*.[2] (emphasis in original)

The *Manifesto* calls for a "theory after Theory ... anchored in MAKING," recognizes "curation" as a scholarly activity, "making arguments through objects as well as words." It calls for political and social engagements of various kinds, but also for "or direct engagement in design and development processes" as, in effect, a form of social and political engagement. And the *Manifesto* begins, sure enough, by acknowledging that, "Digital Humanities is not a unified field but an array of convergent practices."

Everyone in DH will not sign on to every item in the manifesto, but most will, I think, agree with that premise. Stephen Ramsay and Geoffrey Rockwell have addressed the position of those in DH "who have turned to building, hacking, and coding as part of their normal research activity."[3] Anecdotally, they cite Lev Manovich's remark that "a prototype *is* a theory" (77; my emphasis), suggesting that, "'building' may represent an opportunity to correct the discursive and linguistic bias of the humanities" (78), and that we might wish to pose the question, "'What happens when building takes the place of writing?' as a replacement for 'Is building scholarship?'" (83). "Writing is the technology—or better, the methodology—that lies between model and result in humanistic discourse" (82), and other practices, coding and making, for example, can take the place of that methodology in humanities scholarship.

Especially if we open up the DH umbrella to include provocations, parodies, and experiments such as those of Ramsay and Rockwell themselves in their own practice, but also work by Ian Bogost or Limor Fried, for example—or to learn from creative and expressive work such as William Gibson's fiction, for that matter—we get a sense of how making things can do some of the work of theory. But even more conventionally considered, a number of disciplines outside the humanities depend on experiment and practice, even designing, modeling, prototyping, and making things, as integral to their modes of investigation and theory. In this final chapter, I want to take a closer look at how that emphasis on practice (beyond the more conventional part of practice that involves writing and publishing) theorizes the larger context for DH work, the context of the eversion itself.

Beyond the examples I've just cited and have been citing throughout the book, I won't offer a compendium of practices or case studies, here, real or imagined. Such compendia are available elsewhere.[4] In closing, I just want to zoom in on a couple of examples in the work of two representative practitioners whom I encountered at the convention in Boston (although in both cases I knew their work already). My purpose is to call attention to aspects of their work that don't fit the stereotypes of DH projects (tool-building, archiving, text-editing and digitization, data analysis and visualization, mapping, etc.), and so are useful limit-cases for testing the idea of making. But these two examples are, nonetheless, profoundly typical of the *meaning* of practice in the context of the eversion and the new DH, of how acts of making raise theoretical questions and allow practitioners to think through those questions *by* doing things and making things.

I'll start with poetry (*poesis*, after all, is making), with work by writer and artist Amaranth Borsuk, someone who would likely not even self-identify as a digital humanities specialist. Her artists' book was part of the Electronic Literature Exhibit that Sample recommended to conventioneers as among a group of DH-related events outside the usual panels, including a preconference workshop on "Getting Started in DH with DH Commons" and the by-now familiar preconference unconference, a THATCamp. Next, I'll cite a paper presentation *about* practice (which was, of course, also itself a form of practice) delivered by Bethany Nowviskie, who is Director of the Scholars' Lab at the University of Virginia. Her talk was at a very well attended panel session (I arrived late and had to stand leaning against the back wall of the large room), part of MLA president Michael Bérubé's presidential forum. Coincidentally, the session was held in the same wing of the convention center as the Electronic Literature Exhibit—a fact Nowviskie acknowledged in her talk. Aside from the accident of room location, I chose these two examples in order to conclude this book, my extended essay, with a look at what I take to be at the heart of DH practice at the present moment. These examples are typical in the old sense of the term: They are types that figure DH practice, and may well prefigure coming modes of practice, at the two-way intersection of the physical (object, artifact, archive, place) and the digital (code, data, connection, network).

Between Physical and Digital

The massive book exhibit is a traditional part of every MLA convention, and, at the booths in the exhibit hall in Boston 2013, a number of the titles on display were about the digital humanities. In one corner of the hall, a large curtained "booth" was set up more like a theatrical space. With a small stage and screen at one end, it was like the standard presentation booth you might find at any industry convention on technology or video games. It was dedicated to regularly scheduled demonstrations of the newly announced MLA Commons, and Kathleen Fitzpatrick herself was working the booth, as they say, walking the audience through the interface and architecture of the new platform for publishing and scholarly communication. Her purpose was practical. The demos were meant to be gentle introductions, guides to the perplexed. Beta-testers had already been using the platform for weeks. Instead of the kind of theoretical talk Fitzpatrick often gives, about new models of peer review and the nature of publishing, this was a workshop in a booth, really, a demo of a new product, and a chance for people to experience firsthand, with a developer present, a platform they were being called on to use themselves. There have been, for many years, technology-focused demos in the MLA exhibit hall, from hypertexts and CD-ROM textbooks and scholarly editions, to electronic journals. But this was an officer of the MLA itself, evangelizing, as they say, about a platform aimed at the membership as a whole. In many ways, it was for DH a more central event than many of the panels with famous speakers and large audiences.

Located physically in the same peripheral area of the Convention Center, "Avenues of Access: An Exhibit and Online Archive of New 'Born Digital' Literature," curated by Dene Grigar and Kathi Inman Berens, was installed in a medium-sized room of its own.[5] On Friday night, January 4, 2013, the artists in the exhibit performed their works at an offsite event at a local college theatre. Regrettably, I had a schedule conflict and was unable to attend, but I followed on Twitter the responses of a number of digital humanities and media studies scholars in the audience. The exhibit in the convention center included an eclectic mix of genres of electronic and computational creative works, from Ian Bogost's *A Slow Year* and a runnable version of the program that's the focus of the collaborative *10Print* book (both of which had copies of the paper books arranged beside the legacy computer systems associated with them), to a number of other game-based, mobile, and locative works. Characterized in the exhibit's publicity as a "multimodal narrative," Caitlin Fisher's *Circle* is an AR installation that resembles the boxes of objects or "kits" created by Fluxus artists, for example, or the boxes including "feelies" that shipped with early IF games. A large case, open on the table, spills over with a variety of mostly domestic artifacts—small dishes or postcards, etc.—that, when picked up and viewed through a tablet's camera lens, appear to extrude Flash-based popup images, texts, and videos, all of which convey interlinked narratives about a multigenerational family of women. The narratives are random access (you can pick up anything and put it back anywhere on the table or in the case), but the collection is a kind of cabinet of curiosities. Actual and fictive curation is its organizing principle. The things have been arranged and are already loaded with significance, so they feel as if they have auras of meaning already attached to them. The 3D images or video clips somehow don't seem as surprising, therefore, as they might if they were everyday objects distributed out in the world in the style of an ARG or geocache, for example.

Though all the work exhibited was born digital, really almost every piece in the exhibit could also be called "multimodal," from physical objects of *Circle* to the books of poems or codework associated with other works. In the center of the exhibit room, on a table of its own, I found yet another display containing a computer (a laptop in this case) and a book. It was a square-format red book with what looked like a simplified QR code on the cover, Amaranth Borsuk and Brad Bouse's *Between Page and Screen*.[6] The two collaborated to *make* the work—write, program, design, print, and bind it. She's a poet and book artist, he's a programmer and UX (user experience) designer. The result is a compelling artists' book in AR form, a mixed-reality popup book that contains no words,

FIGURE 7.1 Caitlin Fisher, *Circle*

only (after the preliminary pages, title, etc.) one 3-inch square, black and white glyph (which looks like a simplified and enlarged segment of a QR code) printed on each of 16 recto pages (the versos are all blank). When you hold a page up to a Webcam, like the kind built into almost every laptop and many desktop monitors, or the peripheral add-on kind that clips to the top of your screen, you see yourself on the screen holding the book, and the code triggers a Flash animation of text that appears to rise out of the page, each one a little concrete poem made of pixels. Some are just vertically standing "pages" of words that look as if they're printed on a transparent screen, standing perpendicular to the paper page. You can move the book around and even rotate it to see the backwards letters from the back. Animations make the text appear to form and rise up from the page, and moving the page out of camera range makes the text break up and scatter before disappearing. Closing the book collapses the virtual page down into the fold, as if capturing it. Other pages play more explicitly with 3D animations. One produces a circular band of text rotating clockwise, so that its letters form a stream of words, another, four words running down vertically like the sides of a square column, rotating, and yet another is text shaped in the form of a pig (like a butcher's outlined chart), a visual pun on wordplay that builds from "cute" to "charcuterie." Seven of the pages produce prose-poem letters between two main personified characters, signed P[age] and S[creen]. An additional letter is a kind of intervention between the two, signed Pax, and the final "P.S." is a "co-script." The remaining seven glyphs produce lyrical concrete poems. The correspondence between P and S forms a kind of poetic lovers' dialogue (reminiscent of Nick Bantok's *Griffin and Sabine* [1991], as Borsuk has indicated) and also, on another level, a theoretical essay, based on playful deconstructions of etymology, about the competing phenomenologies of reading named in the title.

The paper book is 7 × 7 inches, red, with white and black elements, with the square code-glyph die-cut into the center of the cover. The glyph works as well as the others inside the book: In fact, every time you reload the viewing page online, the cover glyph generates a different text–image. On the exhibit table were sample cards you could take with you with the same generative glyph printed on them. A colophon page at the back—in the space we might expect a note on the typeface—spells out the technology involved. We get that note too (two instances of Helvetica), but the more complicated paragraph reveals the complex stack that underwrites the book's material conditions:

> Between Page and Screen uses the FLARToolkit to project animations in an augmented reality. The application also uses the Robot Legs framework, BetweenAS3 animation library, Papervision 3D engine, and Jiglib physics engine. The source code for this application is available at: between pageandscreen/source.

This is more like what we're used to in the layered software engines and tools used to create a video game than the colophon for a standard print book. But, as I said, it's followed by a statement about the typefaces and is preceded by a credit to the dictionary used to source the etymologies on which the texts spin their improvisational-sounding wordplay.

The key term in the technical colophon is of course augmented reality—used as a name for the space of reading in addition to the mechanism of the book,

FIGURE 7.2 Borsuk and Bouse, *Between Page and Screen*

the space into which the text is, as it says, projected. Borsuk has said that, "augmented reality seemed to me to be tailor-made for this exploratory space where both a page and a screen are necessary to get at the text."[7] You see the animated text only on your computer screen, but you also see the paper book in your hands (as well as on the screen), and the 3D translucence of the blocks of text creates a sense that the words have popped up in the mediated space between your hands and the camera, just as the images in 3D movies seem to

FIGURE 7.3 *Between Page and Screen* being read

occupy the space between the screen and you in your seat. As a blurb by DH scholar and book artist Johanna Drucker puts it, the work "constitute[s] itself across the distributed network of inter-medial relations." Unlike previous Flash poetry, *Between Page and Screen* is as fully committed to the paper-based book as it is to digital text, as physical as it is digital. Its betweenness is its central theme, as well as its formal mandate.

FIGURE 7.4 *Between Page and Screen* being read

Clearly, earlier experiments with the three dimensions of books as physical objects were part of the inspiration, from paper popup books to artists' books that are carved or die-cut, such as Jonathan Safran Foer's *Tree of Codes* (discussed in the previous chapter). The first edition was a limited print-run artist's book that Borsuk herself letterpress-printed and hand bound. Siglio press followed with the mass-market paperbound book (the second printing). Borsuk explains:

For the limited edition version, it was important that the book was in dialogue with the history of book art and fine-press printing. The markers that trigger the animation already reminded me of mid-century book artist Dieter Roth—he did all these beautiful cut books where he would cut out shapes and the pages would layer one on top of the other and you would get different designs. And I knew I wanted to work in a square format— which is also a format he used very often. The paper it's printed on is fine-press paper, letterpress-printed and hand-bound, in order to take part in that tradition.

(Daily Br!nk)

Dieter Roth, an artist (uneasily) associated with the Fluxus movement, makes a particularly suggestive analog muse for Borsuk and Bouse's project, especially a work such as his 1964 *Book AC*, a 16-inch square-format book, with black and white pages with die-cut holes in the form of rectilinear glyphs.[8] It works by exploiting the depth of the book as a physical object. Its layered pages reveal, through their cuts, bits of pages below, so that turning the pages creates a (very) slow-motion flip-book-like experience of morphing composite images. One curator refers to this reading protocol prompted by *Book AC* as "a sequential cut-paper narrative in two-color squares that can be rotated and flipped in all directions. With each turn of the page, a new image is uncovered, offering each reader a unique visual narrative."[9] The spare, monochromatic geometry of Roth's die-cut pages was an obvious graphical inspiration for Borsuk and Bouse, but even more important, I'd argue, is this dynamic, multidimensional reading experience, this self-conscious exploitation of the 3D space of a book, which makes possible a series of transformations to be effected and traversed by the reader. Borsuk and Bouse just move their different version of a dynamic reading experience out a few inches, conceptually, into the augmented space just above the page. Interestingly, Johanna Drucker describes another sculpted, but hand-cut, book by Dieter Roth, *2 bilderbücher* (1957), in this way:

> No element of structure remains neutral in Roth's production since the whole functions only because its parts have been brought into sharp focus in relation to the way they perform. Conventions of bookness become subject matter—a turning page becomes a physical, sculptural element rather than an incidental activity. Linear sequence becomes spatialized. Surface pattern transforms into height and depth, channels of access and areas of blockage, which read simultaneously as a visual pattern and a shaped form. The fact that the work is bound goes beyond mere convenience of constraint and fastening and becomes a means to articulate these relations.[10]

Evert the terms of that description, and you have a sense of how Borsuk and Bouse extend the spatialization of the book into a constructed and sculpted AR space. Instead of taking the reader down into the 3D depth of the codex, they lead the reader up into the 3D reading space "above" the page.

What's most book-like about *Between Page and Screen* is not so much the printed pages and elegant design, but the way it pays tribute to, and models, the reading experience as always already "inter-medial," to use Drucker's term. The particulars of this (e)version, as Drucker says, are "constituted across a distributed network." The work is explicitly, on multiple levels, about the digital and physical dimensions of reading today. In its own mixed realities, the book resists the binary opposition of page and screen, analog and digital, by "projecting" its writing into the space between. ("I regret the fight," S[creen] writes to P[age] at the end of the book, and then concludes, "Don't forget to write.") As one review puts it,

> rather than fret about the rise of e-readers and tablets and the seemingly imminent demise of the book as we know it, book artist and poet Amaranth Borsuk decided to reimagine the digital-versus-paper struggle as a kind of dance, and make it the basis for an artist's book of her own.[11]

Rather than engage in the already tired polemic, Borsuk collaborated with Bouse to make a book that's also an electronic text, Flash poetry that's somehow concrete, electronic literature with a complex body. The result is a kind of theory object, in more than one sense, that embodies the conflict by overwriting the conflict's binary terms.

Because of how it effectively works in an intermedial mixed reality, *Between Page and Screen* is more than just another example of literature in an electronic environment. It's poetry of the eversion. Borsuk has said as much in her general description of "experimental and innovative poetics today," which, she surmises, "hinges on the feeling that invisible text augments the world around us in clouds of information being transmitted electronically from one person to another all the time."[12] And it's not surprising that she and Bouse are reportedly exploring the possibilities of "an immersive, and interactive site-specific poetry experience" using the 3D camera and sensor technology of Microsoft's Xbox Kinect (Daily Br!nk). As I suggested in earlier chapters, that sort of mixed-reality game platform, beginning in 2006 with the Wii, exemplifies the eversion in its shift away from a VR-style immersive game world behind the screen and out into the physical space inhabited by the player's body (Nintendo's idealized "living room"). Nor is it surprising that Borsuk and Bouse say that they became interested in AR when they saw an AR business card in which a "simple geometrical pattern on the card once held up to a camera would turn up the card owner's face."[13] This is essentially the idea behind QR codes themselves, of course, but is also, as I have suggested, vividly illustrated in the AR games on Nintendo's handheld 3DS, in which a code on a paper card triggers a 3D game animation, such as the appearance, as if on your tabletop, of miniature game-IP avatars, little holographic-looking virtual figurines of Mario or your own customized "Mii." Instead of holding the cards up to a screen, one holds the screen as a mobile viewer through which to see the cards + interactive digital animations. In fact, one can imagine AR books, like Borsuk and Bouse's, that could be read using the 3DS, or one's smartphone, or, for that matter, Google Glass.

"Why this mania to name what's between us?"—S writes to P, in *Between Page and Screen*. One answer is that what's between is where we are, now, so it's what we're obsessed with. These specific technologies, and others likely still to emerge, are interesting to us because they're revealing, in glimpses, various possibilities for the everted and augmented, mixed-reality space we already inhabit. Borsuk suggests on her Website (http://amaranthborsuk.com/scholarship) one way to characterize her own practice: It can fit into a lineage of what she calls "a data poetics," an artistic response to the world of ubiquitous data that uses "mediation to access a world of words that is constantly available to be remixed, revised, and re-arranged." Elsewhere, in an essay, she describes our "contemporary landscape" as one "permeated by data on screens, mobile devices, and in the very air we breathe":

> We are indeed living in a world of data-saturation—each object we buy encoded with a rich history of production and delivery, often traceable by simply scanning a barcode. We track our own metadata daily, watching our location on GPS devices or mobile phones, responding to e-mail, organizing our writing into computer folders for easy access, backing up our files to digital servers online or hard drives at home, updating co-workers of our project's status through inter-office microblogging, and informing our friends of personal milestones and daily dramas through social networks. The browsers we use to access the Internet keep a record of every site we visit, and online vendors store our likes and dislikes (as well as those of our friends and others who share our demographic details) in order to recommend products to us.
>
> We increasingly see ourselves as generators of data who are part of a continually flowing datastream or information cloud, spatial metaphors that give shape to invisible pervasive data.[14]

Given this reality, Borsuk says, some artists have strategically constructed "a poetics of collaboration with the flow of information around us." Artists who are creating data visualizations as a form of literature or visual expression, data poetics in general, Borsuk explicitly connects to the practices of *both* graphic designers and "digital humanities researchers." Both, she says, are engaged in pattern recognition, trying to "discern patterns and relationships within the complex network of language." I'd agree, but would generalize the point: The artists she points to (including Borsuk herself in *Between Page and Screen*), like practitioners of the new DH, are responding to the exigencies of the eversion.

From Physical to Digital (and Back Again)

One of the most influential scholars in digital humanities, Bethany Nowviskie, was already active in the early days of humanities computing, working even as a graduate student on important collaborative projects, and she played a leading role in shaping the emergence of the new-model DH ca. 2004–2008. She has also been influential in the creation of the alt-ac movement, and her own work is an example of the paradoxical centrality of DH work being practiced beyond the conventional tenure track, and even beyond the academy and back into it again.

Her talk, as I say, was central to the MLA program as a whole, invited as part of the presidential forum.[15] This is how it began:

> Most mornings, these days—especially when I'm the first to arrive at the Scholars' Lab—I'll start a little something printing on our Replicator. I do this before I dive into my email, head off for consultations and meetings, or (more rarely) settle in to write. There's a grinding whirr as the machine revs up. A harsh, lilac-colored light clicks on above the golden Kapton tape on the platform. Things become hot to the touch, and I walk away. I don't even bother to stay, now, to see the mechanized arms begin a musical slide along paths I've programmed for them, or to watch how the fine filament gets pushed out, melted and microns-thin—additive, architectural—building up, from the bottom, the objects of my command.

The description of using the Replicator, a 3D printer, in her digital humanities center was illustrated on the large screen behind her with slides of a strangely beautiful, abstract object being fabricated. Her given theme, "Avenues of Access," shaped the talk into a meditation on DH tools and the learning curves they often require, and thus on who has access to DH, really, 2009's next big thing, now become an important thread at every annual MLA conference and the focus of a talk at this presidential forum by a deeply engaged practitioner, who, interestingly, talked about (and showed images of) fabrication—one kind of thing made in her center and what that means theoretically:

> Art objects, little mechanisms and technical experiments, cultural artifacts reproduced for teaching or research—cheap 3d-printing is one affirmation that words (those lines of computer code that speak each shape) always readily become things. That they kind of . . . *want to.*
>
> (Ibid.)

DH practice at the Scholars' Lab includes as a central focus acts of tinkering with extruded, everted objects, digital + physical things that are signs of the eversion, and that figure the eversion as a principle of DH practice.

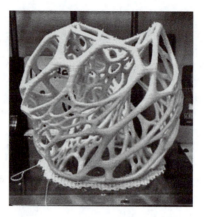

FIGURE 7.5 Abstract 3D print, Nowviskie

When Nowviskie introduced the topic of Google Books and mass digitization, it was in terms of "our collective capacity and will to think clearly about, to steward, and to engage with physical archives," and she then moved to a second "phase change" or "major technological shift," the one signified by 3D printing and fabrication in general: "Momentous cultural and scholarly changes will be brought about not by digitization alone, but by the development of ubiquitous digital-to-physical conversion tools and interfaces." The wider social and technological context signified by those images of the Replicator at work is clearly the same as the one I've been arguing throughout this book: the eversion of the digital network.

> What will humanities research and pedagogy do with consumer-accessible 3d fabrication? With embedded or wearable, responsive and tactile physical computing devices? What will we do with locative and AR technologies that can bring our content off the screen and into our embodied, place-based, mobile lives?

Nowviskie then mentioned, as an example of work already being done in this area, the very Electronic Literature Exhibit next door to her own talk, where Borsuk and Bouse's AR book was on display, along with other multimodal, mixed-reality creative works. Increasing numbers of scholars working in a digital humanities context, Nowviskie suggested, will in future join artists and others in exploring "digital-to-physical conversion . . . the fresh, full circuit of humanities computing—that is, the loop from the physical to the digital to the material text and artifact again." Note that act of definition: Humanities computing, once (and still, sometimes) associated exclusively with acts of digitization, markup, editing of printed texts in the archive, is here recast in a new era as the practice of engaging in and motivating a two-way "circuit" of mixed-reality investigation and play, acts of making with theoretical significance: from the physical to the digital and back again. One of Nowviskie's beautiful, digitally typeset slides spelled it out as a heading: "physical to digital, and back again." As she put it in the talk: "We've come to a moment of unprecedented potential for the material, embodied, and experiential digital humanities."

In an email exchange some weeks after the convention, Bethany Nowviskie responded to my questions about the eversion and the rise of DH in the new millennium.[16] She agreed that the "moment when we stopped thinking of 'cyberspace' as a special, alternate kind of world, and rather as something always interpenetrating our material one" was significant, a moment of a meaningful shift as well in "digital humanities research and production." For her, the shift was characterized not only by "locative and mobile tech, fabrication and wearables, etc.," but also by the rise of social networks as part of everyday communication, which was recognizable when, she observes, "we all started using our real names as a matter of course, across platforms." She speculates that Facebook may be behind this change, but at any rate, it's connected to a growing sense that, "the online world is ubiquitous—that it comes to US now (our sorry selves) rather than being some place we transport a heightened version of ourselves to."

Nowviskie was well aware at the time (about a decade ago) of the changes in the network and people's shifting attitudes toward it, and was among a handful of younger humanities-computing practitioners who helped to shape the new digital humanities as it emerged, who in effect brought the wider eversion to bear on humanities computing. They did so within the ethos of the open-source communities of which they were a part: through what Nowviskie calls acts of "tech transfer."

> I was always trying to keep a pulse on developments outside of academic humanities computing (which was very much in standards- and archive-building mode at the time and doing less with software development, design, and interactivity) so that I could bring those perspectives and ideas to our projects. In part, that was a kind of research-scoping activity for me (thinking about design as a continuum from my book history reading/training), but I'm sure a lot of it was frankly unconscious.

She also attributes her openness to developments outside the academy to the fact that she was "a gamer" who was "teaching game aesthetics and design" at the time, someone "interested in and building some connections to the game developers' community." This was also a period, she recalls, when her friends who left graduate school were likely to look for jobs at tech start-ups. This aspect of her story isn't unique to her experience, but it vividly reveals the ways in which cultural shifts such as the eversion don't happen as the result of invisible hands and impersonal forces. They take place when real people individually and collectively share ideas, approaches, and methods (tech transfer). In Nowviskie's case, a Mellon grant brought a team of software developers into her research and development groups at Virginia, and she ended up collaborating with them and eventually managing them on project teams.

> A couple of game companies—including a branch of EA! [Electronic Arts]—had recently gone out of business in Charlottesville, leaving many good, industry-experienced developers, who had fallen in love with the town, behind. We turned them (at least briefly—some lastingly) into DHers. They were the first developers I had worked with who really came from outside academia, and—now that you've made me think of it—I believe that was the moment when I began to be conscious of . . . an alt-ac identity.

Working with these programmers and game developers who had passed back through the wall into the academy via the alt-ac opening was, she says, "healthily defamiliarizing" and allowed her to "begin to think more consciously about what it meant to import methods, perspectives, even an ethos, from non-academic designers and the FOSS [free and open-source software] community." This approach was cemented for her when she moved to the Library, where she would direct the Scholars' Lab, especially "because library software developers have such a strong sense of their work as being for the common good and their role as being bridge builders between the tech community and the academy."

Nowviskie's personal experience in tech transfer in and out of the academy was important because of its timing, and because she was located at the heart of the emerging new DH, working with Johanna Drucker and Jerome McGann and others in SpecLab, for example, as DH arose from the foundation of electronic textual editing and archive-building at the University of Virginia. Indeed, she was among a group of early DH Makers who did not observe a dividing wall between academic computing and extramural developments, and who therefore helped open humanities computing to the eversion as it was happening in the larger culture. It's clear in her description of her own immersion in the ethos of Maker culture:

> When it comes to the kinds of new technology, methods, approaches, etc. I gravitate toward, a major factor for me is fun, novelty, and a sense of accomplishment from having made something, physical, manipulable, hand-crafted. I tried to hint at that kind of satisfaction in my MLA talk. Wearables, physical computing, 3D fabrication, the Neatline approach to historical map annotation, etc.—all of these are at the intersection of material culture, craft, and play.

The anecdote in her MLA talk about using the Replicator to start her mornings, in other words, and her connecting it to her earlier letterpress printing, is a non-trivial detail. It goes to the heart of understanding the eversion and the new DH, which is *materially symbolized* in 3D printing as it works to move digital files out into the physical world. The eversion is also facilitated within DH by such experimental play (akin to what Nowviskie's one-time colleague at the University of Virginia, Stephen Ramsay, has called "screwmeneutics" when it comes to coding and the data analysis of large corpora[17]) with technologies from outside the humanities, by the general promotion of making and programming, and by the integrating of digital and physical dimensions in humanities research.

3D printing is a good example of the ambiguously symbolic and practical nature of much new DH work, precisely because it may seem practically useless at the present moment—actually the opposite of the instrumentalism and overly practical orientation some critics attribute to DH. Like the QR code out in the culture at large, the 3D printer is, in part, a symbol of a desire to engage with the possibilities opened up by the eversion. So far, for the humanities, its attractions may have been out of proportion to its use value, and some might reasonably suspect that it's more fetish-object than tool. It's also true that 3D printing is surrounded by a kind of geeky hype right now, including, from some quarters, breathless claims for its "disruptive" power to remake manufacturing. And yet the technology is resonant for many in DH and can serve, like Arduino or Raspberry Pi boards, as a gateway to new forms of interdisciplinary engagement (as suggested in Nowviskie's talk). Even though humanities applications may, at first, seem merely speculative, expressive, or symbolic, rather than practical, the same could be said for a good deal of traditional humanities work. Artistic applications of 3D printing are evident enough. Some have experimented with 3D printing for sculpting smaller objects or parts of very large assemblies, especially in complex organic or mathematical forms (see, for example, the work of jewelry designer and sculptor Joshua DeMonte[18]). And, as we've seen, designers and developers, such as the group behind the video game *Skylanders*, use it for making prototypes of objects of art or figurines and toys.

However, to be fair, there is already a good deal of activity using 3D scanning and printing in academic humanities disciplines—in archaeology, for example, or history, or museums in general—wherever material artifacts, many of which are fragile or fragmented, are the explicit focus of research or public interest. For many years, museums have attempted to increase hands-on experiences or opportunities for "object handling." Cheaper digital-to-physical fabrication allows for a much more widely distributed access to surrogates of objects, including objects otherwise off limits even to most researchers. As with digitized surrogates for rare books and manuscripts, 3D copies can be made of rare 3D objects, close-copy models for display and study, even handling and owning. The Smithsonian Institution in Washington, DC, for example, is currently engaged in a program to scan and 3D print models of many of its artifacts (only a tiny fraction of which can ever be on display at once), including a lifemask of Abraham Lincoln by sculptor Clark Mills (1865) and a historical replica of a standing statue of Thomas

Jefferson on display at Monticello.[19] Museums have, of course, always made physical casts of some of the objects in their collections in order to create plaster replicas, but 3D scanning and printing allows for a less invasive and universally applicable method. These humanities applications at the Smithsonian are, in keeping with the institution's broad mandate, combined with natural history applications, the scanning and printing of fossils, for example. This is a reminder of how often it's in the areas of overlap between humanities and the sciences and social sciences that interesting DH applications arise. What Nowviskie calls the "material, embodied, and experiential digital humanities" can also be thought of as a logical extension of an *artifactual* humanities, in an era when all artifacts can be presumed to be amenable to being data-enriched and digitized (in the capacious, layered, two-way sense of the term). One consequence of the humanities' being everted, turning out (again and even more) toward the physical world, is an increased attention to the things of the humanities, of all kinds and at all scales, and 3D printing has obvious potential to help model and remodel such things, in feedback loops that tie malleable software to now-malleable and tagable materials.

Behind the hype, there is a sense that cheap and rapid fabrication has the potential to integrate new digital technologies with traditional humanities teaching and research, including retaining and revitalizing the long-scale interest in exploring the materialities of the archives that convey the heritage of human culture—what has been made. Neil Gershenfeld of MIT's Center for Bits and Atoms has argued (writing even before the current wave of cheaper 3D printers) that the "intersection of 3D scanning, modeling, and printing blurs the boundaries between artist and engineer, architect and builder, designer and developer, bringing together not just what they do but how they think."[20] Fabrication in the advanced classroom, he argues further, can promote "a new physical notion of literacy."

> The common understanding of "literacy" has narrowed down to reading and writing, but when the term emerged in the Renaissance it had a much broader meaning as a mastery of the available means of expression. However, physical fabrication was thrown out as an "illiberal art," pursued for mere commercial gain. These [MIT] students were correcting a historical error, using millions of dollars' worth of machinery for technological expression every bit as eloquent as a sonnet or a painting.
>
> (*Fab*, loc. 126–136)

However simplified the view of Renaissance history this may represent, it does (unfortunately) capture something of more modern, dismissive attitudes among some humanities specialists when it comes to physical fabrication, making things, as either research or pedagogy. In so far as the "two cultures" persist, although they may not be "natural luddites," as C. P. Snow famously suggested, many humanists still adopt an anti-technology ideology as a badge of honor and certificate of membership.[21] The new DH is the everted humanities in this regard, as well. It has deliberately embraced a hands-on, mixed-reality form of practice as a way to resist the ideology of an immaterial, otherworldly humanities. Nothing focuses on and challenges this ideology like an inspiring session turning CAD images into shaped polymer objects, doing work literally "at the intersection of material culture, craft, and play." This is not all heads-down making of concrete things. This aspect of the new DH raises general methodological questions about the future of humanities teaching and research, such as the one Bethany Nowviskie articulated in her MLA talk: "What will we do with locative and augmented reality technologies that can bring our content off the screen and into our embodied, place-based, mobile lives?"

Both of the practitioners I cited in this chapter, Bethany Nowviskie and Amaranth Borsuk, are typical of something crucial to the new DH: They're actively working in the space between the physical and the digital (and back again), experimenting with the layered materialities of AR or 3D printing, as well as the traditional pursuits of textual editing, poetry writing, book arts, book history, bibliography, curation, and archiving. Both practitioners are deeply engaged in exploring the lines of continuity and discontinuity between print culture and digital media, as a way to understand larger humanities questions and practices—by fitting them into a long history and tracing their trajectory going forward. The trajectory is still being plotted, as the data points accumulate, but the general direction of the new digital humanities is evidently turned outward, into the world in all its multidimensional complexities.

★

Notes

1. Mark Sample, "Digital Humanities at MLA 2013," Sample Reality blog, October 17, 2012, http://samplereality.com/2012/10/17/digital-humanities-at-mla-2013.
2. *Digital Humanities Manifesto 2.0*, http://humanitiesblast.com/manifesto/Manifesto_V2.pdf. Reportedly the work of over 100 participants, but it was initiated by Todd Presner, Peter Lunenfeld, and Jeffrey Schnapp. See "Digital Humanities Manifesto 2.0 Launched," Todd Presner's blog, June 22, 2009, http://toddpresner.com/?p=7.
3. Stephen Ramsay and Geoffrey Rockwell, "Developing Things: Notes Toward an Epistemology of Building in the Digital Humanities," in *Debates*, ed. Gold, 75–84.
4. A series of anonymous-composite case studies are available in Anne Burdick et al., *Digital_Humanities*.
5. Dene Grigar and Kathi Inman Berens, curators, "Avenues of Access: An Exhibit & Online Archive of New 'Born Digital' Literature," http://dtc-wsuv.org/elit/mla2013/index.html.
6. Amaranth Borsuk and Brad Bouse, *Between Page and Screen* (Los Angeles: Siglio, 2012).
7. Danielle Oliver, "Amaranth Borsuk: Digital Poet," Daily Br!nk, n.d., http://dailybrink.com/?p=1934.
8. Dieter Roth, *Book AC 1958–64* (New Haven, CT: Ives-Sillman, 1964). Copy as described and imaged on the Princeton University Library Graphic Arts blog, Julie L.

Mellby, "Dieter Roth's *Book AC*," Princeton University Library Graphic Arts blog, http://blogs.princeton.edu/graphicarts/2011/02/dieter_roths_ac.html.

9. Mellby, "Dieter Roth's *Book AC*."

10. Johanna Drucker, *The Century of Artists' Books* (New York: Granary Books, 1995), 74.

11. Edward Moyer, "Digital Pop-Up Book Gets Poetic With QR Codes," Cnet (February 9, 2012), http://news.cnet.com/8301–17938_105–57373708–1/digital-pop-up-book-gets-poetic-with-qr-codes.

12. Amaranth Borsuk, "The Upright Script: Modernist Mediations and Contemporary Data Poetics," author's Website, http://amaranthborsuk.com/scholarship.

13. Joann Pan, "Can Augmented Reality Save the Printed Page?," Mashable (February 3, 2012), http://mashable.com/2012/02/03/augmented-reality-book-between-page-and-screen.

14. Amaranth Borsuk, "The Upright Script: Words in Space and On the Page," *Journal of Electronic Publishing* 14.2 (Fall 2011), http://quod.lib.umich.edu/cgi/t/text/text-idx?c=jep;view=text;rgn=main;idno=3336451.0014.212.

15. Bethany Nowviskie, "Resistance in the Materials," author's blog, January 4, 2013, http://nowviskie.org/2013/resistance-in-the-materials.

16. Email interview with Bethany Nowviskie, January 23, 2013.

17. Stephen Ramsay, "The Hermeneutics of Screwing Around; or, What Do You Do With a Million Books?," April 17, 2010, http://playingwithhistory.com/wp-content/uploads/2010/04/hermeneutics.pdf.

18. Smithsonian Channel, "40 under 40: The Art of 3D Printing," http://smithsonianchannel.com/site/sn/video/player/latest-videos/the-art-of-3d-printing/2069940943001.

19. See the Smithsonian's Digitization Team's Facebook page, http://facebook.com/photo.php?v=504110162961157.

20. Neil Gershenfeld, *Fab: The Coming Revolution on Your Desktop—from Personal Computers to Personal Fabrication* (New York: Basic Books, 2008), Kindle edition, loc. 1278.

21. C. P. Snow, *The Two Cultures: And a Second Look* (Cambridge, UK: Cambridge University Press, 1979).

SELECTED BIBLIOGRAPHY

Abelson, Hal, Ken Ledeen, and Harry Lewis. *Blown to Bits: Your Life, Liberty, and Happiness After the Digital Explosion*. New York: Addison-Wesley Professional, 2008.

Anderson, Chris. *Makers: The New Industrial Revolution*. New York: Crown Business, 2012. Kindle edition.

Ashton, Kevin. "That 'Internet of Things' Thing." *RFID Journal* (July 22, 2009): http://rfidjournal.com/article/view/4986.

Barthes, Roland. *Mythologies*. New York: The Noonday Press, 1972.

Benjamin, Walter. *The Arcades Project*. Translated by Howard Eiland and Kevin McLaughlin. Cambridge, MA, and London: Belknap Press of Harvard University Press, 1999.

Bilton, Nick. "One on One: Robin Sloan, Author and 'Media Inventor'." *The New York Times* (October 12, 2012): http://bits.blogs.nytimes.com/2012/10/12/one-on-one-robin-sloan-author-and-media-inventor.

Birkerts, Sven. *The Gutenberg Elegies: The Fate of Reading in an Electronic Age*. London: Faber & Faber, 1994.

Bissell, Tom. "One Night in *Skyrim* Makes a Strong Man Crumble." *Grantland* (November 29, 2011): http://grantland.com/story/_/id/7290527/one-night-in-skyrim-makes-strong-man-crumble.

Blum, Andrew. *Tubes: A Journey to the Center of the Internet*. New York: Ecco/Harper Collins, 2012. Kindle edition.

Bogost, Ian. *A Slow Year*. Highlands Ranch, CO: Open Texture, 2010.

Bogost, Ian. *Alien Phenomeology, Or What It's Like to Be a Thing*. Minneapolis and London: University Press of Minnesota, 2012. Kindle edition.

Bogost, Ian. "Beyond the Elbow-patched Playground." Author's blog (August 23 and 25, 2011): http://bogo.st/xy.

Bogost, Ian. "Gamification is Bullshit." Author's blog (August 8, 2011): http://bogost.com/blog/gamification_is_bullshit.shtml.

Bogost, Ian, and Nick Montfort. *Racing the Beam: The Atari Video Computer System*. Cambridge, MA: MIT Press, 2009.

Bolter, Jay David, and Richard Grusin. *Remediation: Understanding New Media*. Cambridge, MA: MIT Press, 2000.

Borsuk, Amaranth. "The Upright Script: Modernist Mediations and Contemporary Data Poetics." Author's Website: http://amaranthborsuk.com/scholarship.

Borsuk, Amaranth. "The Upright Script: Words in Space and On the Page." *Journal of Electronic Publishing* 14.2 (Fall 2011): http://quod.lib.umich.edu/cgi/t/text/text-idx?c=jep;view=text;rgn=main;idno=3336451.0014.212.

Borsuk, Amaranth and Brad Bouse. *Between Page and Screen*. Los Angeles: Siglio, 2012.

Braid. Jonathan Blow, 2008.

Brown, Bill. "Thing Theory." *Critical Inquiry* 28.1 (Autumn 2001): 1–22.

Bryant, Levi. "Alien Phenomenology, Idealism, and Materialism." Larval Subjects blog (August 22, 2012): http://larvalsubjects.wordpress.com/2012/08/22/alien-phenomenology-idealism-and-materialism.

Burdick, Anne, Johanna Drucker, Peter Lunenfeld, Todd Presner, and Jeffrey Schnapp. *Digital_Humanities*. Cambridge, MA and London, UK: MIT Press, 2012.

Cangeloso, Sal. "*Fez* soundtrack Is Full of Secrets." Geek.com (April 20, 2012): http://geek.com/articles/games/fez-soundtrack-contains-hidden-information-20120420.

Carr, Nicholas. *The Shallows: What the Internet Is Doing to Our Brains*. New York: Norton, 2010.

Carmody, Tim. "A Bookfuturist Manifesto." *The Atlantic* (August 11, 2010): http://theatlantic.com/technology/archive/2010/08/a-bookfuturist-manifesto/61231.

Carmody, Tim, and Robin Sloan, eds. *New Liberal Arts*. Snarkmarket/Revelator Press: http://snarkmarket.com/nla/new-liberal-arts.html.

Chacon, Scott. *Pro Git*. New York: Apress, 2009: http://git-scm.com/book.

Cline, Ernest. *Ready Player One*. New York: Crown, 2011. Kindle edition.

Coleman, B. *Hello Avatar: Rise of the Networked Generation*. Cambridge, MA and London, UK: MIT Press, 2011.

Crane, Gregory. "What Do You Do With a Million Books?" *D-Lib Magazine* 12.3 (March 2006): http://dlib.org/dlib/march06/crane/03crane.html.

Digital Humanities Manifesto 2.0, http://humanitiesblast.com/manifesto/Manifesto_V2.pdf.

Drucker, Johanna. *The Century of Artists' Books*. New York: Granary Books, 1995.

Drucker, Johanna. "Humanistic Theory and Digital Scholarship." In *Debates in the Digital Humanities*, edited by Matthew K. Gold, 85–95. Minneapolis and London: University of Minnesota Press, 2012.

Drucker, Johanna. "The Virtual Codex from Page Space to E-space." In *A Companion to Digital Literary Studies*, edited by Susan Schreibman and Ray Siemens. Oxford: Blackwell, 2008. http://digitalhumanities.org/companionDLS.

Dunne, Anthony. *Hertzian Tales: Electronic Products, Aesthetic Experience, and Critical Design*. Cambridge, MA: MIT Press, 2006.

Eisenstein, Elizabeth. *The Printing Press as Agent of Change*. Cambridge: Cambridge University Press, 1980.

Farman, Jason. *Mobile Interface Theory: Embodied Space and Locative Media*. New York and London: Routledge, 2011.

Fez. Phil Fish, 2007.

Fitzpatrick, Kathleen. *Planned Obsolescence: Publishing, Technology, and the Future of the Academy*. New York: New York University Press, 2011.

Fleishman, Glenn. "How the iPhone Knows Where You Are." *Macworld* (April 28, 2011): http://macworld.com/article/1159528/how_iphone_location_works.html.

Fraistat, Neil, and Steven E. Jones. "Immersive Textuality." TEXT 15 (2003): 69–82.

Fried, Limor. "Social Defense Mechanisms: Tools for Reclaiming our Personal Space," MS Thesis, MIT, 2005, http://ladyada.net/media/pub/thesis.pdf.

Galey, Alan. "The Enkindling Reciter: E-Books in the Bibliographical Imagination." *Book History* 15 (2012): 210–47. doi: 10.1353/bh.2012.0008.

Gardiner, Eileen, and Ronald G. Musto. "The Electronic Book." In *The Oxford Companion to the Book*, edited by Michael F. Suarez and H. R. Woudhuysen, 164–71. Oxford: Oxford University Press, 2010.

Gay, Roxane. "Bookworms and Apples." *The New York Times* (December 14, 2012): http://nytimes.com/2012/12/16/books/review/mr-penumbras-24-hour-bookstore-by-robin-sloan.html?ref=books&_r=1&.

Gershenfeld, Neil. *Fab: The Coming Revolution on Your Desktop—From Personal Computers to Personal Fabrication*. New York: Basic Books, 2008. Kindle edition.

Gershenfeld, Neil, Raffi Krikorian, and Danny Cohen. "The Internet of Things." *Scientific American* (December 4, 2009): 76–81.

Gibson, William. "The Art of Fiction No. 211: William Gibson." *The Paris Review* 197 (Summer 2011): 106–49.

Gibson, William. "Google's Earth," *New York Times* (August 31, 2010): http://nytimes.com/2010/09/01/opinion/01gibson.html.

Gibson, William. *Neuromancer*. New York: Ace Books, 1984.

Gibson, William. *Spook Country*. New York: Putnam's, 2007.

Gibson, William and Denis Ashbaugh. *Agrippa (A Book of the Dead)*. New York: Kevin Begos, Jr., 1992.

Gitelman, Lisa. *Always Already New: Media, History, and the Data of Culture*. Cambridge, MA: MIT Press, 2006.

Gordon, Eric, and Adriana de Souza e Silva. *Net Locality: Why Location Matters in a Networked World*. Chichester, West Sussex, UK: Wiley-Blackwell, 2011.

Grafton, Anthony, and Lisa Jardine. *From Humanism to the Humanities: Education and the Liberal Arts in Fifteenth- and Sixteenth-Century Europe*. Cambridge, MA: Harvard University Press, 1986.

Greenblatt, Stephen. *The Swerve: How the World Became Modern*. New York and London: W. W. Norton & Co, 2011.

Greenfield, Adam. *Everyware: The Dawning Age of Ubiquitous Computing*. Berkeley, CA: New Riders, 2006.

Hale, Constance, ed. *Wired Style: Principles of English Usage in the Digital Age*. New York: Hardwired, 1996.

Halttunen, Karen. "Groundwork: American Studies in Place—Presidential Address to the American Studies Association, November 4, 2005." *American Quarterly* 58.1 (March 2006): 1–15.

Hayles, N. Katherine. "Cybernetics." In *Critical Terms for Media Studies*, edited by W. J. T. Mitchell and Mark B. N. Hansen, 144–56. Chicago: University of Chicago Press, 2010.

Hayles, N. Katherine. *Electronic Literature: New Horizons for the Literary*. Notre Dame: Notre Dame University Press, 2008.

Hayles, N. Katherine. *How We Became Posthuman: Virtual Bodies in Cybernetics, Literature, and Informatics*. Chicago: University of Chicago Press, 1999.

Heath, Dan, and Chip Heath. *The Myth of the Garage and Other Minor Surprises*. New York: Crown Business, 2011.

Heidegger, Martin. *Being and Time*. New York: Harper Perennial, 2008.

Howard, Jennifer. "Digital Materiality; or Learning to Love Our Machines." Wired Campus blog at *The Chronicle of Higher Education* (August 22, 2012): http://chronicle.com/blogs/wiredcampus/digital-materiality-or-learning-to-love-our-machines/38982.

Huizinga, Johan. *Homo Ludens: A Study of the Play Element in Culture*. Boston: The Beacon Press, 1950.

Jagoda, Patrick. "Fabulously Procedural: *Braid*, History, and the Videogame Sensorium." *American Literature*. Forthcoming, 2013.

Jockers, Matthew L. *Macroanalysis: Digital Methods and Literary History*. Champaign: University of Illinois Press, 2013.

Jockers, Matthew L. "On Distant Reading and Macroanalysis." Author's blog (July 1, 2011): http://matthewjockers.net/2011/07/01/on-distant-reading-and-macroanalysis.

Jockers, Matthew L. "Unigrams, and Bigrams, and Trigrams, Oh My." Author's blog (December 22, 2010): http://matthewjockers.net/2010/12/22/unigrams-and-bigrams-and-trigrams-oh-my.

Johns, Adrian. *The Nature of the Book: Print and Knowledge in the Making*. Chicago: University of Chicago Press, 1998.

Johnson, Steven. "The Long Zoom." *The New York Times Magazine* (October 8, 2006): http://nytimes.com/2006/10/08/magazine/08games.html?pagewanted=all&_r=0.

Jones, Steven E. *Against Technology: From the Luddites to Neo-Luddism*. New York: Routledge, 2006.

Jones, Steven E. *The Meaning of Video Games*. New York: Routledge, 2008.

Jones, Steven E. "MYST and the Late Age of Print." *Post Modern Culture* 7.2 (1997): http://pmc.iath.virginia.edu/text-only/issue.197/jones.197.

Jones, Steven E., and George K. Thiruvathukal. *Codename Revolution: The Nintendo Wii Platform*. Cambridge, MA: MIT Press, 2012.

Judkis, Maura. "QR Code Tattoo Signals End of the QR Code?" *Washington Post* Style Blog (December 19, 2011): http://washingtonpost.com/blogs/arts-post/post/qr-code-tattoo-signals-end-of-the-qr-code/2011/12/19/gIQAJW7y4O_blog.html.

Jurgenson, Nathan. "Digital Dualism versus Augmented Reality." Cyborgology blog (February 24, 2011): http://thesocietypages.org/cyborgology/2011/02/24/digital-dualism-versus-augmented-reality.

Jurgenson, Nathan. "The IRL Fetish." *The New Inquiry* (June 28, 2012): http://thenewinquiry.com/essays/the-irl-fetish.

Jurgenson, Nathan. "We Need a Word for That Thing Where a Digital Thing Appears in the Physical World." *The Atlantic* (July 9, 2012): http://theatlantic.com/technology/archive/2012/07/we-need-a-word-for-that-thing-where-a-digital-thing-appears-in-the-physical-world/259570/.

Juul, Jesper. *A Casual Revolution: Reinventing Video Games and Their Players*. Cambridge, MA: MIT Press, 2009.

Kirschenbaum, Matthew G. "Digital Humanities As/Is a Tactical Term." In *Debates in the Digital Humanities*, edited by Matthew K. Gold, 415–28. Minneapolis and London: University of Minnesota Press, 2012.

Kirschenbaum, Matthew G. *Mechanisms: New Media and the Forensic Imagination*. Cambridge, MA: MIT Press, 2008.

Kirschenbaum, Matthew G. "What is Digital Humanities." In *Debates in the Digital Humanities*, edited by Matthew Gold. Minneapolis, University of Minnesota Press, 2012, 3–7.

Kohler, Chris. "Disney's Biggest Stars Join Forces for *Skylanders*-Style Gaming Mash-up." *Wired* (January 15, 2013): http://wired.com/gamelife/2013/01/disney-infinity.

Kolowich, Steve. "Authors of 'Bill of Rights' for Online Learners Face Criticism." *Chronicle of Higher Education*, Wired Campus (January 25, 2013): http://chronicle.com/blogs/wiredcampus/authors-of-bill-of-rights-for-online-learners-face-criticism/41971.

Kraus, Kari. "Introduction: Rough Cuts: Media and Design in Process," The New Everyday (July 28, 2012): http://mediacommons.futureofthebook.org/tne/pieces/introduction.

Kuhn, Thomas S. *The Structure of Scientific Revolutions*. Chicago: University of Chicago Press, 1962.

Lanier, Jaron. *You Are Not a Gadget: A Manifesto*. New York: Vintage, 2010.

LeMieux, Patrick, and Stephanie Boluk. "Eccentric Spaces and Filmic Traces: Portals in Aperture Laboratories and New York City." *Proceedings of the 8th Digital Arts and Culture Conference, After Media: Embodiment and Context*. Irvine, CA: University of California Press, 2009.

Liu, Alan. "Is Digital Humanities a Field?—An Answer From the Point of View of Language." Author's blog (March 6, 2013): http://liu.english.ucsb.edu/is-digital-humanities-a-field-an-answer-from-the-point-of-view-of-language.

Liu, Alan, Paxton Hehmeyer, James J. Hodge, Kimberly Knight, David Roh, Elizabeth Swanstrom, and Matthew G. Kirschenbaum, eds. The Agrippa Files, http://agrippa.english.ucsb.edu/.

McCarty, Willard. "Modeling: A Study in Words and Meanings." In *A Companion to Digital Humanities*, edited by Susan Schreibman, Ray Siemens, and John Unsworth. Oxford: Blackwell, 2004, http://digitalhumanities.org/companion.

McCarty, Willard, and Elijah Meeks. "proof," Humanist List Archives (January 13–14, 2012): http://dhhumanist.org/Archives/Current/Humanist.vol25.txt.

McGann, Jerome J. "Marking Texts of Many Dimensions." In *A Companion to Digital Humanities*, edited by Susan Schreibman, Ray Siemens, and John Unsworth. Oxford: Blackwell, 2004.

McGann, Jerome J. *Radiant Textuality: Literature After the World Wide Web*. New York: Palgrave, 2001.

Meeks, Elijah. "TVTropes Pt. 1: The Weird Geometry of the Internet." Stanford University Libraries & Academic Information Resources, Digital Humanities Specialist blog (December 21, 2011): https://dhs.stanford.edu/social-media-literacy/tvtropes-pt-1-the-weird-geometry-of-the-internet.

Miéville, China. *The City & The City*. New York: Random House Digital, 2011. Kindle edition.

Minecraft. Markus Persson/Mojang, 2009.

Montfort, Nick. "Beyond the Journal and the Blog: The Technical Report for Communication in the Humanities." *Amodern* 1 (2013): http://amodern.net/article/beyond-the-journal-and-the-blog-the-technical-report-for-communication-in-the-humanities.

Montfort, Nick. *Twisty Little Passages: An Approach to Interactive Fiction*. Cambridge, MA: MIT Press, 2003.

Moretti, Franco. *Atlas of the European Novel, 1800–1900*. New York: Verso, 1999.

Moretti, Franco. *Graphs, Maps, Trees: Abstract Models for a Literary History*. London and New York: Verso, 2005.

Moyer, Edward. "Digital Pop-Up Book Gets Poetic With QR Codes." Cnet (February 9, 2012): http://news.cnet.com/8301-17938_105-57373708-1/digital-pop-up-book-gets-poetic-with-qr-codes.

Mueller, Martin. "Collaboratively Curating Early Modern English Texts." Project Bamboo wiki draft (August, 9, 2011): https://wiki.projectbamboo.org/plugins/viewsource/viewpagesrc.action?pageId=24648795.

New York Times series, "Humanities 2.0," November 17, 2010–July 27, 2011, http://topics.nytimes.com/top/features/books/series/humanities_20/index.html.

Novak, Marcos. "Everson: Brushing Against Avatars, Aliens, and Angels." In *From Energy to Information: Representation in Science and Technology, Art and Literature*, edited by Bruce Clarke and Linda Dalrymple Henderson, 309–23. Stanford: Stanford University Press, 2002.

Nowviskie, Bethany. "Eternal September of the Digital Humanities." In *Debates in the Digital Humanities*, edited by Matthew K. Gold, 243–48. Minneapolis and London: University of Minnesota Press, 2012.

Nowviskie, Bethany. "Resistance in the Materials." Author's blog (January 4, 2013): http://nowviskie.org/2013/resistance-in-the-materials.

Nunan, Timothy. "Sticking a 'Fork' in the Humanities? Some Thoughts on Digital Humanities." Author's blog (July 16, 2011): http://timothynunan.com/2011/07/16/sticking-a-fork-in-the-humanities-some-thoughts-on-digital-humanities.

O'Reilly, Tim. "What is Web 2.0: Design Patterns and Business Models for the Next Generation of Software." Author's blog (September 30, 2005): http://oreilly.com/web2/archive/what-is-web-20.html.

Pan, Joann. "Can Augmented Reality Save the Printed Page?" Mashable (February 3, 2012): http://mashable.com/2012/02/03/augmented-reality-book-between-page-and-screen.

Pannapacker, William. "The MLA and the Digital Humanities," *The Chronicle of Higher Education* Brainstorm blog (December 28, 2009): http://chronicle.com/blogPost/The-MLAthe-Digital/19468.

Parikka, Jussi. *What Is Media Archaeology?* Cambridge, UK: Polity Press, 2012.

Petroski, Henry. *Evolution of Useful Things: How Everyday Artifacts—From Forks and Pins to Paper Clips and Zippers—Came to Be as They Are*. New York: Vintage, 1994.

Petroski, Henry. *The Pencil: A History of Design and Circumstance*. New York: Knopf, 1992.

Petroski, Henry. *The Toothpick: Technology and Culture*. New York: Knopf, 2007.

Piper, Andrew. *Book Was There: Reading in Electronic Times*. Chicago: University of Chicago Press, 2012. Kindle edition.

Portal. Valve, 2007.

Ramsay, Stephen. "The Hermeneutics of Screwing Around; or, What Do You Do With a Million Books?" (April 17, 2010): http://playingwithhistory.com/wp-content/uploads/2010/04/hermeneutics.pdf.

Ramsay, Stephen. "On Building." Author's blog (January 11, 2011): http://stephenramsay.us/text/2011/01/11/on-building.html.

Ramsay, Stephen. *Reading Machines: Toward an Algorithmic Criticism*. Champaign: University of Illinois Press, 2011.

Ramsay, Stephen, and Geoffrey Rockwell. "Developing Things: Notes Toward an Epistemology of Building in the Digital Humanities." In *Debates in the Digital Humanities*, edited by Matthew K. Gold, 75–84. Minneapolis and London: University of Minnesota Press, 2012.

Robertson, Adi. "Oculus Rift Virtual Reality Gaming Goggles Launched on Kickstarter (Update: Funded)." *The Verge* (August 1, 2012): http://theverge.com/2012/8/1/3212895/oculus-rift-virtual-reality-head-mounted-display-kickstarter.

Robertson, Stephen. "Putting Harlem on the Map." In *Writing History in the Digital Age*, edited by Jack Dougherty and Kristen Nawrotzki: http://writinghistory.trincoll.edu/evidence/robertson-2012-spring.

Rogers, Mikeal. "The GitHub Generation: Why We're All in Open Source Now." *Wired* (March 7, 2013): http://wired.com/opinion/2013/03/github.

Roth, Dieter. *Book AC 1958–64*. New Haven, CT: Ives-Sillman, 1964.

Rushkoff, Douglas. *Program or Be Programmed: Ten Commands for a Digital Age*. New York: OR Books, 2010. Kindle edition.

Salen, Katie, and Eric Zimmerman. *Rules of Play: Game Design Fundamentals*. Cambridge, MA: MIT Press, 2004.

Sample, Mark. "Digital Humanities at MLA 2013." Sample Reality blog (October 17, 2012): http://samplereality.com/2012/10/17/digital-humanities-at-mla-2013.

Sample, Mark. "Haunts: Place, Play, and Trauma." Sample Reality blog (June 1, 2010): http://samplereality.com/2010/06/01/haunts-place-play-and-trauma.

Scheinfedlt, Tom, and Dan Cohen, eds. *Hacking the Academy*. http://hackingtheacademy.org/what-this-is-and-how-to-contribute.

Schell, Jesse. "Design Outside the Box." Presentation at DICE (Design, Innovate, Communicate, Entertain) (February 18, 2010): http://g4tv.com/videos/44277/DICE-2010-Design-Outside-the-Box-Presentation.

Schreibman, Susan, Ray Siemens, and John Unsworth, eds. *A Companion to Digital Humanities*. Oxford: Blackwell, 2004: http://digitalhumanities.org/companion.

Shelley, Mary Wollstonecraft. *Frankenstein; or, The Modern Prometheus*. Peterborough, Ontario, CA: Broadview. 2012 [first published 1818].

Shirky, Clay. *Here Comes Everybody: The Power of Organizing Without Organizations*. New York: Penguin Press, 2008.

Skylanders: Spyro's Adventure. Toys for Bob/Activision, 2011.

Skyrim, The Elder Rolls V. Bethesda Game Studios, 2011.

Snow, C. P. *The Two Cultures: And A Second Look*. Cambridge, UK: Cambridge University Press, 1979.

Spore. Redwood City, CA: Maxis/Electronic Arts, 2008.

Stephenson, Neal. "Mother Earth Mother Board." *Wired* 4.12 (December 1996): 97–160. Reprinted in *Some Remarks: Essays and Other Writing*. New York: William Morrow/Harper Collins, 2012. Kindle edition, loc. 1783–3616.

Stephenson, Neal. *Reamde*. New York: Harper Collins, 2011. Kindle edition.

Stephenson, Neal. *Snow Crash*. New York: Bantam, 1992.

Sterling, Bruce. "An Essay on the New Aesthetic." Beyond The Beyond blog (April 22, 2012): http://wired.com/beyond_the_beyond/2012/04/an-essay-on-the-new-aesthetic.

Sterling, Bruce. *Shaping Things*. Cambridge, MA: MIT Press, 2005.

Striphas, Ted. *The Late Age of Print: Everyday Book Culture From Consumerism to Control*. New York: Columbia University Press, 2009.

Svensson, Patrik. "Humanities Computing as Digital Humanities." *DHQ* 3.3 (2009): http://digitalhumanities.org/dhq/vol/3/3/000065/000065.html.

Tanz, Jason. "The Curse of Cow-Clicker: How a Cheeky Satire Became a Video-Game Hit." *Wired* 20.1 (December 20, 2011): http://wired.com/magazine/2011/12/ff_cowclicker.

Topolsky, Joshua. "I Used Google Glass: The Future, With Monthly Updates." *The Verge* (February 22, 2013): http://theverge.com/2013/2/22/4013406/i-used-google-glass-its-the-future-with-monthly-updates.

Tufte, Edward R. *The Visual Display of Quantitative Information*. Cheshire, CT: Graphics Press, 1983.

Turkle, Sherry. *Alone Together: Why We Expect More From Technology and Less From Each Other*. New York: Basic Books, 2012.

Turkel, William J. "Intervention: Hacking History, From Analogue To Digital and Back Again." *Rethinking History* 15.2 (June 2011): 287–96.

Vinge, Vernor. "True Names." First published in *Dell Binary Star* 5 (1981). Reprinted in *True Names and the Opening of the Cyberspace Frontier*, edited by James Frenkel, 239–330. New York: Tom Doherty Associates, TOR, 2001.

Virilio, Paul. *The Lost Dimension*. Translated by Daniel Moshenberg. New York: Semiotext(e), 1991.

Walker, Rob. "Freaks, Geeks and Micrososft." *New York Times* (May 31, 2012): http://nytimes.com/2012/06/03/magazine/how-kinect-spawned-a-commercial-ecosystem.html?pagewanted=all.

Wiener, Norbert. *Cybernetics: Or Control and Communication in the Animal and the Machine*. Cambridge, MA: MIT Press, 1948.

Williford, Christa, and Charles Henry. *One Culture: Computationally Intensive Research in the Humanities and Social Sciences: A Report on the Experiences of First Respondents to the Digging Into Data Challenge*. Washington, DC: Council on Library and Information Resources, 2012.

Zone, Ray. *Stereoscopic Cinema & the Origins of 3-D Film, 1838–1952*. Lexington: The University Press of Kentucky, 2007.

INDEX